PRAISE FOR *Straight*

"An engrossing read that will not only equip you with lots of interesting trivia for your next cocktail party but also probably challenge your personal beliefs."
—LAURA ANNE STUART, *Express Milwaukee*

"Readers won't unquestioningly think 'straight' again."
—*Ms. Magazine*

"In her refreshingly jargon-free new book, Blank uses her relationship as a way of showing the words 'homosexuality' and 'heterosexuality' are just that—words that limit, shape and constrain the world as much as they describe it. She deftly reveals the shifts and anxieties in western culture that led to the invention of 'straight' fewer than 150 years ago."
—SARAH BARMAK, *Toronto Star*

"Blank's style is clear, confident, and lively. To translate her findings from the depths of academia, she offers a good teacher's knack for clear comparisons and lucid explanation. She's also given to catchy opening sentences that send you racing ahead."
—SONDRA GUTTMAN, *Urbanite*

"This book begs to be pondered. . . . If you're heterosexual (or know one), reading *Straight* is a good decision."
—TERRI SCHLICHENMEYER, *Washington Blade*

"Using wit and wisdom, Blank substantiates her argument that love and passion are not defined by biology."
—WINNIE MCCROY, *Edge*

"On its face, *Straight* is a book about the history of sex, but it is really a book about the history of knowledge. . . . Michel Foucault and others have treaded this ground before, but Blank's thorough and witty book is the first to target these known unknowns squarely at a popular audience."

—CHLOE ANGYAL, *GOOD Magazine*

"A lively, accessible synthesis of decades of scholarship on the history and sociology of sexuality . . . highly recommended."

—J. M. IRVINE, *Choice*

"Witty in her defamiliarization of the heterosexual . . . Blank argues that sexuality is too complex, variable and manifold to be contained within a simple binary framework."

—ELAINE SHOWALTER, *Washington Post*

"*Straight* comes at an opportune time, as the nation struggles to define marriage and the rights of those who identify as anything other than classically straight. Blank ultimately concludes that heterosexuality is a concept invented by society, and society thus has the power to re-define it. Both supporters and opponents of the gay rights movement would do well to read this book with an open mind; Blank's words bring some sober clarity to a battle that often feels vitriolic and rooted in uninformed prejudice."

—LAURA DATTARO, *Baltimore City Paper*

"Hanne Blank has rendered a meticulously researched romp through the history of 'heterosexuality'—that pesky orthodoxy still looming over Western culture like smog. Her sweeping synthesis takes on everything from Freud to Larry Craig, expertly weaving this untold history with insight and a refreshing dose of irreverence."

—LISA M. DIAMOND, author of *Sexual Fluidity*

"What would it mean to dispense with our current categories of sexual identity? Writing with grace and wit, Hanne Blank demonstrates that what sounds like a radical proposition is also historically inevitable."

—LAURA KIPNIS, author of
How to Become a Scandal and *Against Love*

STRAIGHT

STRAIGHT

THE SURPRISINGLY SHORT HISTORY
OF HETEROSEXUALITY

HANNE BLANK

Beacon Press · Boston

For Malcolm

Beacon Press
25 Beacon Street
Boston, Massachusetts 02108-2892
www.beacon.org

Beacon Press books
are published under the auspices of
the Unitarian Universalist Association of Congregations.

15 14 13 12   8 7 6 5 4 3 2 1

This book is printed on acid-free paper that meets the uncoated paper
ANSI/NISO specifications for permanence as revised in 1992.

Text design by Wilsted & Taylor Publishing Services

Library of Congress Cataloging-in-Publication Data

Blank, Hanne.
Straight : the surprisingly short history
of heterosexuality / Hanne Blank.
p. cm.
Includes bibliographical references and index.
ISBN 978-0-8070-4459-9 (paperback : alk. paper)
1. Heterosexuality—History.
2. Homosexuality—History. I. Title.
HQ23.B56 2012
306.76'409—dc23   2011031432

CONTENTS

INTRODUCTION

Sexual Disorientation

Every time I go to the doctor, I end up questioning my sexual orientation. On some of its forms, the clinic I visit includes five little boxes, a small matter of demographic bookkeeping. Next to the boxes are the options "gay," "lesbian," "bisexual," "transgender," or "heterosexual." You're supposed to check one.

You might not think this would pose a difficulty. I am a fairly garden-variety female human being, after all, and I am in a long-term monogamous relationship, well into our second decade together, with someone who has male genitalia. But does this make us, or our relationship, straight? This turns out to be a good question, because there is more to my relationship—and much, much more to heterosexuality—than easily meets the eye.

There's biology, for one thing. My partner was diagnosed male at birth because he was born with, and indeed still has, a fully functioning penis. But, as the ancient Romans used to say, *barba non facit philosophum*—a beard does not make one a philosopher. Neither does having a genital outie necessarily make one male. Indeed, of the two sex chromosomes—XY—which would be found in the genes of a typical male, and XX, which is the hallmark of the genetically typical female—my partner's DNA has all three: XXY, a pattern that is simultaneously male, female, and neither.

This particular genetic pattern, XXY, is the signature of Kleinfelter Syndrome, one of the most common sex-chromosome anomalies. XXY often goes undiagnosed because the people who have it often look perfectly normal from the outside. In many cases, XXY individuals do not find out about their chromosomal anomaly unless they try to have children and end up seeing a fertility doctor, who ultimately orders an image called a karyotype, essentially a photo of the person's chromosomes made with a very powerful microscope. In a karyotype, the trisomy, or three-chromosome grouping, is instantly revealed. As genetic anomalies go, this particular trisomy is not a cause for major alarm (aside from infertility, it causes few significant problems), which is a good thing, since it is fairly common. The estimates vary, in part because diagnosis is so haphazard, but it is believed that as many as one in every two thousand people who are declared male at birth may in fact be XXY. At minimum, there are about half a million Americans whose genetics are this way, most of whom will never know it.

What does an unusual sexual biology mean for sexual orientation? Is it even *possible* for XXY people to have a sexual orientation in the way we usually think about sexual orientation? What about their lovers, partners, and spouses? "Heterosexual," "homosexual," and "bisexual" are all dependent on the idea that there are two, and only two, biological sexes. What happens when biology refuses to fit neatly into this scheme? If I'm attracted to, and in love with, someone who is technically speaking neither male nor female, does that make me heterosexual, homosexual, bisexual, or something else altogether? Who gets to decide? And, more to the point, on what grounds?

Some would argue that genetics aren't as important as anatomy and bodily functions. After all, you can't see chromosomes with the naked eye. But here, too, I run into problems. Part of what makes a man, as we are all taught from childhood, is that he has a penis and testicles that produce sperm, which in turn are necessary to fertilize a female's egg cells and conceive a fetus. The ability to sire a child has been considered proof of masculinity for thousands of years. This is something my partner cannot do. His external plumbing looks and acts pretty much like any genetically typical male's, but, in the words of one of my partner's vasectomied coworkers, "he shoots blanks." In my partner's case, no vasectomy was required. His testicles do not produce viable sperm. They never have and never will. This is part of the territory for most people who have XXY sex chromosomes.

So if heterosexuality is by definition, as some of our right-wing brothers and sisters like to claim, about the making of babies, then there is no possible way for my partner and me to be construed as heterosexual. But even the Bible recognizes that infertility exists. The notoriously procreation-fixated Catholic Church permits marriage, and marital sex, between people known to be infertile. Curiously, whether or not reproduction is a cornerstone of heterosexuality seems to depend on whom you ask, and in what circumstances.

Not that it really matters in practice. At this point in time contraception is more the rule than the exception for sexual activity between different-sex partners throughout the first world. Many people, including members of committed male/female couples, don't have children or plan to have them, yet somehow this doesn't stop them from feeling quite certain that they know what their sexual orientations are. They consider sexual orientation as being rooted in a calculus of subjective attraction and biological sameness. The Greek "hetero" means "other" or "different," after all, and biological men and women do differ from one another. We make use of these biological differences every day without thinking every time we look at people and identify them as either male or female, ask whether a baby or a dog is a boy or a girl, or determine the sexes of the members of a couple we spot on the street and assign them sexual orientations in our minds.

Surely such informal, man-in-the-street diagnostics ought to apply just as well to my partner and me. Or perhaps not. As an XXY individual who has chosen not to take hormone supplements, my partner's naturally occurring sex hormones take a middle path. His estrogen levels hang out a little lower than mine, his testosterone levels a little higher. As a result, my partner, like other XXY people who don't take exogenous hormones, has an androgynous appearance, with little to no facial and body hair, a fine smooth complexion, and a tendency to develop small breasts and slightly rounded hips if he puts on a little weight.[1] When we lived in a LGBT-heavy neighborhood in Boston, my partner and I were often identified by others as lesbians. We were regularly referred to as "ladies" by shopkeepers, door-to-door Mormons, and parents trying to prevent their kids from crowding us at the zoo. Lesbian couples we encountered in passing often shot us little conspiratorial smiles of recognition. (We always smiled back. Still do.) But it wasn't all pleasantries. Once while walking together we had bottles thrown at us from a car, its occupants screaming "Fuckin' dykes!" out the windows as they sped away. Assumptions of sexual orientation are never merely innocent perceptions, because these perceptions shape behavior.

Assumptions about biology and gender are complicated, fraught, and by no means clear or unambiguous. The ways people have identified my partner's biological sex, and therefore not only the nature of our relationship to one another but also our respective sexual orientations, have run an extraordinary gamut that might be distressing if we hadn't long ago learned to laugh at it all. My partner's physical androgyny—the minimal facial hair, refined complexion, and elegant, long-limbed build that are common side effects of his genetic anomaly—has led some people to assume that he is a female-to-male transsexual who is early in the transition process, still more hormonally female than male. I have heard him identified as a "passing butch." Once, at a party, I overheard a woman stating with assurance that my partner was a very feminine gay man who had "made an exception" for me. At other times I have been assumed to be the one making the exception, a "hasbian" who turned from dating women to seeing a gentle, feminine straight man. By the same token, these reactions have changed as we've aged and our styles of dress and grooming have changed. For the past several years, with my partner usually dressing in corporate-office menswear and sporting a dashing haircut modeled on the young Cole Porter's, we have typically, though not always, been read as heterosexual. If the range of responses we've had can tell me anything about what my sexual orientation is supposed to be, it's that other people don't necessarily know what box I should be checking off on those clinic forms either.

My own sense of sexual identity is, incidentally, no help. I have no deep personal attachment to labeling myself in terms of sexual orientation, nor do I have the sensation of "being" heterosexual or homosexual or anything but a human being who loves and desires other human beings. I have been romantically and sexually involved with people of a variety of biological sexes and social genders over the course of my adult life. When pressed, I am most likely to declare my "sexual identity" as "taken." This option, however much it might be the best fit, is not available to me on most forms that ask this sort of question.

I could, I suppose, resort to legal documents to sort out the question of what my orientation is, and what the orientation of my relationship with my partner might be. Here at last it is uncomplicated. Based on our birth certificates, my partner and I and our relationship could be defined as uncomplicatedly heterosexual. But there's a caveat, and it's a big one: our sexes were diagnosed at birth on the basis of a visual check of our genitals, on the assumption that external genitals are an infallible indicator of biological sex. This is the assumption behind every "it's a boy" or "it's a girl," not just historically but every day around the world. Thanks to the publicity given to cases like that of intersex South African athlete Caster Semenya in 2009, and indeed to the ink I am spilling here, however, mainstream culture is gradually becoming aware that this assumption is not necessarily warranted. Many biologists, including Brown University biologist Anne Fausto-Sterling, have eloquently testified that humans have at least five major sexes—of which typical male and typical female are merely the most numerous—and that furthermore, human chromosomes, gonads, internal sexual organs, external genitals, sex hormones, and secondary sexual characteristics can appear in many different guises.

The law, however, still acknowledges only two sexes. It does not always or necessarily acknowledge sexual orientation at all. On the occasions when it does recognize sexual orientation, it typically acknowledges only two of them as well, heterosexual and homosexual. (Once in a while bisexuality is included, but often not.) All of these sexual orientations are wholly dependent upon—and could not be conceptualized without—the general consensus that there are two and only two human biological sexes. But as we now know, and as is demonstrated so charmingly in the person of my very own beloved, this is not necessarily so. Rather, the convenient sorting of human beings into two biological sexes and a correspondingly limited number of sexual orientations is an artifact of a historical system that was formed at a time when medicine, biology, and social theory were capable of far less than they are now. We are still using a very limited nineteenth-century set of ideas and terminology to talk about a decidedly more expansive twenty-first-century landscape of biology, medicine, law, social theory, and human behavior.

—

It has, in point of actual fact, only been possible to be a heterosexual since 1869.[2] Prior to that time, men and women got married, had sex, had children, formed families, and sometimes even fell in love, but they were categorically not heterosexuals. They didn't identify themselves as "being" something called "heterosexual." They didn't think of themselves as having a "straight" sexual identity, or indeed have any awareness that something called a "sexual identity" even existed. They couldn't have. Neither the terms nor the ideas that they express existed yet.

"Heterosexual" and "heterosexuality" are creations of a particular, distinct, well-documented time and place. They are words, and ideas, developed by people whose names are known to us and whose handwritten letters we can still read. Their adoption and integration into Western culture was a remarkable process that historian Jonathan Ned Katz, the first to chronicle it, has aptly called "the invention of heterosexuality."

It was an invention whose time had clearly come, for it took less than a century for "heterosexual" and "heterosexuality" to leap out of the honestly rather obscure medical and legal backwaters where they were born and become part of a vast and opaque umbrella sheltering an enormous amount of social, economic, scientific, legal, political, and cultural activity. Exactly how this happened is a complicated, diffuse story that takes place on many different stages at roughly the same time, over a span of time measured in decades.

We need not, however, labor under the delusion that "heterosexual" became such a culture-transforming success because it represented the long-awaited discovery of a vital and inescapable scientific truth. It wasn't. As we shall see, the original creation of "heterosexual" and "homosexual" had nothing to do with scientists or science at all. Nor did it have anything to do with biology or medicine. "Heterosexual" (and "homosexual") originated in a quasi-legal context, a term of art designed to argue a philosophical point of legislature.

Perhaps this should not surprise us. Indeed, it can be argued that the biomedical business of sexuality has nothing to do with sexual orientation or sexual identity anyway. The materials and physiology of sexual activities are, on a strictly mechanical level, a separate problem from the subjective mechanics of attraction or desire, as rape— something that can and does happen to people without regard to biological sex, age, condition, or consent—attests with such brutal efficiency. Separate from human sexual orientation or identity in a different way are the chemistry and alchemy of human conception, which can, after all, take place in a petri dish. There is, biomedically speaking, nothing about what human beings do sexually that requires that something like what we now think of as "sexual orientation" exists. If there were, and the attribute we now call "heterosexuality" were a prerequisite for people to engage in sex acts or procreate, chances are excellent that we would not have waited until the late nineteenth century to figure out that it was there.

"Heterosexual" became a success, in other words, not because it represented a new scientific verity or capital-T Truth. It succeeded because it was *useful*. At a time when moral authority was shifting from religion to the secular society at a precipitous pace, "heterosexual" offered a way to dress old religious priorities in immaculate white coats that looked just like the ones worn among the new power hierarchy of scientists. At a historical moment when the waters of anxiety about family, nation, class, gender, and empire were at a rather hysterical high, "heterosexual" seemed to offer a dry, firm place for authority to stand. This new concept, gussied up in a mangled mix of impressive-sounding dead languages,[3] gave old orthodoxies a new and vibrant lease on life by suggesting, in authoritative tones, that science had effectively pronounced them natural, inevitable, and innate.

What does all this have to do with me, my partner, and the unanswered question of which multiple-choice box I should tick? Plenty. The history of "the heterosexual" lurks unexamined not just in our beliefs about our inmost private selves, but also in our beliefs about our bodies, our social interactions, our romances, our family lives, the way we raise our children, and, of course, in our sex lives. Virtually everyone alive today, especially in the developed world, has lived their entire lives in a culture of sexuality that assumes that "heterosexual" and "homosexual" are objectively real elements of nature.

As a result of this pervasiveness, heterosexuality is like air, all around us and yet invisible. But as we all know, the fact that we can see through air doesn't mean it can't exert force, push things around, and create friction. In the process of asking questions about my own life, I have had to learn to think about heterosexuality like an aircraft pilot thinks about the air: as something with a real, tangible presence, something that is not only capable of but is constantly in the process of influencing if not dictating thoughts, actions, and reactions. If I, or any of us, are to be able to decide whether or not we or our relationships qualify as "heterosexual," it behooves us to understand what that means. This history represents the attempt to begin to comprehend what exactly this invisible wind is, where it comes from, what it's made of, and where it might be pushing you and me and all of us.

———

For something that has such a monolithic aura of inevitability and authority about it, it often seems that we have a difficult time saying for sure exactly what, and who, is heterosexual. Recently we have witnessed a wave of loudly, politically heterosexual Larry Craigs, Mark Foleys, and Bob Allens all neck-deep in scandal over secretive same-sex liaisons. In 2004, the phrase "on the down low" entered the national vocabulary thanks to Oprah Winfrey's bully pulpit, instantly familiarizing and frightening a generation with the phenomenon of the heterosexually identified married man who has surreptitious sex with other men.

This shouldn't have shocked anyone, really. We've known full well since Kinsey that a large minority—survey numbers vary, but Kinsey claimed 37 percent, and other surveys have agreed that it is at least that high—of men have at least one same-sex sexual experience in their lives. And even this should have been predictable, given the vast evidence from centuries past of married men who were known to enjoy sexual liaisons with other men. Indeed, they were often punished for it, which is how we know.

There have, in other words, been hundreds of thousands, probably millions of married men whose intimate lives could be characterized as simultaneously straight and not. The question is, Are these husbands heterosexual? And how do we decide?

The answer, of course, depends on where you draw your lines. In turn, where we draw the lines is not a legal question or a medical question or a scientific question or even a moral question. It's a social question. There is no ultimate high council in charge of heterosexuality, not even an *Académie française* whose uniformed experts determine its official usages and rules. No act of Congress or Parliament exists anywhere that defines exactly what heterosexuality is or regulates exactly how it is to be enacted. On the subject of the parameters and qualifications of straightness, the International Standards Organization has been conspicuously silent. What heterosexuality "is" is not handed down to us from on high, and it is far from concrete or monolithic.

Historically, what heterosexuality "is" has been a synonym for "sexually normal." Early in the history of the term, it was even used interchangeably with the term "normal-sexual." And there, as they say, is the rub. "Normal" is not a mode of eternal truth; it's a way to describe commonness and conformity with expectations. But what is most common and expected, in terms of our sexual lives or any other aspect of the human condition, does not always remain the same.

Sexual expectations and behaviors, like all other social expectations and behaviors, change over time. Within living memory there have been massive shifts on questions like whether women were supposed to feel sexual desire or have orgasms, whether sex outside of marriage could ever be openly acceptable, and the permissibility and desirability of sex acts other than penis-in-vagina intercourse. Casting further back in time, historians have tracked major shifts in other aspects of what was considered common or "normal" in sex and relationships: Was marriage ideally an emotional relationship, or an economic and pragmatic one? Was romantic love desirable, and did it even really exist? Should young people choose their own spouses, or should marriage partners be selected by family and friends? Even assuming that we speak only of interactions and relationships between males and females, these relationships have simply not always been the same, nor have the people participating in them been expected to do, think, feel, or experience the same sorts of things. What "normal–sexual" is, above anything else, is *relative*.

A similar situation holds in regard to the beliefs that are held about why it should be that women feel desire for men and vice versa. Beyond the old tired tug-of-war over nature and nurture, there are numerous other contestants vying for pride of place as being The One True Reason that men and women want anything to do with one another in the first place. The religious often make claims that different-sex attractions are "God-given," others that they are "universal." With an eye to sexual dimorphism, some determinists announce that an interest in a different-sex sexual partner is "biological." Dozens of scientists and pseudoscientists in dozens of fields have hurried to supply their own, ever more specialized, hypotheses. The cacophony of opinion on this does not appear to have reduced anyone's faith that there must, inevitably, be a right answer to be found. Having decided that heterosexuality exists, we maintain a correspondingly unshakable faith that it exists for a reason. Hardly anyone seems to notice or care that we go back and forth, and then back and forth some more, about what that reason might be.

Nor do we seem to achieve consensus on where to place heterosexuality's limits, or even how best to police them. Often, points of damage or destruction—the places where a thing becomes not *this* but *that*—are useful places to look for the boundaries that limn definitions. Not here. At various times and in various places, people have believed that heterosexuality (or normal-sexuality) could be destroyed by, among other things, becoming a Catholic monk, reading novels, not moving your bowels often enough, cross-dressing (including women wearing pants), too much education, not enough religion, divorce, improper ejaculation, masturbation, the abolition of slavery, women's working for pay, and too much leisure time for anyone.

Even if we are not inclined to paranoia about heterosexuality's potential destruction by the literary, the constipated, and the apostate, we still have to reckon with situational homosexuality. Sometimes, even the most devoutly heterosexual find themselves in circumstances where their normal pattern of being sexually interested in different-sex partners seems to go right out the window. As unnumbered sailors, prisoners, and boarding-school boys have demonstrated, whether one behaves heterosexually or homosexually sometimes seems like little more than a matter of circumstance. Does the experience of situational homosexuality fundamentally change whether a person is heterosexual or "normal-sexual"? Unsurprisingly, the answers are all over the map, as are the explanations for why a phenomenon like situational homosexuality should exist in the first place.

Despite the fact that most of us use the term "heterosexual" with enormous (and cavalier!) certainty, there seems to be no aspect of "heterosexual" for which a truly iron-clad definition has been established. There seems to be general agreement that "heterosexual" has to do with men and women and the approved sorts of sexual, emotional, social, familial, and economic attractions and activities that might go on between them, but the overall picture is ambiguous and the details change depending on who you ask and when in time you look. There is a Heisenbergian quality about defining "heterosexual": the more precisely the term is being defined, the more likely it is that the term is only being defined by the lights of a single moment in time and space.

Similarly telling in their grand and vexing ambiguities are two other things we inevitably talk about when we talk about heterosexuality: gender and sex, both in the sense of "having sex" and in terms of biology.

"To have sex" can mean lots of things. It might mean "to be a creature with a biological sex." Or it could mean "to be gendered," as in "androgynous fashions," "male pipe fittings," "chick flicks." It can mean having a libido, in the sense of "oversexed" or "undersexed," or simply having genitals, as when we refer to the vulva and all its parts as "a woman's sex." Colloquially, we most often use it to mean "to engage in sexual activity," but what this in turn denotes is alas far from clear. It could simply mean "to engage in erotic activity," but it could as easily mean "to engage in penis-in-vagina penetration," "to attempt to procreate," or "to engage in erotic activity leading to orgasm." Any, or indeed all, of these things could be true and relevant when talking about heterosexuality. This is why we can't assume that "having sex" only means one thing, even if we're operating on the assumption that we're talking about sexual activity between partners of different biological sexes. Only one of the many sex acts of which our species is capable, after all, requires the simultaneous engagement of both a penis and a vagina.

When it comes to "sex," context is king: its three tiny letters wear an awful lot of hats. This is true even within fairly narrow and strict-seeming fields, such as biology. The thing we call "biological sex" is the diagnosis of physical sex made according to the observation of bodily characteristics, and also the constellation of bodily characteristics that are observed to make that diagnosis. The late Johns Hopkins sexologist John Money identified seven different criteria for a diagnosis of biological sex in humans, including genetic or chromosomal sex, internal anatomy, external anatomy, sex hormones, and the type of gonads an individual possesses. This is extremely useful, as it emphasizes the very real possibility that in any given individual, these criteria will not all necessarily point to the same diagnosis. Sex chromosome anomalies, "ambiguous" genitalia that in some way or other blur the difference between male- and female-typical genitals, hormone levels that are far from textbook, and gonads that are somewhere between ovary and testis are all fairly common and naturally occurring.

There is little agreement, however, about how these atypical biologies should be identified. Nor is there consensus on how they might best fit in, socially and psychologically, to a binary system that traditionally has no space for them. Attempts to force people with nonbinary biology to fit into the binary mold of male and female have had highly mixed results and have created enormous controversy, not least for sexologists like John Money.[4] The usual biological sexes recognized by biomedical science are female, male, and, for conditions like my partner's XXY chromosomes, intersex. But, as should be clear from the fact that my partner's body, neither male nor female in so many major biological ways, was uncontroversially diagnosed as male when he was born, even these lines are frequently blurry.

One reason that biological sex may not be as clear-cut as it may seem it should be is that biology can change. Some changes in sexual biology are spontaneous, such as ejacularche (the onset of the ability to ejaculate) or menopause (the cessation of the ability to menstruate). Others are induced, such as hysterectomy, which is a surgery removing the uterus (and often ovaries as well). Not coincidentally, hysterectomy may also present an incidence of induced menopause if performed on a premenopausal woman.

Biological and bodily changes may—or may not—affect how we diagnose or think of a person's biological sex. We don't think of women as no longer being women just because they have hysterectomies. A man who has his testicles surgically removed because of testicular cancer is still considered male (and will likely be firmly reassured of this by his doctors). On the other hand, if the same surgeries—removal of the uterus/ovaries or testes—are done as part of sex reassignment, then these biological changes suddenly become fundamental in terms of giving a basis to a diagnosis of a new sex. The organs removed may be biologically identical, but the surgeries' effects on "biological sex" can be light years apart. Biology is a science, but it does not exist in a vacuum.

———

Gender, or "social sex," is alas no less complex. Gender refers to all the manifestations of masculinity or femininity that are not immediately, demonstrably biological. These include mannerisms, conventions of dress and grooming, social roles, speech patterns, and much more. A useful way to think about it is that we *have* biological sex—it is inherently present in our physical bodies—but we *do* gender.

Beliefs about the relationship between biological sex and gender are varied and complex; our understanding of it is decidedly incomplete. For most of our past, people did not typically perceive any difference between sex and gender at all. The contention was that biological sex created gender because gender was essentially biological—or to put it another way, there was some "essence" associated with being biologically female that generated characteristics we call femininity, and some "essence" of maleness that did the same with regard to masculinity. Until quite recently this was a mainstream, commonly accepted view. In the past century or so, however, the gender essentialism model has been heavily criticized and largely disproven. Whether or not gender is influenced by biology, and to what degree if so, is now the subject of intense scientific debate.

The role of gender socialization, on the other hand, is uncontroversial and can be easily observed. We begin teaching gender beginning at birth, for instance by swaddling baby boys in blue while girls are given pink, by adorning baby girls with frills and lace while baby boys are dressed in less ornamented, more utilitarian clothes. In these and innumerable other ways, people learn how to "do gender" according to the expectations of the cultures and subcultures in which they live. For the most part we are socialized to do gender so that we are "gender typical" or "cisgendered," meaning that the way we do gender matches up with our culture's expectations of what someone of our biological sex is supposed to be like: masculine males and feminine females. But gender is not uniform. "Masculine" and "feminine" can be highly nuanced, with different styles that make social statements about a person's socioeconomic class, ethnicity, religion, education, subcultures, and aesthetics. This is all the more relevant because people often don't perceive themselves as doing gender consciously. Many people believe that their masculinity or femininity, and the ways they express it, is "just who they are."

Gender is indeed part of how we express our personalities. It isn't as automatic or as inevitable as it may feel. One way we can see gender as a mode of self-expression in action is in the ways that styles of gender performance change over time and from one subgroup of people to the next. Masculinity does not look, sound, dress, or act the same for a rapper as for an Orthodox Jewish rabbinical student; a California surfer chick does femininity very differently from a New York City lady-who-lunches. At the same time, these ways of doing gender can be changed . . . and learned. A California surfer chick could learn how to do femininity in ways that would let her fit right in at New York's toniest tables, if she wanted to.

Styles of doing gender are mixable and mutable, and so are genders themselves. Masculinity, femininity, and androgyny are not mutually exclusive characteristics. Being big, burly, and bearded is no barrier, for one of my friends, to also being a tender and caring registered nurse. Being petite and pretty doesn't exclude Danica Patrick from being a ferociously aggressive race-car driver. There are no such things as "opposite" genders, any more than a strawberry is the "opposite" of a plum. They are merely different. Describing any two sexes or genders as "opposite" is not fact; it is merely an outdated and inaccurate custom.

Whether or not we are aware of it, the ways we do gender are a primary mode of self-expression and social signaling. Our gender performance tells other people a great deal not just about who we are, but who we want other people to perceive us to be. This is particularly relevant because gender is so much a matter of performance, and because it is so separable from biology. A person's gender may or may not have a conventional relationship to his or her biology. There is, after all, no reason it has to.

For all these reasons, we have to look carefully at who and what we're talking about when we discuss heterosexuality. Heterosexuality, as we understand it, is rooted in relationships between people of particular sexes, genders, and biologies. Yet sex and gender and biology encompass a wide variety of things. When we take all this into account, it becomes somewhat easier to understand just why and how it has come to pass that we don't, in fact, have a complete and valid universal definition for "heterosexual."

———

Would that defining "heterosexual" were as simple a problem as defining a particular type of sexual desire or activity. Alas, human sexual interests and behaviors are every bit as ambiguous and complicated as biology and gender. Science has not been able, at this point, to supply a definitive answer to the question of why and how our sexual interests and desires arise. What the available evidence suggests is that sexual desires are partly intrinsic to the individual and partly learned or acquired from culture. How intrinsic and learned desires relate to one another, however, and the actual mechanisms that cause a given person to desire one thing or person but not another, remain an utter mystery.

Many of the things that people frequently find sexually desirable can be linked to reproductive success. Clear skin and good teeth are signs of health. Curvy female hips are a signal of sexual maturity and suggest that a woman will bear children easily. But there is huge variety in what can be found sexually appealing, and quite a bit of it has no meaningful bearing on reproductive success whatsoever. Long lean bodies, short fleshy bodies, pale skin, dark skin, blue eyes, brown eyes, red hair, black hair, moustaches, and hands with long thin fingers all have their ardent partisans, although none of these characteristics are necessary in order to make happy, healthy babies. Why should "gentlemen prefer blondes," as some assuredly do? Or redheads? Why should women find cleft chins appealing? What's the percentage in being besotted by freckles? Hard to say. There doesn't appear to be any obvious biological benefit in it. And, of course, sexual desires are not limited to human beings or their bodies. History tells us that people can and sometimes do feel sexual desire for, among rather a lot of other things, shoes, urine, barnyard animals, latex rubber, and trees. The so-called "reproductive imperative," in other words, is not necessarily what is driving the bus when it comes to our experiences of sexual desire, not even when what we desire is a human being of a different biological sex than ourselves.

The staggering variety of things we can and do desire is only exceeded by the number of things we do with them. How do we define a sexual activity as being a sexual activity, and what does it mean to engage in one? Historically, the criteria for what constituted "sexual activity" for most scientific purposes have been remarkably narrow, confined solely to the act of penis-in-vagina intercourse. Philosopher Marilyn Frye, in a 1988 essay entitled "Lesbian 'Sex,'" noted that in most sexological research, this was additionally narrowed to describe only the experiences of males. What this means is that for many decades, for the purposes of biomedical science, the sex act of record consisted of the insertion of an erect penis into a vagina, the thrusting of that penis within the vagina, and the ejaculation of semen from the penis followed by withdrawing the penis from the vagina.

You'd never know it from the insert-thrust-squirt-remove trajectory that serves as a description of this activity, but penis-in-vagina intercourse actually involves two people. Their genitals are very different, they engage in different physical activities during this type of intercourse, and they have different sensory experiences of it. Neither would you guess that human sexual activity included many other options, performable by many different combinations of participants of various biological sexes. This has been a very real problem in both the study and the popular discussion of sexual activity: a single lopsided model of a single activity is held up not just as the baseline from which all else departs, but as the alpha and omega of human sexual behavior.

The resulting picture we have developed of sexuality and its workings has historically been severely biased. Surely if we are trying to understand just what sexual activity and heterosexuality have to do with one another, and how that relationship might work, it is incumbent upon us likewise to consider that "sexual activity" doesn't look the same for everyone. As Lisa Diamond and Michael Bailey have begun to argue, the narrowly male-oriented focus of so much sexological research means that when it comes to sexual orientation, models developed on the basis of male-oriented research might not even be appropriate tools to use to help figure out how sexuality works for women.[5] The implications, insofar as the applicability of our current system of understanding and classifying sexuality, are staggering.

Another way in which our understanding-sexuality toolbox is often lacking concerns the variety of functions that sexual activity fulfills. People often attempt to justify the heterosexual/homosexual scheme on the basis of the fact that while different-sex couples can engage in reproductive sex, same-sex couples cannot. But reproduction is hardly the only reason different-sex couples engage in sexual activity. It cannot be. For purely mechanical reasons—because a specific sexual act must be performed by two fertile people of different biological sexes at the right time of the menstrual cycle for conception to even be possible—procreative sexual activity can only possibly account for a small subset of all sexual activity between women and men.

In truth, sexual activity is social activity. Our culture is often loath to recognize this, although we do embrace the idea that sexual activity can be about the social functions of expressing affection and intensifying social and emotional bonds. Indeed, many people believe that sex is only justified by love. But sexual activity has many other social roles to play. It can be a reward, a mode of exchange, a way to affirm loyalty, or an appeasement. It can be a commodity, a way of providing reassurance, and a rite of passage. As a source of pleasure it has few equals. It's an age-old means of asserting dominance and a visceral mode by which to demonstrate submission. It can furthermore be a means of gaining control, a way to humiliate and violate, and a way to punish. And any given sex act, no matter who engages in it, can and often will involve more than one of these dynamics.

The subjective experience of the erotic and of pleasure is, per-haps unsurprisingly, also enormously variable. It's not just that desires differ from one person to the next, or that some sexual episodes are transcendent and others are only so-so, but that identical objects or actions can provoke entirely different reactions depending on circum-stances. Not everything that is potentially desirable is *actually* desir-able. Not all "sex" is sexy. A lover we once found irresistible becomes repulsive after a nasty breakup. A sex act we enjoyed with one partner may just not do it for us when we try it with another. Some argue that it may not even be appropriate to call some examples of "sexual acts"—rape, for example—sexual at all.

All of this brings us back around to the issue of heterosexual-ity and what we must take into account if we are going to illuminate it in any way. Human sexuality, as should be clear by now, encom-passes much more than the ways that the biological sex(es) or so-cial gender(s) of the people we fancy compare to our own. Whom we choose as erotic-activity partners is just one aspect of what we do sexually. Words like "heterosexual" may hint at, but do not accurately denote, all the complexities (or vagaries, or ambiguities) of an indi-vidual's actual lived experience of sexuality.

Because there is so much inbuilt variability where sexuality is concerned, there are five caveats worth keeping in mind for any explo-ration of sexual orientation. First, the biological sex and social gender of a prospective partner are only two of many characteristics in which an individual may take a sexual interest, and their relative impor-tance is subjective and variable. Second, sexual desire (what we like or want) and sexual behavior (what we actually do) are not the same thing, and may or may not be related. Third, sexual and/or erotic ac-tivity take on considerably more forms than we may be personally accustomed to recognize, and certainly more forms exist overall than are sanctioned by any given culture. Fourth, we have to remember that all sexual activity is social activity, while only a small subset of all sex-ual activity is also reproductive activity. This means that it behooves us to think about sexual activity first as social, and only consider it as (potentially) reproductive when it actually is. And last, we must bear in mind that the relationships between perception, thought, emotion, and behavior are neither automatic nor consistent. In many cases they are demonstrably affected or directed by culture and socialization. We don't just want what we want because we want it; we want what we want because that's what we've learned to want.

With this in mind, we can proceed to take a look at the history of heterosexuality. As we should, because whether we like it or not, the idea of heterosexuality is embedded in each of us, in our actions and reactions, our emotional responses, and our intellectual assertions. We can see its distinctive imprint in the things we believe about love, in the ways we pursue pleasure, in the things we expect from our relationships, our work, our government, and our genitals. This concept we call "heterosexuality" doesn't just shape our sex lives; it shapes the ways we understand the world to work and, consequently, the ways it does. Heterosexuality reaches too far beyond the merely personal, and in too many profound and pervasive ways, for us to write it off as a simple matter of biology or nature or even Divine plan. It cannot be reduced to economics, the search for pleasure, or even to true love. It certainly cannot be reduced to a few checkboxes on a clinic form. All of these things may play a part in what we think of when we think about heterosexuality, but none of these things *are* heterosexuality.

CHAPTER ONE

The Love That Could Not Speak Its Name

One of the "top ten new species" of 2007, according to the International Institute for Species Exploration at Arizona State University, was a fish by the delightful name of *Electrolux addisoni*. But was *Electrolux* actually new? The ornate sleeper ray was familiar to the scuba divers and snorkelers who were sometimes greeted by it as they swam its home waters off the South African coast. Doubtless local fishermen had known about it even longer. But in another sense, *Electrolux* was genuinely novel. It became "new" on the day a biologist confirmed that it hadn't previously been documented, gave it a name, and triumphantly added it to the rosters of official, openly shared, systemic human knowledge.

As the case of *Electrolux* demonstrates, there is a difference between simply *being* and *being known*. No one would attempt to argue that this fish had no existence prior to the time it was given a scientific name. Yet suddenly, in 2007, it was "new." Written documentation of a particular kind, by an authority figure of a particular kind, was what turned *Electrolux addisoni* from a thing that just *was,* whether anyone knew about it or not, into a thing that *was known.*

In the nineteenth century, a similar thing happened to heterosexuals. Prior to 1868, there were no heterosexuals. There were no homosexuals either, for that matter. For most of human history, love might have been romantic or platonic, brotherly or maternal, *eros* or *agape*, but it was definitively not heterosexual or homosexual, straight or gay. The names did not exist, nor did the categories they now describe. In the mid-nineteenth century, Western people in general were only beginning to think or speak in terms of there being different types of human beings who were differentiated from one another by the kinds of love or sexual desire they experienced.[1]

Specific sexual behaviors, to be sure, were named, categorized, and judged. This was nothing new. They had been for more than a thousand years. The most famous example of this is the term "sodomy." As a term and an idea, if not as a practice, "sodomy" arose from the Catholic Church, which for much of Western history was the highest authority on matters of behavior and morals (among rather a lot else) in the West. The Catholic Church has historically disapproved, on principle, of all sexual activity that is not potentially procreative. This is the broadest definition of "sodomy."

Sodomy was sodomy no matter whom it involved. Sodomy could take place between a man and a woman, two men, two women, or some other combination of participants. A "sodomite" was not a kind of person but a person who committed a particular type of sin. In the same way that a usurer committed the act of moneylending or a murderer committed the act of killing, a sodomite committed the act of sodomy. It was not an identity label but a rap sheet.

Part of the Catholic understanding of "sodomy" was an awareness that sexual sin was something that could happen to anyone. Simply feeling desire put one at risk. Sexual misbehavior was not a marker of some sort of constitutional difference but merely evidence of temptation unsuccessfully resisted.

This sensibility is a large part of why, prior to the nineteenth century, Western culture did not include the concept that all people were split into two sexual camps. It is also why there does not seem to have been much sense, prior to the eighteenth century, of people thinking in terms of a hierarchy of sexual "types." The tendency instead was to think in terms of people who, openly or covertly, occasionally or habitually, engaged in a variety of sexual acts. Some of those acts were more sinful than others. The only sex act that was not considered sinful in the eyes of the Catholic Church was potentially procreative penis-in-vagina intercourse performed within the context of a valid marriage, and even that had to be performed in particular ways and limited to specific times.

Much has changed. We are now so used to thinking of sexuality in terms of orientations and identities, "deviant" versus "normal," that it hardly occurs to us that there might be workable alternatives to our customary ways of thinking. But history shows that there are actually many such alternatives. The desire for sexual activity has been thought about, as in classic Catholic dogma, as a manifestation of the unruly appetites of the earthly body, possibly goaded on by forces of evil. But the desire for sexual activity has also been imagined simply as a biological function, like eating or elimination, a common concept in both Classical thought and in the neoclassical thought of the intellectual eighteenth century.

Our modern habit of interpreting sexual desire as a manifestation of our identities, part and parcel of our individual human selves, is merely one more option. But since the nineteenth century, this has been the option our culture has chosen more than any other. As French philosopher Michel Foucault famously put it in his *History of Sexuality,* a particular sexual type became "a personage, a past, a case history, and a childhood, in addition to being a type of life, a life form, and a morphology. . . . It was consubstantial with him, less as a habitual sin than as a singular nature." This is the view upon which the existence of "heterosexual" depends.

This was not an overnight shift but a process. Although it had its roots in earlier changes in philosophy and science and law, the nineteenth century became the era in which the decisive shift occurred. By the end of the nineteenth century, Western culture had learned to view sexual desire and activity not as a unified field on its own, but as a collection of specific and distinctive desires and activities, each of which had a role to play in helping to define a specific and distinctive subtype of human being. Many different desires and acts were given official names in this period, making the momentous shift from merely *being* to *being known.* As these desires and acts were defined and characterized and written down in the right authoritative ways by the right authoritative people, they were used to help create another set of known entities: sexual types. Of these, the most powerful and important, and certainly the most enduring and culture-altering, were "homosexual" and "heterosexual."

Because the terms have become ubiquitous, we forget that "homosexual" and "heterosexual" come from this very particular time and place. Every era has its own catchphrases and neologisms. Our world is not static, and as new ideas and objects enter the culture so do new words and phrases, even as old ways of thinking and outmoded vocabulary fade. We happily and knowledgeably chat about computer geeks and geneticists, but no longer about alchemists or natural philosophers. We would consider it rather stilted to speak of bluestockings, jesters, and foundlings, but we are quite comfortable speaking of women intellectuals, comedians, and children who have been put up for adoption. Such changes in language can convey far more than just dictionary meanings. For instance, "Negro," "colored," "black," "African American," and "person of color" could all technically be used to refer to the same person. But their historical freight gives each of these words different associations, so much so that we have strong preferences about which ones we would willingly choose. Words and the ways we use them are always rooted in time and in place.

This is particularly important when we consider "heterosexual." What Jonathan Ned Katz has called "the invention of heterosexuality" took place at a specific point in history, in a unique intertwining of historical and cultural streams. Put simply, these terms came to exist because a need was perceived to identify people as representatives of generic types distinguished on the basis of their tendencies to behave sexually in particular ways. The story of how this need arose is a story of industrialization and urbanization, the rise of the middle classes, the complications of empire, and the scientific and philosophical legacies of the Enlightenment, all of which contributed to creating a world in which the idea of a type of human being called "heterosexual" made a specific and useful kind of sense.

SEX AND SIN IN THE NEW CITY

In the nineteenth century, the cities of Europe and North America began to swell at a previously unimaginable pace. By 1835 London reached a population of one million, while its nearest Continental rival, Paris, hit the million mark in 1846. Urban growth took place at exponential rates: New York City boasted 60,515 residents in the 1800 census . . . and a whopping 3,437,202 in 1900.

Behind the urban explosion lay newly mechanized and rapidly growing industry and its rapacious appetite for laborers—not to mention all the goods and services that a swelling population requires. The promise of steady work and steady pay lured the rural working classes out of the hinterlands by the hundreds of thousands in a twin process of urbanization and corresponding rural population drain that continues around the world even today. It is impossible to overstate, and nearly impossible to imagine for those of us who have always lived in a world with enormous industrialized cities, how dramatically the modern metropolis has altered human culture.

These hugely increased, unprecedentedly dense populations transformed urban experience. All sorts of common but unorthodox sexual activities like prostitution, sexual violence, and same-sex eroticism seemed suddenly more frequent, more random, and more out of control than they had been when the cities and their populations were both much smaller. Certainly, by comparison to rural towns and villages, the cities seemed like hotbeds of sexual misconduct and excess. It also appeared to many that people not only engaged in more sexual misconduct in the cities, but that they were more likely to get away with it. This was often true, since city populations frequently lacked the social unity and interdependence of the smaller villages and towns, making community enforcement of proper behavior both less possible and less likely. Some rural modes of policing sexual behavior survived in the cities, at least for a while. The charivari, a gritty mob of people banging pots and pans, tooting horns, and singing gleefully filthy songs under the windows of an illicit couple, for instance, survived in both the United Kingdom and the United States until at least the First World War. But neither rowdy noisemaking nor shotgun weddings, nor even the odd spot of vigilante justice, could conceivably address all of the sexual crimes that took place in a big city.

This might, in theory, have been a job for the police. In reality, policing as a branch of civil service was still in its infancy, with City of London police chartered by statute in 1839 and New York City forming a police force only in 1845. The responsibilities and reach of city police forces took time to work themselves out, and the law and the courts would similarly scramble for decades to catch up with the regulatory and disciplinary needs of the swelling cities. To those who lived in cities—and even to those who only heard stories about them—the urban world was a frightening, dirty, dangerous place, especially from a sexual standpoint, full of prostitutes and predators.

Urban sexual misconduct was typically, if inaccurately, blamed on the lower classes. Because the fastest-growing groups in the new city were the working class and the poor, it often appeared that the rising rates of sexual misconduct reflected the socioeconomic class of these new urbanites rather than merely the larger overall population. The middle and upper classes, who prided themselves on their moral rectitude (and had the additional advantage of enjoying all the discretion money could buy), had no trouble ascribing disproportionate, even innate, degeneracy to their socioeconomic inferiors.

This was not a new idea. Western Europe had long held to the idea that all creatures belonged to a grand overarching hierarchy. Since the medieval era, a central notion of Western thought was the idea of the *scala naturae* or Great Chain of Being, the concept that all living beings had a place in a strict hierarchy that led inexorably upward from dirt to plants to animals to humans to the angels and ultimately to God. As one ascended this natural ladder, one ascended in perfection. Wealth, health, moral uprightness, and social dominance were all considered proofs of superiority, while inferiority betrayed itself in poverty, sickness, immorality, and powerlessness. All men were automatically higher than all women, white-skinned people automatically higher than dark-skinned, and Christians above those of other faiths. The Great Chain thus furnished a conceptual framework that would be important later: the idea that inherent or quasi-inherent "imperfections," such as particular sexual habits, could be part of the intrinsic makeup of whole classes of people.

As the nineteenth century wore on, the Great Chain of Being acquired a sort of slantwise sibling in evolutionary theory. Charles Darwin himself never asserted that evolution represented the same sort of grand ladder of ascending perfection. Indeed, the fact that the notion of progress toward an ultimate Godly perfection was entirely excluded from Darwin's characterization of natural selection was part of what made his theories so controversial. But this did not stop people from applying the teleology of the Great Chain to the principles of natural selection and evolution. In particular, the "science" of eugenics recasts the basic principles of the Great Chain onto natural selection in a particularly poisonous way. (Eugenics and Darwinism were related in a literal way as well as a figurative one: as a field, eugenics was pioneered by Darwin's cousin, Sir Francis Galton.) Eugenicists believed that human evolution had a goal, and that this goal was to produce ever better and fitter human beings. Therefore, they reasoned, a lack of moral or physical virtue directly reflected a hereditary deficit. For instance, the "moral imbecile." "Moral imbeciles," in the eyes of eugenicists, were simply born without the ability to feel or act morally, just as an imbecile—what we would now call a developmentally disabled person—was born without the ability to think or reason normally. Eugenicists saw both kinds of imbeciles as examples of evolutionary error, and of undesirable clutter in the gene pool.

At the same time as Darwin's theories were enthusiastically seized upon by eugenicists, "social Darwinists," and other champions of the hierarchy of life encapsulated in the Great Chain of Being, they also helped to facilitate a wholesale questioning of the whole notion of a fixed human hierarchy. Egalitarianism and universal human rights were relatively new concepts at the turn of the nineteenth century, brought to the attention of most as a result of the French and American revolutions of the late eighteenth century. At the time of the rise of the monster cities of the West, these progressive ideas by no means dominated the scene. The idea that birth was worth, and that one's place in the Great Chain was not really something one could change, was still common even as people began to simultaneously entertain the notions that perhaps this should not matter and that a civil society might have an interest in behaving as if it mattered less, or perhaps not at all.

As the cities grew, the pragmatic value of civil egalitarianism became increasingly evident. Whether a country was headed by a king or a president, whether it maintained a formal aristocracy or insisted upon equality of citizenship, the intense population pressure of the cities made it increasingly apparent that the masses required some sort of management. Merely asserting old hierarchies of class was not going to get the job done either, because in the new industrial economy hierarchies of class were changing, too. What was required were systematic, reproducible, universally applicable systems for social management that could be implemented on a large scale.

It is no coincidence that we first see this happening with regard to sex in early Napoleonic France. Beginning as early as 1802, when the French government began regulating and registering Parisian prostitutes via the Bureau des Moeurs (Bureau of Morals) and Bureau Sanitaire (Bureau of Health), the policing of the sexual activity of the general public increasingly became a problem for the state. Many efforts focused on specific problem behaviors like prostitution, or health problems like venereal diseases. In England, the infamous Contagious Diseases Acts (enacted in 1864) attempted to stem the tide of the latter by rigidly controlling the former, complete with compulsory gynecological exams. Other early attempts at managing the sexuality of the masses were more philosophical in nature, such as the campaign to raise the age of consent that became such a hot-button issue in the English 1870s.[2]

The law was integral to this effort to impose greater control over the sexual behavior of citizens. Central to this legal effort, in turn, was the process of creating a body of work that helped to support the law and aid it in doing its managerial work. The new secular state required secular justification for its laws, and professionals in many fields began to apply themselves to the task of providing it. Physicians like Richard von Krafft-Ebing would do this in a particular and distinctive way. Drawing on an Enlightenment legacy of scientific naming, a variety of sexual behaviors and characteristics were suddenly made both "new" and "known" thanks to Krafft-Ebing's classification and assignment of scholarly names. Krafft-Ebing's book *Psychopathia Sexualis* (1886) was a pioneering, and highly problematic, index to disorders of the "sexual instinct" and the human types subject to them.

As with the ornate sleeper ray that became *Electrolux addisoni* in 2007, none of the actual behaviors Krafft-Ebing catalogued were new to the annals of human experience. Krafft-Ebing no more "discovered" the various sexual peccadilloes of the human race than he could've "discovered" his own grandfather. But he did apply a formal taxonomy to the sexual actions and actors he described. Although he was not the one who coined the word, his taxonomic vocabulary also included the word "heterosexual," its first adoption in the medical literature.

WHAT'S IN A NAME

Naming and cataloging can be real and powerful science. They can also be real and powerful cultural magic. This is precisely why we have to be wary of who is in charge of naming and cataloging things, what their motivations are in doing so, and how they go about doing it. If the right person with the right qualifications names a thing or a phenomenon in the right way, chances are excellent that other people will accept unquestioningly that that thing or phenomenon is a real scientific (which is to say objective and material) entity. By the mid-nineteenth century, when the word "heterosexual" was first coined—in a letter written May 6, 1868, by a writer named Karl Maria Kertbeny—scientific naming was a ritual that had the weight of more than a hundred years of authority behind it. But the process of scientific naming was not always as objective, or as material, as we often suppose.

Science is at root a social effort. As a discipline, material science—whether physical or biological—is a collective effort carried out by a large, loosely affiliated group of people for the greater good, and it is subject to a certain amount of human bias no matter what we do. We are simply not capable of omniscience, and so we must choose what we will pay attention to at any given instant, what qualities of an object we will decide are important enough to observe, characterize, and record. This alone is enough to show our hand.

The history of taxonomy bears this out to a degree that is frankly astonishing, and which hints at some of the human prejudice to come later in the cataloging and naming of human sexuality. Carolus Linnaeus, the brilliant Swedish father of scientific naming and self-anointed "prince of botanists," was an ardently Christian academic who wrote lengthy compendiums in scholarly Latin. He was also a bit of a sexual obsessive. Once Linnaeus had finished with them, all plants known to him had been classed according to the number and function of their sex organs, and many of them had been named for genitals as well. With a decided knack for the unsavory image, he

named a stinkhorn fungus *Phallus daemonicum,* and a perfectly in-
nocuous North American shrub commonly called the Jamaica caper
became *Capparis cynophallophora*—the caper that bears a dog's penis.
Even during his lifetime, Linnaeus's relentless sexualizing of his subject matter often raised critical eyebrows and occasionally inspired
tirades in print. Linnaeus, in turn, immortalized his critics by naming
ugly or noxious plants after them. The most famous example of this
is the unattractive little relative of the aster called *Siegesbeckia,* named
for Johann Siegesbeck, an academic who took strong exception to the
"loathsome harlotry" of Linnaeus's work.

We can perhaps understand why others might've been frustrated.
Linnaeus's system was more than a little offbeat and decidedly arbitrary in what it chose to describe: the *nuptiae plantarum,* or marriages of plants. He did not mean this as a euphemism. A world of
human social and sexual expectations was encoded in his categories.
Monandria were one-husbanded plants, tidily monogamous, with a
single pistil (female sex organ) and a single stamen (male sex organ)
in a given flower. *Dodecandria,* on the other hand, had a disturbingly
numerous twelve "husbands" per bloom. Linnaeus's assumption was
that all plants "married." He did not presume that plants like mosses,
whose "weddings" he could not observe, were simply not the "marrying type"; it would take later observers to realize that many mosses
actually reproduce asexually. Linnaeus could not bear the thought
of it and so consigned them to the class of *cryptogamia,* those who
married in secret.

Linnaeus and his sex-obsessed work would almost be laughable
if they hadn't been so influential. Linnaeus's taxonomic principles—if
not necessarily his sexual focus in applying them—became the basis
for a breathtakingly prolific discipline. The 1735 first edition of Linnaeus's *Systema Naturae* was a mere eleven pages, but by the thirteenth
and last edition in 1767, the book had grown to over three thousand
pages. (Currently, the Species 2000 initiative database project based at
University of Reading is working toward a valid checklist of all known
species of organism, and their rolls included, as of 2009, more than
one million species.)

The cataloging of known things, and the establishment of names
for those things, remains a central project of science. The fact that it is

a profoundly human endeavor, saturated with human values and prejudices, is one of science's open secrets, betrayed in the very language that is used to name things. Dead languages cannot remove human fingerprints. "Phallus daemonicum" is as overt a cultural reference as "Electrolux."[3] Or, as we shall soon see, as "heterosexual."

Cataloging and naming human characteristics is but an extension of the principle of cataloging and naming natural objects and phenomena. When nineteenth-century culture began to perceive a need to manage sexual behavior on a civic level, it also had to devise language and concepts with which to talk about them. The language that already existed for doing this lay mostly within the realm of religion—the syntax of sin and sinners, virtue and saints. Neither that language nor the Church authority on which it rested were terribly desirable to the new secular state. The practice of scientific naming provided a logical place to turn. The physical and biological sciences (including medicine) could claim a politically valuable neutrality: the objects that science investigated were not the works of man but the works of nature. Scientists could claim that they merely looked at what *was*. It was the right tool at the right time. But as we have seen, much might depend on what was chosen for observation and by whom.

It can scarcely come as a surprise that much of what was chosen for observation, when human sexuality became the object of study, was chosen because it was perceived as troublesome. Nor can it come as a surprise that those who decided to take upon themselves the task of cataloging and naming these troublesome sexual behaviors had very strong opinions about the objects of their investigation, opinions that influenced their work. Sexuality had, after all, become a pressing public issue, and it wanted effective handling by people who understood just how serious an issue it was. Nothing less than the fate of the family—and even the nation—was at stake.

FOCUS ON THE FAMILY

If the morally grey, sexually suspect world of the working-class city was the realm of public concern and state regulation, the private and eminently respectable realm of the middle-class family was one of the primary things all that regulation was intended to protect. Beginning in the late eighteenth century, a new "focus on the family" emerged as a primary concern for the newly fledged middle classes whose reach, ranks, and social power were on the rise.

Unlike inherited aristocratic wealth, middle-class money came from work in the professions, from trade, or, increasingly, from ownership and management of industry. Just as with the aristocracy, tight control over marriages, families, and children was key to protecting and increasing this wealth and security. But the middle classes did this in their own distinctive ways. Where the aristocracy (or indeed a traditional rural working household) would base its ideas of family and lineage on the management of hereditary rank and property, the middle classes, as historian Lawrence Stone has explained, organized themselves around four central and distinctively modern features: intense emotional bonds, a brash new emphasis on personal autonomy, an unprecedented interest in privacy, and an intensified interest in sex.[4]

This last point may seem surprising, but it shouldn't. The stereotypical Victorian prude, and the Victorian lady of scrupulous sexual ignorance and passivity, did exist—their modern-day analogues do too—but there was far more to Victorian sexuality than this. Victorians, including women, talked more and in greater detail about sexual issues than any previous generation we know of.

It was an era of wide-ranging and often extreme opinions on all aspects of sex. Some Victorians were indeed sex-phobic, misogynist, and prudish, even priggish. Physicians like William Acton famously made statements like "the majority of women are (happily for them) not very much troubled with sexual feeling of any kind," and British gynecologist Isaac Baker Brown did advocate, and perform, surgical removal of the clitoris as a cure for female masturbation.[5] But even among his colleagues, Acton was known as an illogical extremist, and Baker Brown was eventually drummed out of the profession.

Other Victorians' views of sex were quite progressive. Political publisher Richard Carlile professed a belief that women "had an almost constant desire for copulation," and only social constraints kept them from acting on it. Wishful thinking, perhaps, given the lack of both social approval and reliable contraception, but others were similarly bold about giving sexuality pride of place in human affairs.

"Sexual matters," wrote the popular physician and advisor Henry Guernsey, "are so thoroughly interwoven with the highest destinies of the human race, physically, mentally, and spiritually, there is scarcely any function of higher import."[6]

Most nineteenth-century middle-class individuals struggled to find a sexual middle ground—not as negative and harsh as the views of Acton or Baker Brown, but probably not as openly enthusiastic as those of Carlile or Guernsey either—where they could feel comfortable, respectable, and safe. This was no small task. The bourgeois family, with its hothouse emotions and its pigeon-hole privacies, was supposed to be a fortress and a shield, providing a buffer zone of respectability that protected its members from aristocratic decadence on the one side and the horrors of the teeming city on the other. The purpose of this family was the generation and formation of people—specifically men—who would form an unassailable backbone for the state.

The deliberate formation of a solid, respectable, and powerful middle-class culture was more than a reaction against the aristocracy or, in the New World, an effort to embody the "more perfect union" envisioned by America's founding fathers. It was also an effort to create a strong national core that could survive increasing exposure to the world. By the mid-nineteenth century, the United States, Great Britain, and nearly all of the European states had extended their reach, as well as their armies and economies, to the far corners of the globe. Whether in British India, the Belgian Congo, German East Africa, French Cambodia, or any of the legion other European or American appropriations, successful empires required adept management of far-flung possessions inconveniently populated by vast numbers of people who didn't look, think, or act like their colonial overlords. "Natives" were often thought of as primitive or childlike, in dire need of the civilizing influence of the superior European. (Fear of a brown planet is, in other words, nothing new. Nor is the racist, paternalistic sentiment well summarized as "what these people need is a honky.") But the elite and the aristocracy did not have the numbers to provide more than the uppermost layer of top brass. The majority of colonial personnel came out of the middle classes. A powerful middle class allowed European and European-descended whites to maintain their sense of themselves as standard-bearers, those whose "fitness to rule" equipped them for empire.

The question on everyone's mind was whether the middle classes would prove equal to the task. There was a pervasive fear that the bourgeoisie, with their comfortable houses and citified ways, were creating men who were hopelessly enervated, dissipated, weak, and diseased. Neurasthenia was a rather vague "illness" first characterized in 1869 by American physician George Miller Beard. It afflicted men with fatigue, anxiety, headache, depression, and sexual impotence, to which they succumbed when an insufficiently sturdy constitution was subjected to an overly stressful and stimulating world. To many it seemed as if "respectable," strong, competent white masculinity was disappearing, creating the looming specter of what Theodore Roosevelt would later call "race suicide." As Darwin's evolutionary theory became popular, some began to wonder if perhaps it was happening backwards, the respectable classes eroding generation by generation, perhaps to the point where they might become indistinguishable from those troublesome teeming masses. When British army major-general Sir Frederick Maurice worried publicly about the problem of "where to get Men,"[7] it wasn't the problem of finding males that concerned him. Paranoia and pessimism about manhood were so intense that Daniel Carter Beard, the highly influential founder of the American Boy Scouts, entitled his 1939 autobiography *Hardly a Man Is Now Alive*.

Manliness, in turn, was tightly linked to sexuality. "Real men" were virile, but virility meant both sexual potency and its strict and well-socialized control. Any form of "deviance," including masturbation, was not only morally wrong; it was also believed to drain men's bodies of vital essences and cause illness. Sylvester Graham, he of the eponymous health-food cracker, claimed that a man who could make it to the age of thirty without giving in to the temptations of his sexual urges would be a veritable god. Historian Angus McLaren devotes an entire book, *The Trials of Masculinity*, to looking at the ways in which unorthodox sexuality—whether real or imagined, harmless or hurtful—was used from the mid-nineteenth century through the 1930s as a way to separate the "real men" from the "degenerates" and "perverts." It was a terrifically effective strategy. As William James noted an 1895 essay entitled "Degeneration and Genius," "Call a man a 'cad' and you've settled his social status. Call him a 'degenerate,' and you've grouped him with the most loathsome specimens of the race."[8]

Sexual degeneracy became a yardstick with which to take the measure of a man. Pimps and procurers, exhibitionists, effeminates, pornographers, and bigamists, as well as more exotic creatures like sadists, fetishists, and necrophiles, came under intense scrutiny. So too, notably, did men who had sex with other men. Rapists and those who preyed sexually on young women, however, were often ignored on the basis that they were more unmannerly or uncivil than they were abnormal or "degenerate." Journalistic muckraker W. T. Stead noted with some truth during the 1895 Oscar Wilde trial that if Wilde, "instead of indulging in dirty tricks with boys and men, had ruined the lives of half a dozen simpletons of girls, or had broken up the home of his friend's wife, no one would have laid a finger on him."

The desire to identify and weed out these "degenerates" and "deviants" had, by the middle third of the nineteenth century, become a pressing one. How it was to be done, on the other hand, and how exactly to describe and define the kinds of "degeneracy" in question, was far from clear. Laws concerning sexuality, mostly inherited from the canon law of the Catholic Church, tended to be vaguely worded and imprecise. Other disciplines were no better. Little wonder that the gap was not long left empty, given the pressure on the middle-class male to form the right kind of family, be the right kind of man, and, moreover, be able to specify what made him so.

THE INVENTION OF HETEROSEXUALITY

Had the German-speaking world not been going through some legislative growing pains in the 1860s, we might still live in a world without heterosexuals. Germany came together in 1866 along geographic lines that are more or less familiar to us today, an amalgamation of the multiple German-speaking kingdoms, duchies, and principalities of the North German Confederation joined together under a generally Prussian leadership. Like many civil governments, Germany was still wrestling with the implications of the French Revolution, as well as feeling the aftershocks of its own revolutionary conflicts in 1848. The new ideals of secular and civil government compelled German law-makers, as they revised their legal codes to suit a new, composite nation, to figure out what to do with inherited collections of sex-related laws that were often more or less identical to old Church decrees.

It was a fraught process. Paragraph 143 of the Prussian Penal Code of April 14, 1851, in particular, provoked significant protest. P. 143 stipulated harsh punishments, consisting of up to five years at hard labor and accompanied by the loss of civil rights during the period of punishment, for anyone convicted of "unnatural fornication between people and animals, as well as between persons of the male sex." The rationale given for this law, and the severity of its consequences, was that "such behavior is a demonstration of especial degeneration and degradation of the person, and is so dangerous to morality."[9] The law, clearly written to sound dispassionate, nonetheless sounds the old familiar religious gong of morality and sin. As befitting a post-Enlightenment, science-respecting culture, the law invoked Nature as both a stand-in for God and a dispassionate secular authority. The addition of degeneracy made it au courant with fears of a decaying race. Taken all together, P. 143 provided highly effective leverage against sexual misconduct for the government. It also, inevitably, provided the same for blackmailers. Officially or unofficially, it was a law to ruin lives with.

Among the individuals who stepped forward to oppose the law were Karl Ulrichs and Karl-Maria Kertbeny. They were not friends, though they corresponded for a while, and only Ulrichs is known to have been attracted to men. But both shared the conviction that P. 143 was unjust, and it is due to their work that we have the word and the concept of the "heterosexual."

Ulrichs's devoted opposition to P. 143 stemmed from his having been sacked from a promising bureaucratic career when his attractions to men were discovered. The injustice led him to devote his life to arguing, as logically and as rigorously as he could, that same-sex sexuality was natural, inborn, and unchangeable, and therefore ought not to be punished. Ulrichs was no scientist, but he scoured the medical literature for insights into his own sexual condition. Impressed by medical literature about hermaphrodites, he developed a theory that he too was a type of hermaphrodite. Where hermaphrodites' bodies encompassed both male-typical and female-typical organs in the same body, Ulrichs claimed that the *Urning*, or man who loved men, had a male body but a female mind. (The notion that gender—the social aspects of sexuality—might be separable from biological sex did not become widespread until the second half of the twentieth century.) Ulrichs's theory of "sexual inversion," rigorously logical by the standards of the day, was presented in 1864 in a pair of pseudonymously self-published pamphlets. Ulrichs hoped that his pamphlets would persuade German legislators to change their minds, and thus the law.

Austro-Hungarian Karl Maria Kertbeny shared Ulrichs's conviction that the Prussian law was unjust. A friend and coworker's suicide, committed because a blackmailer threatened to expose the young man's "abnormal tastes," had opened Kertbeny's eyes to the problems inherent in a law that made it illegal for two men to engage in activities that a man and a woman could partake of together without consequence. Kertbeny produced two strongly worded, anonymously published pamphlets arguing against Paragraph 143 that employed the notion of human rights as derived from the French Declaration of the Rights of Man and Citizen.

Ulrichs's and Kertbeny's approaches differed in many ways. While Ulrichs leaned on the innate femininity of the *Urning* psyche in order to emphasize the involuntary character of same-sex desires, Kertbeny insisted that men who loved men were typically manly and virile and deserving of full citizenship in the modern state. Ulrichs's approach, with its insistence that men who loved men were on some level not male, implicitly endorsed the idea that biological sex could be legitimate grounds for different treatment under the law. Kertbeny, by contrast, took a leaf from English philosopher Jeremy Bentham's book and argued simply that it was wrong to punish actions that harmed no one and all the more unethical to punish them selectively according to the biological sexes of the participants. The two men shared a moderately sized correspondence, but Kertbeny never adopted Ulrichs's models or his terminology. He preferred his own system of classification, first explicated in a letter to Ulrichs on May 6, 1868, in which he opposed "homosexuals" to "heterosexuals" as two parallel and, he implied, equal types of human beings.

As it turned out neither man's argument, nor their associated terminology, made any dent in the law. Paragraph 143 and similar laws were retained through multiple incarnations of the German legal code, later becoming P. 175 in 1871 when Germany was fully united. Later, and infamously, Hitler used this law to legitimize the incarceration and murder of thousands of *Schwülen,* or "faggots," in the concentration camps. The law was not removed from the books until 1969. By that time, the "heterosexual" and "homosexual" terminology of those who had so stalwartly resisted it in the beginning had won out, and so for the most part had the view of sexuality those terms implied.[10] The rise of "heterosexual" was hardly instantaneous, however. Moreover, it had virtually nothing to do with Ulrichs or Kertbeny at all.

A SEXUALITY CALLED NORMAL

Thus we return to Krafft-Ebing and *Psychopathia Sexualis.* The popularization of the word "heterosexual" was far from being Krafft-Ebing's goal in writing his book. Like Kertbeny and Ulrichs, Krafft-Ebing's interests did not really lie with the sexually typical or the heterosexual, but again with the heterodox, the outlier, and the sexual "deviant." Although Krafft-Ebing did inadvertently establish "heterosexual" and "heterosexuality" as biomedical terms in its pages, his actual purpose for creating *Psychopathia Sexualis* was the systematic observation, description, naming, and categorization of sexual deviance for the sake of the law. In the 1886 introduction to the first edition, Krafft-Ebing wrote that he hoped the catalog would be of aid to the judges and legislators compelled to issue rulings in cases of sexual misconduct.

Psychopathia Sexualis was unquestionably groundbreaking. At the same time it was derivative—Krafft-Ebing does not acknowledge his debts to either Ulrichs or Kertbeny, among others—and not very well organized. But it was the earliest known attempt at compiling a comprehensive list of disorders of the "sexual instinct." In the grand Linnaean tradition, it is a compendium of exotic "new" species of human being, classified according to their particular sexual quirks or pathologies and given names predominantly formulated, per the well-established ritual, from bits of dead languages.

If we read between the lines of Krafft-Ebing's terminology, we get a pretty clear idea of what he was willing to characterize as appropriate, healthy sexuality: potentially procreative intercourse and very little else. Krafft-Ebing's views were rather akin to those of the Catholic Church: anything that did not lead to the ultimate goal of procreation was inappropriate, if not outright pathological. Even at that, Krafft-Ebing held, one had to engage in this potentially procreative inter-course at the right time of life. Those who were sexual at the wrong time—during childhood or old age—suffered from *paradoxia*. One additionally had to do it with the right attitude. Too much interest in sex and you had a case of *hyperaesthesia*, too little and it was *anaesthesia*. There seemed to be an endless number of ways in which one could deviate just a bit too much from wholesome sexuality.

Newly christened and described, these and a variety of other het-erodox behaviors and characteristics, including sadism, masochism, and fetishism, entered the lexicons and the communal imaginations not just of medicine but also of law, government, and the general pub-lic. Krafft-Ebing's book was highly academic, and he went out of his way to pen the really juicy bits in Latin on the theory that it would limit the consumption of potentially titillating information. This di-minished the readership not at all, since most middle-class European men of the day were sufficiently well educated that a little bit of Latin posed no obstacle. In any event, there were soon translations aplenty, including the first American English edition in 1893. So much for the old catchalls of sodomy and "crimes against nature"; the increas-ingly widely understood message was that the modern sexual deviant *specialized*.

None of these specialized behaviors, it bears repeating, were new to the annals of human experience. Many had well-established slang names. "The game at flatts," for instance, was an Enlightenment-era English phrase referring to sex between women, both of whom had "flat" genitals. But a formal taxonomy made these activities, and those who engaged in them, real in a whole new way. Nowhere was this truer than in the case of the word "heterosexual," twenty-four appear-ances of which are scattered throughout Krafft-Ebing's book.

Like its sibling "homosexual," the word "heterosexual" is a stitched-together Frankenstein's monster of a term, half Latin, half Greek. In Krafft-Ebing, it is used alongside "normal-sexual" without much apparent preference for one over the other. It seems to have been only after *Psychopathia Sexualis* became a standard text, and its terminology began to see further use in the medical literature, that the more scholarly sounding "heterosexual" finally found its niche.

As Jonathan Ned Katz writes in his *The Invention of Heterosexuality,* Krafft-Ebing's "disturbing (and fascinating) examples of a sex called sick began quietly to define a new idea of a sex perceived as healthy." That healthy sexuality centered around reproduction, but Krafft-Ebing grudgingly acknowledged that it also encompassed the desire for and pursuit of erotic pleasure. This was a watershed. After Krafft-Ebing, the "sexual instinct" could refer to erotic desire as well as reproductive potential.

"Heterosexual" did not, however, spring forth as a household word with a single uncontested meaning. For a few years, it was used as a term of pathology. The first time the word appeared in English, predating the English translation of *Psychopathia Sexualis* by a year, was in an 1892 journal article by Chicago physician James G. Kiernan. Kiernan and a few contemporaries employed "heterosexual" using a different understanding of the Greek "hetero," or "different," to mean "both." Kiernan's "heterosexuals" were people we would now call bisexual. *Dorland's Medical Dictionary* of 1901 repeats this, but additionally defines the term to mean an "abnormal or perverted appetite toward the opposite sex." That definition was echoed in the Merriam-Webster *New International Dictionary* of 1923. The early use of "heterosexual" to describe behaviors that were considered pathological reflects, more than anything else, a deep-seated anxiety about sexual desire. It took English sexologist Havelock Ellis to resolve these anxieties and to stabilize "heterosexual" with a meaning that approaches the way we use the word today. By 1915, Ellis had begun to use the word "heterosexual" as shorthand for a type of relationship between male/female pairs that simultaneously included the ennobling emotion of love, the potential for procreation, and the experience of erotic pleasure.

By the time the unabridged second edition of the Merriam-Webster dictionary was published in 1934, "heterosexual" had appeared in mainstream print in both England and the United States.[11] The 1934 definition of the term, according to Merriam-Webster, was "manifestation of sexual passion for one of the opposite sex; normal sexuality." The normal-sexual was the heterosexual, and the heterosexual was normally, typically, acceptably, even laudably sexual. With the help of good old-fashioned scientific taxonomy, a model for sexual desire and activity between men and women had not only been legitimized; it had been made emblematic of an inherent physical and psychological normalcy that suited both respectable middle-class families and the well-regulated secular state. The modern heterosexual had officially been born.

CHAPTER TWO

Carnal Knowledge

Imagine yourself poking around the attic of your grandmother's house. Breathing the dusty, close air under the eaves, you open an old trunk to find several diaries bound in old, cracked leather, all written in the same gracefully looping hand. The name written on the flyleaf is familiar, a great-great uncle's. Intrigued, you flip through the yellowed pages, only to stop when something catches your eye, a passage in which your long-dead ancestor wrote that he and a friend named William "retired early and in each other's arms did friendship sink peacefully to sleep."[1]

You look back a few pages. It seems that this is an old boarding school friend of your great-great uncle's he's talking about, who came to visit him at home several years after they had both graduated. They would both have been grown men by then, though still on the young side, early twenties, perhaps. These two were sharing a bed? Falling asleep in each other's arms? Hmmm. Maybe it was just a figure of speech.

Next you sift through a bundle of letters addressed to your great-great-grandfather, each still tucked into its brittle old envelope. You open one, a long, chatty missive from one of his law school classmates, commiserating with your great-great-grandfather about the difficulties of starting a law practice in a strange town. Maybe, the letter writer ventures, it would be easier if they could cooperate somehow. Then you turn the page. "Yes, James, I must come; we will yoke together again; your little bed is just wide enough; we will practise at the same bar, and be as friendly a pair of single fellows as ever cracked a nut."[2]

What would you think if you stumbled across these family heirlooms? Would you think you came from a long line of closet cases? Would you assume, based on the available evidence, that your great-great-grandfather must have been bisexual at the very least? It would make sense if you did. Men don't generally share beds unless they're sexually involved with one another, after all. Everybody knows what sleeping together means.

Or do we? To us today, sleeping together almost invariably means sexual activity. But as it turns out this assumption is of fairly recent vintage. For most of human history it just meant sharing a bed, a pragmatic solution to the problem of expensive beds, bed linens, and bedrooms. In an era before central heat, sharing a bed also meant you'd be warm at night. To be sure, bed sharing wasn't always pleasant, as letters written by travelers sharing inn-house beds with lousy, farty, unmannerly strangers attest. But in many people's lives, bed sharing, which always involved members of the same biological sex, represented not only a common but an emotionally intimate refuge, so tender that Herman Melville compared it, in the pages of *Moby Dick,* to the intimacy of long-married couples.

By and large, our ancestors seem to have appreciated sharing their beds. Even younger siblings, who we might think would've welcomed finally having a bed to themselves after an older sibling they'd had to share with left home, sometimes missed it terribly. The teenaged Elisha Whittlesey, later a US congressman during Abraham Lincoln's term, wrote to his older brother William, "I never knew what it was before to be separated from a dear Brother. . . . You and I was always together. . . . I miss you most when I go to bed." Indeed, Lincoln himself is well known to have been a bed sharer, a fact on which many speculations about his sexuality have been based. As a penniless law student, he rented lodgings whose low cost was partly due to the fact that the bed was shared. The man with whom Lincoln shared that bed, Joshua Speed, became one of Lincoln's closest and dearest friends. Both male and female same-sex friends frequently shared beds out of affection, with women friends sometimes even, as historian Carroll

Smith-Rosenberg notes, "dislodging husbands from their beds and bedrooms so that dear friends might spend every hour of every day together" during visits.

No responsible historian would claim that all bed sharing, always, was strictly nonsexual. It would be naive to think that proximity and opportunity never led to things going bump in the night. Some relationships we would now describe as "homosexual" or "homoerotic" undoubtedly flourished without comment behind the scrim of propriety granted by this unremarkably common practice. But the fact is that bed sharing *was* common, and it *was* seen as proper. The simple fact that bed sharing was assumed to be an unremarkable, nonsexual experience suggests that this, in the vast majority of cases, is exactly what it was.

Clearly, what "everybody knows" about sharing a bed has changed. Once what "everybody knows" was that it was commonplace for friends, family members, and fellow travelers to share beds on a regular basis, and that sharing a bed was all there was to it. Now, what "everybody knows" is that "let's spend the night together" has only one unequivocal meaning—to the point that the Rolling Stones were forbidden to sing the original lyrics on *The Ed Sullivan Show* in 1967 and from performing it altogether in their first appearance in China in 2006.

Although the things "everyone knows" seem like common-sense realities, inevitable and unshakable facts, the truth is that they aren't. They change. But if what "everyone knows" can change, then how is it that everybody still seems to know it? How do we know what we know about sex? How do we arrive at our expectations, our interpretations of words and behaviors and appearances, our opinions of ourselves and of others where sexuality is concerned? Does it matter?

KNOWING WHAT TO THINK

When anthropologists talk about this "stuff everyone knows," they use the term *doxa*.[3] Doxa comes from the Greek for "common knowledge," and that's a pretty good description of what it is: the understanding we absorb from our native culture that we use to make sense of the world. Doxa is, quite literally in most cases, the stuff that "goes without saying," the assumptions and presumptions and "common

sense" ideas we have about our world and how it works. Virtually everything we know about sexuality, and heterosexuality, we know—
or think we know—because of doxa. Perhaps the best way for me to
express the power of doxa is that it is the reason that, even as you
read these words, some of you are probably secretly telling yourselves
that it doesn't matter what some silly historian says, those sentimental
gentlemen sleeping in one another's arms were *clearly* gay.

Absorbing a culture's doxa, very much including its doxa regarding sexuality, is an inescapable cultural process that starts at birth.
Doxa influences virtually everything we do, including the ways in
which we handle infants. For instance, the crying of baby boys is more
likely to be perceived by caregivers as being "excessive," whereas the
crying of baby girls is more likely to be perceived as normal. Baby
boys are therefore more likely to be punished for excessive crying, not
because they actually cry excessively but because they are boys.[4]

This is simultaneously an expression and a teaching of doxa. Baby
boys do not know that they are learning doxa when they are punished for crying. The big brothers and sisters of those baby boys don't
know they are learning doxa when they see it happen. Caregivers are
not necessarily aware that they are teaching doxa to children, or that
they are treating boy children differently than girl children because
doxa has taught them to. People don't experience doxa as an external force; they experience it as internal knowledge: the stuff that "everyone knows." Yet if what "everyone knows" is that "boys don't cry,"
then the likelihood that boys will be punished if they do cry becomes
greater. And if "everyone knows" that boys who cry are punished, the
likelihood is that boys won't cry if they can possibly help it.

"Doxa" may, in its unfamiliar Greek, sound like abstruse ivory-
tower theory, but it's just a name for a very real, mundane, routinely
overlooked everyday process. "Boys don't cry" is doxa. But it is not
just an abstract belief; it is also a daily influence on how people think,
speak, and act. This is precisely how doxa becomes seamless and invisible and, for better or worse, "just the way things are." Knowingly
and unknowingly, willingly and unwillingly, we participate in doxa
because it is how we know what is desirable and undesirable to the
people we deal with daily, what is acceptable and unacceptable, what
will get us punished and what will get us praised. Doxa is made up of

all the things we need to know reflexively if we are to succeed in navigating the expectations of our culture.

At the same time, doxa needs us. Doxa does not, and cannot, exist without people or culture. And as people change and cultures change, so, as we've seen with the example of bed sharing, does doxa. But doxa does not change because some top-down authority tells it to. Our big cultural authorities—organized religion, medicine, the sciences, the law, the media, and so on—can exert a lot of influence on doxa, but they cannot simply create it from nothing. The creation of doxa is a folk process. We all create it, together, mostly unintentionally.

The folk process of doxa becomes very clear to us when we look at the different ways that the things "everyone knows" about heterosexuality have been created. Whether it involves assimilating information that originates with authority figures, creating marked categories, invoking God and nature, or interpreting statistics with a decidedly populist bent, we take part in a large cultural conversation that selects, shapes, and distributes knowledge. In these ways and many others, we participate—and are always participating, whether we realize it or not—in the process of creating what "everyone knows" about heterosexuality.

HOMEOPATHIC FREUD

The process by which cultures create doxa is noisy. It relies on the existence of many different voices, a vast cloud of information and opinion and back-and-forth with a decidedly low ratio of signal to noise. Noisy, however, does not mean random. If you are familiar with the social media platform Twitter, you have probably already seen the phenomenon of a large cultural conversation taking on distinct moods and subjects at specific times, simply by glancing at Twitter's automatically generated "trending topics" list. "Heterosexual" gained prominence in our thinking and our vocabulary in pretty much the same way as a trending topic does online: more and more people started talking about it until finally it came into its own.

Before this could happen, however, "heterosexual" had to get into the conversational flow. For Kertbeny and Krafft-Ebing, you will recall, "heterosexual" was nothing more than an experiment in classification, an attempt to define and categorize something that had not previously had a name. For us, "heterosexual" is not an experiment but a cornerstone of how we organize our ideology of sex. As a culture, we believe that a thing called "heterosexuality" exists, inherent and irreducible. We believe it produces certain kinds of desires, behaviors, and relationships. In the late 1800s, hardly anyone had heard of such a thing as a "heterosexual." By 1950, "heterosexuals" were everywhere, and most people firmly believed they always had been. Quite a bit had to happen in the intervening decades in order for "heterosexual" to go from being just an awkward neologism to being a primary and unquestioned tenet of sexuality doxa. One of the major forces in this transition was Sigmund Freud and, more importantly, the popularization of his work.

Freud was simultaneously a simplistic and a highly critical thinker when it came to heterosexuality. More than once he admitted that the "exclusive sexual interest felt by men for women is also a problem that needs elucidating and is not a self-evident fact based on an attraction that is ultimately of a chemical nature,"[5] and acknowledged, in an equally radical insight, that heterosexuality required just as much restriction in its choice of object as homosexuality. But at the same time as he made these incisive observations about the complexity of sexual desires, he also accepted without reservation that heterosexuality existed. Freud's belief that heterosexuality was a genuine human phenomenon and a normative characteristic of human behavior is reflected throughout his work. It was this large-scale Freudianism—and not the nuanced asides—that made Freud's name in the English-speaking world, especially in America.

Freudian theories on sex began to percolate through the European and American intelligentsia in the 1910s and '20s, gaining momentum and visibility to the point where they more or less ruled the psychological roost well into the second half of the twentieth century. Freud's premise that adult sexuality was developed via a long succession of social interactions that began in infancy was particularly popular and influential. Every person, Freud argued, was born with an intrinsic sexual capacity as part of their physical and psychological makeup. What became of this innate sexual potential was dependent on a devilishly complicated equation with a terrifying number of shadowy and often lurid variables that could as easily go wrong as right.

Being a properly constituted heterosexual thus became an achievement. In Freud's world it was not merely nature or God's will that made a person sexually "normal." Upbringing and family were murky, treacherous waters that had to be navigated correctly to arrive at adult heterosexuality's safe harbor. Freudian theory implicated the middle-class nuclear household and the world of relatives, friends, school, and strangers as well in the creation of adult sexual personae. Parent-child relationships were particularly important, and woe betide the parent who unwittingly failed a child at any point in this fraught endeavor.

The result of achieving a proper sexual trajectory, from a Freudian point of view, was not only that a person would feel sexual desire for a partner of the "correct" biological sex but that he or she would arrive at adulthood with a whole array of specific desires, propensities, and awareness. Men would have learned to divert their Oedipal longings for their mothers onto other women, as well as to channel their rampant progenitive desires into more socially acceptable forms of creativity such as architecture and farming. They would desire sex for sex's sake, themselves, but instinctively know how to classify women on the Madonna/whore continuum.[6] As for women, they would have overcome their childhood desires to sleep with their own mothers . . . and their own fathers . . . and learned how to desire sex with their husbands in the name of a subconscious desire for children. A woman would also develop the magical (and automatic) ability to imprint on the man to whom she lost her virginity, an experience that would forever color her relationship both to that man and to the sexual act.

The transformation of the polymorphously perverse child into a properly functioning heterosexual adult was exceedingly complicated, making "normal" heterosexuality dependent on the success of many delicate and entwined operations. Few psychologists still subscribe to such literal Freudian theories of sexuality formation, but their influence lingers in the public imagination. Even today, people often assume that non-heterosexuality has to do with a person's parents or upbringing, some kind of sexual trauma, or some condition of arrested psychological development.

After Freud, as Jonathan Ned Katz puts it, it was clear that "heterosexuals were *made,* not born." But even Freud did not simply reach down and bestow this sensibility upon us like some grandiose god. He couldn't have. Even in Freud's heyday, relatively few people actually read his works. Freud's influence on us is due to what amounts to a gigantic, culture-wide game of Telephone. Authors of marriage manuals and sexual self-help titles were particularly prone to leaning on, if not always leaping aboard, the Freudian bandwagon.

In the early decades of the twentieth century, for instance, British women's reproductive-health crusader Marie Stopes was among the authoritative voices repeating Freudian notions such as the idea that the way a woman loses her virginity will automatically and permanently color her attitudes toward sex. Freud had given this notion his scholarly and medical imprimatur in his *Three Essays on the Theory of Sexuality* in 1905. Stopes reinforced it in 1918 in her best-selling *Married Love,* explaining that husbands who were too eager and selfish to be tender on their wedding nights were creating wives who would always dislike sex and resent their husbands' imposition.

The depth of Freud's influence shows all the more clearly when it emerges in the work of writers like the influential Theodor van de Velde, who ordinarily steered clear of psychology in favor of physiological verities. Van de Velde's 1926 *Ideal Marriage* was the *Joy of Sex* of its day, going through forty-six printings in its original edition before being reissued in 1965. (*The Joy of Sex* dates from 1972.) In its pages, van de Velde calmly endorsed Freudian claims that "the longing for maternity" was a primary motivator of sexual interest "in the majority of women," as well as passing along other Freudian shibboleths, such as warning of the dangers of sexual neurosis and "psychic impotence" among men who were "brain workers."

Through such repetition Freud's theories became truisms, and the truisms, echoed over and over, read by thousands and discussed by thousands more, gradually became incorporated into our thinking on a grand scale. Before long, they emerged as doxa. The process was doubtless hastened both by the internal logic of Freud's theoretical framework and by the fact that Freud's theories were invented as clinical observations made of people's recollections of their experiences. Particularly in the large outlines in which popular sources typically handed them down, they were easily adapted for self-analytical use.[7] Because psychoanalysis and self-analysis were automatically transactional and participatory, Freud's theories on sexuality were uniquely available to the public conversation. By the time of World War II, a basically Freudian understanding of sexuality had become a cultural commonplace, a sex doxa that has contributed not only to the now-laughable notion that comic books turn young people into juvenile delinquents and sexual deviants, but which continues to influence the ideology of American government-mandated "abstinence-only" sex education.[8]

At this point, Freud's presence in our sexuality doxa often seems weirdly indirect, diffuse, almost homeopathic. This is precisely the point: when ideas thoroughly permeate a culture they emerge as doxa. The widespread and dramatic simplification of Freudian ideas is what gave them their power to shape thought and action. Freud never set out to influence millions of people who never read a word he wrote. He never could have. Repetition and diffusion, on the other hand, did a dandy job of making his ideas into integral parts of what "everyone knows" about sex.

THE OPPOSITE OF SLUT

Another way doxa gets shaped, transmitted, and put into practice is through language. Consider, for example, the word "slut." Calling a woman a slut singles her out. It labels her as not just doing something wrong, but doing quite a bit of it. She breaks the rules, runs right over the boundaries of sexual propriety, goes overboard in a direction a respectable woman isn't supposed to admit to. "Slut" is clearly part of the doxa of sex, in that it informs us of a boundary in regard to how sexual a person, specifically a woman, is supposed to be.

But if a "slut" is the exception, what is the rule? What is the opposite of "slut"? "Slut" is an example of what social scientists call a "marked category," meaning a term that signifies something that transgresses or contradicts the expected or the doxic.[9] The differences between "nurse" and "male nurse" or "bishop" and "female bishop" are the modifiers that mark the differences between the typical and the atypical, the expected and the startling. We see the same effect at work in words like "disabled" and "disfigured," and indeed in "retarded," all of which imply the existence of some comparatively better or more perfect state that the person or thing in question has deviated from or failed to achieve.

Through these implied or direct comparisons, marked categories clearly indicate what is considered foundational, the baseline from which everything else is a divergence. Consider the phrase "people of color." This might be considered a politically correct phrase these days, but what is its unmarked equivalent? It should be "colorless people," but it isn't: there is no such thing as a colorless person. "People who are not 'of color'" are the baseline, the default, the unexceptional, the normal. The unmarked category against which "people of color" are tacitly opposed are "not-colored" people; in other words, whites.

Marked categories are, we quickly apprehend, a particularly efficient way to communicate doxa. Marked categories like "people of color," with no clearly defined corresponding unmarked category, tend to be the most socially potent of all. When the unmarked, expected, normative "default" category is unnamed and invisible, all the focus falls on the marked category: there is nothing that is opposite and equal. What *do* we call people who are at the other end of the spectrum from sluts? Prudes, perhaps. But "prude" too is a marked category, the extreme at the other end of the bell curve. There is no meaningful word for the middle of that bell curve, the space that fits comfortably inside the boundaries of doxa, the space that most people occupy most of the time. Nameless and characterless, the space we can loosely characterize as "normal" is almost completely undefined.

This is why "slut" and "prude," "pervert" and "deviant" all work so well as insults and as ways to police the boundaries of sex doxa. The labels are effortless to deploy and hard, even impossible, to defend against. As any woman who has been the subject of slut-shaming knows all too well—and about two out of three American women deal with this while they are still in high school, according to a 1993 study done by the American Association of University Women—the victim has no traction.[10] The facts of her sexual existence are immaterial, all that matters is that she has been painted in the bright Technicolor of the marked category and cannot disappear into the amorphous invisibility of "normal." The opposite of "slut" is *someone who has not been labeled a slut,* someone who has never been charged with violating doxa. The opposite of "pervert" is exactly the same: *someone who has never been charged with being one.*

This makes it doubly fascinating, and doubly relevant, that the word "heterosexual" exists. For many thousands of years, as you recall, there was no word for it, illustrating how things that are doxic and typical are usually not singled out with names; they just *are*. Kertbeny coined "heterosexual" and "homosexual" as a pair on purpose: having two marked categories instead of only one generates a certain amount of equality, which was precisely his point. The paired words suggest that both "homo" and "hetero" are marked categories whose specialization sets them off from the unmarked human universal, the undifferentiated "sexual." The idea of a primitive, undifferentiated sexuality that developed into a more structured and bounded sexual persona was central to Freud's theory of sexuality, and a belief in this developmental process has become part of our doxa. Yet at the same time, there is a great deal about "heterosexual" that remains amorphous and undefined until we cross a line and become a prude, a pervert, a deviant, or a slut. Marked language gives us our sexuality doxa not by carefully defining what is expected of us, what will be accepted by our families and friends, but by marking out—with the linguistic equivalent of a scarlet letter—what will not.

IT'S ONLY NATURAL

Nature, the physical universe, is the baseline of our reality. It encompasses everything that exists that is not made by human hands, and it encompasses the humans—and their hands—as well. All the physical forces that cause natural phenomena to happen are also nature, from the weak nuclear force that helps hold atoms together to the mysterious spark that makes the difference between life and death. Nature exists spontaneously, without our having to do anything; it was here when we got here and it will be here when we leave. This is precisely why people so often attempt to rationalize doxa, their expectations and assumptions regarding human behavior, based on what exists or fails to exist in nature.

This is particularly true when it comes to sex, and nature arguments in regard to sexual activity between men and women in particular have been around for a very long time. Reproduction is a particularly dramatic and impressive natural phenomenon, and doubly impressive because it is what perpetuates the species. For early

Christians, it was the only thing sufficiently important to justify either sexual desire or sexual activity. Every sexual behavior and every sexual desire that could not lead directly to conception soon became labeled with the fateful phrase *contra naturam,* against nature. The sexes of the participants were not the limiting factor in whether a sex act was "against nature," the potential for reproduction was. Even for a duly married man and woman, any time "someone obtains or consents that semen be spilled elsewhere than in the place deputed by nature," as medieval cleric William Peraldus put it, the Church labeled it *contra naturam.*[11]

Fascinatingly, though, by the time Peraldus was writing in the early thirteenth century, the Church was labeling as *contra naturam* even some sexual activity that would have seemed, on the surface, to play by the potentially reproductive rules. Historian Ruth Mazo Karras points out that "against nature" was openly used to condemn behaviors that are clearly *not* contrary to nature, notably including rear-entry vaginal penetration. Any medieval man or woman would have been well aware that there was nothing unnatural whatsoever about penis-in-vagina intercourse in this posture, having seen animals do it. Yet it, along with any position other than what later became known as the "missionary," was decried as being "against nature in terms of the manner." The Church wanted, and indeed insisted upon, a version of what was "natural" that was identical to the doxa the Church endorsed. What churchmen were willing to condone on the basis of its being "natural" was a pretty severely edited version of actual nature.

Such opportunistic and specific embraces of "nature" are common . . . and telling. When, for instance, psychotherapist Richard Cohen advocated "reparative therapy"[12] in 2000 to a group called "Parents and Friends of Ex-Gays," he claimed that "there is no scientific data that substantiates a genetic or biologic basis for same-sex attraction." (Cohen's claim is correct as far as it goes. However, as we shall see in the next chapter, there is no scientific data that substantiates a genetic or biologic basis for sexual orientation, period.) Only willful human perversity, he implied, could explain the existence of something that is not biologically predestined.[13] On the flip side, it has been strongly suggested in many quarters, not least the august pages of *National Geographic,* that same-sex sexual relationships among ani-mals provide a legitimating natural origin, and possibly even evidence of a natural purpose, for same-sex sexuality among human beings. As University of Liverpool evolutionary psychologist Robin Dunbar put it, "Anything that happens in other primates, and particularly other apes, is likely to have strong evolutionary continuity with what happens in humans."[14]

The fact that opposing viewpoints can both lay claim to natural support for their views on human sexuality should come as no surprise. Nature is vast and contains multitudes. The only genuinely consistent aspect of the claims we make about the relationship between what happens in nature and our beliefs in terms of what should happen in human sexuality is that human beings are the ones making the claims.

We would do well to consider the source. It is not nature that is so keen to tell us what is true or right or legitimate in terms of human sexuality. "What exists in nature," after all, encompasses an extraordinary variety of sexual activities, routinely including polygamy, polyandry, gang rape, incest, cannibalizing one's mates, and the injection of sperm packets (spermatophores) into a mate's bodily flesh.[15] It's often rather horrifying by human standards, but that's precisely the point: nature isn't so choosy as we are. When human beings cherry-pick examples of sexual behavior in nature to buttress their own beliefs about the way sexuality is or should be among humans, it is virtually never an accurate reflection of what nature demonstrates. As a reflection of human beliefs and values, on the other hand, it is inevitably spot on.

NUMBERS RACKET

Within months of the 1948 publication of the first Kinsey report, *Sexual Behavior in the Human Male,* Kinsey's statistical approach to sexuality was so much on people's minds that it showed up on Broadway.

> *According to the Kinsey Report*
> *Every average man you know*
> *Much prefers his lovey-dovey to court*
> *When the temperature is low*

In *Kiss Me, Kate,* Cole Porter's sassy, slightly risqué lyrics for "Too Darn Hot" were not just a reference to an unprecedented and controversial piece of research, but testament to a whole new way of thinking about sex.

Statistics, a seventeenth-century invention, had already merged with the nineteenth-century notion of demographics by the time Kinsey began his study of human sexuality in Indiana in the late 1930s. Kinsey was not the first or only person to apply a numbers-oriented approach to sexuality. Little remembered now, pre-Kinsey researchers such as Dorothy Dunbar Bromley, Lewis Terman, George Henry, and Carney Landis had already done pioneering work on topics like the sex lives of college students, attitudes about sex and marriage, same-sex sexual behavior, and gender roles. With their interviews, questionnaires, statistics, and demographic correlations, they created a whole new mode for research on sex. The profoundly subjective theoretical approaches of psychoanalysts like Freud were based on one-on-one case studies. The pathological catalogs of Krafft-Ebing and his ilk dealt only with people who had already been defined as sick, perverted, or damaged. Quantitative research on sexuality, by contrast, gave researchers a window into the generic everyday.

Like Linnaeus's quest to document every organism in God's creation, the new sexology sought to document the range of what existed. What researchers discovered was that a lot more people were having a lot more sex of a lot more kinds and varieties than anyone had previously suspected. And these people—5,300 men in the 1948 Kinsey report; 5,940 women in the 1953—were of a type that could not be easily ignored. Mostly middle-class, predominantly college-educated, typically white men and women, Kinsey's subjects were exactly the sort of people who dominated the culture of the day.

What was so remarkable about Kinsey was his relentless insistence that everyday sexual activity was a legitimate phenomenon of the natural world and a proper subject for classic bench-science observation and documentation. By regarding sexual behavior as just one more phenomenon that science could observe, Kinsey was able to reduce the effects doxa had on his ability to gather information. This dispassionate approach to sexual behavior, devoid of value judgments or moralist crusading, was an important and lasting contribution to sexology.

Kinsey's attempts to keep doxic judgment out of his data collection did nothing, however, to prevent his audience from interpreting his data through doxa's lens. Far from it. Kinsey's methods, combined with his large sample sizes, made it possible for readers to begin thinking about sexuality not just demographically, but as a sort of representation of cultural consensus. His data, collected in a spirit of inclusivity and transparency, was often interpreted as evidence of a sort of majority rule.

This was particularly relevant because Kinsey's research indicated that, for a significant majority, the boundaries of then-current doxa and the boundaries of sexual experience matched fairly well. Anal intercourse and oral sex *were* genuinely uncommon in male/female relationships. Most penis-in-vagina intercourse *did* take place with the man on top. Men *did* report being more easily and frequently aroused than women, and people whose sexual lives exclusively involved other-sex partners *were* in the vast majority. General readers, as well as doctors, lawyers, and the media, didn't hesitate to use Kinsey's work as proof that doxa was right, that all these things were every bit as correct, right, and normative as they had always been claimed to be.

Then again, Kinsey's work also documented a great deal of heterodox sexuality. The first report's revelations of substantial amounts of masturbation, adultery, same-sex activity, premarital sex, and other transgressive activity in the general population created shockwaves. The sexually orthodox could, and most assuredly did, find affirmation and a sense of solidarity in the Kinsey reports. But so could the heterodox outliers. Contemporary sexual identity politics became possible, in part, because the sexually unorthodox could point to Kinsey's statistics as proof that they were not alone. Rather than being marginalized as "sick" or "deviant," unorthodox sexual activities and those who practiced them could simply be characterized in mathematical terms as minorities.

This was a powerful option in those early days of the civil rights movement. The US military was racially desegregated by presidential executive order in 1948, the same year the first Kinsey report appeared, and the landmark *Brown v. Board of Education* verdict was given in 1954, the year after the second Kinsey report. Early gay liberationists enthusiastically took up similar strategies to those fighting

racial injustice and began to develop their own formal identity politics. The now-canonical slogan "one in ten," used to claim that one in
ten people are homosexual, was derived from Kinsey's work by Harry
Hay, founder of the pioneering gay rights organization the Mattachine
Society, who used it to lobby for inclusion and rights.

Both the status quo and the nascent agenda of sexual liberation
found data they could use in Kinsey's research. The use of statistics
for doxical ends hasn't slowed since. Quantitative research on sexual
behavior not only continues to be a major stream of sexology, but sta-
tistically oriented sex surveys have become a mass-market standard.
National periodicals like *Men's Health, Glamour, Cosmopolitan,* and
even the youth-focused *Seventeen* sponsor or administer sex surveys
with almost the frequency of universities or government agencies,
and often in conjunction with them.[16]

Through this kind of intensively mainstreamed quantitative research, the general public has learned to rely on the sex survey as a
means of gauging sexual performance. What "every average man you
know" thinks, likes, or does sexually—or at least what he claims he
does when researchers ask—is used both as proof of "how things are"
in a general sense and as a yardstick for measuring individual lives.

This is somewhat problematic, because the quality of sex research
is notoriously difficult to gauge. Like almost all research on human
subjects, it is prone to problems like sampling bias and leading word-
ing in questionnaires, but it is also significantly prone to problems of
exaggeration and omission in respondents' answers. A 2009 study in
the *Journal of Sex Research* showed that when 376 heterosexually active men and women were asked to complete separate daily and retrospective reports of how often they had engaged in penis-in-vagina
intercourse over a two-month period, the reports often didn't match.
When called on to recall their sex lives over the previous two months,
subjects commonly reported having had more sex than their daily reports indicated had actually taken place.[17] This was not deliberate de-
ception, just typical variability in terms of memory and expectations.
These are endemic problems of sexuality research, and they mean that
even when data is provided and collected with the best of methodol-
ogy and intentions, the numbers that a sex survey generates simply
may not be very accurate. Yet researchers and readers alike tend to

ignore this. The numbers themselves achieve a sort of authority all their own. Even to researchers who should know better, sometimes statistics seem to create their own realities, from which people derive new rules, new expectations, and new doxa about what is required to be sexually "normal."

Without our even noticing it, we assist in creating sexuality doxa, perform the work of passing it along, and use it in our own lives and in our interactions with other people—including when we inadvertently adjust our accountings of our sex lives to make ourselves look better or just "more normal" when we are interviewed by sexologists. Our doxa of sex influences how we experience it, teaching us what makes good sex good and bad sex bad, standards that also, as we shall see, change over time especially for women. Doxa affects what and whom we are comfortable (movie stars) and uncomfortable (our parents) considering as sexual entities. It teaches us what desires we can express publicly without much fear of censure, and which desires we'd better make sure no one else finds out about if we don't want to get beaten up.

Doxa not only shapes how we think, feel, and act with regard to sex; it also influences what things we are capable of talking about, feeling, and thinking. Without doxa that establishes, in an "everyone knows" sort of way, that heterosexuality exists, it would be unlikely that anyone would simply claim out of the blue that it did. It is only because we live in a culture where virtually everyone *does* agree that a quality called "heterosexuality" is real that people have experiences or emotions they are capable of identifying as "heterosexual." For most of human history, as you will recall, no one did anything of the kind. People had sexual and emotional experiences, to be sure. Perhaps they felt excited by them, or scared, or bored, or enlightened, or embarrassed. But we may be certain that it was not until after "everyone knew" that "heterosexual" was a thing one could be and experience themselves being that anyone had the experience of "feeling heterosexual."

There is, of course, a level on which sexual activity is not a matter of doxa and meaning but merely an issue of bodies and mechanics. But we do not, as much as we might like to believe in "no strings" sex, actually engage in sexual activity on that purely mechanical level. All sexual behavior between human beings is social, and socially meaningful. Note that I do not say that all sexual behavior is important. Importance is not the same thing as meaning. But sexual activities, even masturbation, are social activities, and all have at least some cultural significance. As David Halperin puts it, "Sexuality is not a somatic fact; it is a cultural effect."[18] Doxa is both the medium that creates this thing we call "sexuality" and, simultaneously, the rulebook by which we figure out what "sexuality" means for ourselves and for everyone else.

CHAPTER THREE

Straight Science

Scientifically speaking, we don't know much about heterosexuality. No one knows whether heterosexuality is the result of nature or nurture, caused by inaccessible subconscious developments, or just what happens when impressionable young people come under the influence of older heterosexuals. We do not know whether heterosexuals have different anatomy or physiology compared to non-heterosexuals. Our knowledge of any potential differences in terms of how heterosexuals' nervous systems respond to sexual stimulus, compared to non-heterosexuals, is nonexistent.

This isn't too surprising. We haven't been looking. No dedicated neurologist has ever hunched over microscope slides of brain tissue teasing out telltale details that make a "heterosexual brain" heterosexual. Endocrinologists cannot give us the hormonal recipe for the biochemical cocktail that makes a person straight, nor have geneticists even tried to locate such a thing as a "straight gene," except insofar as they often assume that genes are "straight" unless they are something else. Sociobiologists have yet to register any definitive statements on questions like whether being the firstborn, or perhaps having a lot of older sisters, or maybe being an only child, increase one's odds of growing up to be heterosexual. Dozens, even hundreds of scientists have made careers, sometimes quite influential and lucrative ones, in attempting to answer exactly these and similar questions where homosexuality is concerned. But somehow heterosexuality seems always to be left out in the cold, with no one to show the slightest concern for its nature or workings.

Interestingly enough, science has yet to prove that heterosexuality—or indeed any sexuality—exists in any way that is relevant to material science. For this to be the case, heterosexuality would have to be demonstrated to have a physical and objective existence. It would have to be quantifiable, in grams or nanometers or angstroms or amperes or joules or milliliters. And it would have to be measurable in some way not dependent on having a human being, with human biases, be the judge of whether or not it exists—that is, it would register a weight on a scale, produce a chemical reaction in a test tube, give off light or heat, and so on.

This is the nature of the searching that lies behind much of the research that looks for things like "gay genes" or "gay hormones." The theory is that if physical scientific evidence of homosexuality could be found, it would provide an objective foundation for sexual orientation, making it a legitimate object for the empirical sciences.

The same should be true of heterosexuality. After all, in order for there to be the marked category "gay brain," there must be an opposed unmarked non-gay brain. The confirmation of the existence of the marked category would simultaneously have to confirm the existence of the unmarked one. Neither one, however, has yet been confirmed to exist.

This is not for lack of trying. Many scientists have claimed to find evidence of homosexuality in the body, in anatomy and genetics and hormones, but none has so far held up to scrutiny: when we look for proof that our "gay" bit of the body is genuinely different from a default "straight" model, the evidence tends to fall apart. In the face of more than a century of failing to find an empirical basis for sexual orientation, the depth of the faith scientists continue to maintain that they will find such a thing is almost touching. It is also very telling: there are a lot of people out there who very badly want the doxa of sexual orientation, in which we all have an enormous social investment, to have a physical, demonstrable existence. But the fact remains that scientists often look for evidence of non-heterosexuality, what we consider the exception to the rule, while assuming that the heterosexual rule itself requires no evidence. Scientifically speaking, this is precisely backwards. In science, it should technically not be possible to even begin considering whether there might be exceptions to a rule until you have proven that the rule exists.

The fact that researchers have repeatedly assumed a material scientific validity for heterosexuality without seeking verification is simultaneously problematic and completely unsurprising. That heterosexuality exists is doxa: "everyone knows" that heterosexuality is real. But what is real from the standpoint of culture is not always or necessarily real from the standpoint of physical science, as the example of phlogiston eloquently attests. Phlogiston was the name given in 1703 to something that learned scientific men had long assumed had to exist for the world to function as it did: a colorless, odorless, tasteless, insubstantial substance that was capable of burning. Anything that could be burnt, it followed, contained phlogiston, and anything that contained phlogiston could have its phlogiston removed by burning off the phlogiston. It was not until the 1780s that experiments by the French chemist Anton Lavoisier proved that phlogiston did not and in fact could not exist.[1] Nevertheless, some very fine scientists, notably Joseph Priestley, the man who discovered oxygen, continued to cling to the phlogiston theory for the very good reason that it was familiar, consistent, and explained lots of things that scientists had observed in experiments.

It is possible that, from the perspective of the physical sciences, including biomedicine, "heterosexuality" and "homosexuality" may be rather like phlogiston. No matter how formal the name sounds, heterosexuality was not, after all, developed as a scientific concept or according to anything like scientific principles. As we recall, the idea of something called the "heterosexual" was developed by non-scientists, specifically for use in the non-scientific milieu of the law. From its very inception, "heterosexual" was about people as social entities, participating in social and sexual interactions with one another, in the larger context of their society and their nations and national legal codes. There is nothing about the concept of heterosexuality that suggests, or has ever suggested, that it must of necessity be an objective physical quality with a measurable physical existence.

When "heterosexual" caught on in the sciences, it was through psychiatry, the branch of medical science to which the social is of maximum importance. Early psychiatry in particular was essentially non-biological in its orientation. Its practitioners did study medicine, but as we know from the work of Freud and his contemporaries, the state of the psychiatric art of that day had to do with memories and repression, dreams and the unconscious. The sorts of sophisticated biomedical models we use today in talking about mental and behavioral medicine—neuroanatomy, biochemistry, neuropharmacology—simply did not yet exist. At the time when "heterosexual" was in its infancy, the existence of hormones was just being deduced (the word "hormone" dates from 1905), and the earth-shattering news from the world of brain anatomy was the discovery of the location of the Broca's (1868) and Wernicke's (1874) areas, two of the regions in the brain responsible for language. The application of even the crudest physical biomedical experimentation to the problem of sexual response would not happen until after 1910.

Early psychiatry was part of the material-science field of biomedicine by convention and because its practitioners had studied medicine, not because the actual practice of early psychiatry had much to do with biomedical physical science. "Heterosexual," coined by a layman who was just trying to articulate a protest against an unjust law, became "scientific" and "medical" because it was adopted and used by men who had scientific educations, not because it had been revealed or proven by experimentation and research.

As a psychiatric inheritance, "heterosexual" was promptly enshrined in medical practice as a standard of normalcy and proper function. There it has remained. The overwhelming assumption, among natural scientists who work on sexual orientation, appears to be that heterosexuality simply must exist as a physical-science reality. Were it not, the myriad attempts to explain homosexuality on biomedical grounds would not make much sense. But the truth is, no one has yet established—or, to my knowledge, attempted to establish—that a quality called heterosexuality exists not as a social phenomenon among humans, but as a spontaneously appearing material entity in nature. They only behave as if they had.

THE DEGENERATE IN THE MIRROR

The early days of "heterosexual" were also the early days of sexual science. As nineteenth-century race, gender, and class insecurity found a point of focus in sexual deviance, it came to seem imperative that "degenerates" be managed, lest they place the upright and respectable at risk of falling pell-mell down the crumbling rungs of the evolutionary ladder. A vast body of what can be described as medico-legal and medico-moral literature began to appear, including *Psychopathia Sexualis.* Such texts were intended to help doctors, lawyers, and other specialists understand and deal with these dangerous deviants.

Out of these writings emerged two major subtexts that reflected not only on the deviant few, but also on the "normal-sexual" many: conformity with gender role, and conformity with the principle of procreativity. Two additional concepts, the notion of a sexual orientation and the more subjective notion of a sexual identity, both grew out of the obsession with determining the parameters of deviance.

Procreativity was a fairly straightforward standard. For early sexology, as it was for the Catholic Church, the only defensible sexual act was a potentially procreative sexual act. The further that sexual activity took one from the potential for procreation, the less defensible and more "perverse" it was. Acts between same-sex partners fell clearly and decisively into the nonprocreative category. But so too did the use of contraception, which was widely viewed as morally wrong despite its growing popularity behind closed doors.

Newly named dynamics like masochism, sadism, and fetishism, however suspect they might have been, were not automatically beyond the pale. A certain masochistic tendency was considered psychologically normal in women and a corresponding sadistic tendency normal in men. Early British sexologist Havelock Ellis claimed this was a legacy of a fundamental, less complicated pre-civilization sexuality in which males seized women for sex, and women accepted such aggression. In modern people, he thought, such aggression and submission were quite normal as long as they were not excessive. Freud held a similar view, taking the fairly liberal tack that an act had to turn completely away from procreation before it became a perversion. But most people, and most writers, seem not to have been so tolerant as Freud or Ellis. Virtually all of what we would today term "foreplay"—another concept for which we must thank Freud—could be and often was considered too nonprocreative to be widely accepted. As late as 1920, sex advisors like Walter Robie had to vigorously reassure couples that it was all right to do noncoital things that generated mutual pleasure, cheerleading husbands to such outré lengths as to "Kiss without shame, for she desires it!"[2]

Nonprocreative sex was seen as problematic not only because it was sterile. It also defied, or appeared to defy, gender norms. According to the doctrine of sexual complementarity, developed in the late Enlightenment, the male was to be active to the female's passive, desiring to the female's desired, pleasure-seeking to women's maternity-seeking, and so on. A woman who submitted passively to intercourse with her husband was normal, while a woman who took an active role, like getting on top, was not. Neither, for that matter, was a husband who willingly tolerated such things. Any man who voluntarily took on a sexual role other than what Angus McLaren has characterized as "the impenetrable penetrator" was considered at least suspect, if not outright deviant. Men who performed oral sex on their female partners, for instance, were considered passive and effeminate. The women who allowed or, worse, requested such a thing, remarkably enough, might be credited with sadism. Many early sexologists and their colleagues believed such dangerous cross-gendered behavior could represent the beginning of a slippery slope: once he became inclined to the "passivist" act of performing oral sex on women, a man might continue to become more and more passive until he became the lowest of the low, a fellator of other men.

By far the era's favorite phantasm of deviance and ruin was spermatorrhea, or the "excessive" loss of semen. This fictitious disease was usually blamed on masturbation, the ultimate in nonreproductive sexual activity. Avoiding and preventing masturbation became a pervasive and urgently felt concern, giving rise to numerous books, pamphlets, treatment regimes, and a few lucrative careers. In addition to well-known preventatives like Bible study, cold-water baths, dietary fiber, and Boy Scouting, other remedies like chastity belts, tying children's hands to the bedposts, and hard manual labor were indicated to assist the masturbator in conquering his addiction to self-abuse. The masturbator who could or would not refrain courted consequences ranging from nervous exhaustion, insanity, syphilis, bed-wetting, impotence, sterility, effeminacy, loss of vitality, homosexuality, and perhaps even death.[3]

Anything and everything, it seemed, could spur one to the dissipating, morally degenerate, vitality-sapping practice of self-stimulation. Reading novels was considered a high-risk activity, encouraging fantasy and laziness. Constipation was judged to excite the nerves of the pelvis and encourage insalubrious behavior; both Sylvester Graham's eponymous cracker and John Kellogg's breakfast cereals were part of the effort to ensure regular, healthy bowel movements that would not cause undue stimulation to sensitive bits of the anatomy. Some believed the use of the vaginal speculum by gynecologists would make women sex-mad and lead not just to masturbation but nymphomania—associated with unseemly "masculine" levels of sexual interest—and perhaps even to prostitution. Even thumb-sucking was an enemy of sexual propriety and was vilified in high scientific medico-moral style in pediatric literature from the 1870s until the 1950s as encouraging masturbation and causing an ugly, telltale dental deformity to boot.[4]

Most dangerous was the foreskin of the penis. Merely to have one could rouse a man to deviant thoughts and actions as the foreskin moved over the head of the penis during everyday movements. To prevent this, doctors sometimes pierced the foreskin and infibulated it, holding it closed with loops of wire. Much more often the foreskin was simply removed.[5] The routine circumcision of baby boys at birth, championed heavily in the United States by pioneering pediatrician Abraham Jacobi, was viewed as a reasonable precaution against masturbation and its destructive effects on health, morals, and the ability to have a normal married life. The practice continues today in US hospitals, its original aims swept discreetly under the rug, justified now by controversial claims that it improves genital hygiene and may lessen risks of certain infections.[6]

Frighteningly, it was not only sexual misconduct that presented a threat to procreativity and proper gender. Noisy and complicated, crowded and stressful, the new urban, industrial world likewise ground away at one's constitution with its newspapers, train journeys, and dissipating entertainments. A man who could not withstand the pressures of modern life could easily become a hysterical, feminized, and impotent "neurasthenic." Too feeble to perform properly as heterosexuals, neurasthenics and other "psychic impotents" might turn to fetishes, voyeurism, exhibitionism, masochism, or even other men in order to get enough stimulation to overcome their debilitated state. Such sexual enervation, Austrian psychologist and sexologist Wilhelm Stekel argued, could even lead to murder, with the dagger or bullet becoming a stand-in for the penis that could no longer penetrate.

Deviance, it was clear, was everywhere. It was subversive and subtle and lurked even in the private and mysterious realms of thoughts and emotions. As people were made more and more aware of all the many ways in which deviance could infiltrate their lives, an undercurrent of sexual self-consciousness and self-examination became an increasingly commonplace experience. The mandate to avoid degeneracy meant knowing at all times that what one desired and how one behaved were above suspicion. Even the subconscious mind—a Freudian, and thus a contemporary, invention—was to be thoroughly interrogated with the help of psychoanalysis, lest it harbor hidden monstrosities. At any moment, it seemed, one could look into the mirror and find a degenerate looking back.

This is different in several important ways from the proto-gay subculture that formed around urban undergrounds of men who desired and had sex with men. In the entertaining and enlightening *Mother Clap's Molly House: The Gay Subculture in England 1700–1830*, historian Rictor Norton reveals that well before any medical professional or lawmaker had a notion of something called a "homosexual" or a "heterosexual," there were men spontaneously self-identifying and forming community based on their shared sexual desire for other men. These men were not only aware of their sexual commonality; they built culture around it: they called themselves "mollies" and called one another by feminine "maiden names," dealt with what we would now call gay bashing and police harassment, and sometimes called upon priests known to be one of their own to perform funeral services for men who had been hanged as sodomites. Simultaneously informal and established, visible and underground, mollies and their subculture clearly existed.

This does not, however, make them the equivalent of modern-day gays. And it certainly does not make their non-molly contemporaries the equivalent of modern-day heterosexuals. The fact that small groups of eighteenth-century urbanites understood themselves to be sexually different from the norm, and understood their sexual desires and preferences to have particular social significance, does not mean that those outside this subculture had any similar understanding of theirs. It particularly does not mean that those outside the molly subculture had any sense of themselves as being "not-mollies." Indeed, why would they?

Yet this is precisely what it means to have the sense that one "is heterosexual": to understand one's self to be part of a specific, distinctive sexual culture. The self-identification of small numbers of sexually non-normative individuals was not something that generated a sensibility of "the heterosexual" or "the normal-sexual" in the rest of the population. What generated this sensibility in the mainstream was the increasingly common experience of looking in the mirror to see if a deviant or degenerate looked back.

This self-inspection was not the result of a spontaneous inner desire to "know thyself" that was magically, simultaneously experienced organically by huge swathes of the European and North American middle and upper classes. It was triggered socially, by fear. Becoming sexually self-aware was a matter of pure old-fashioned self-defense.

Western culture acquired sexual self-consciousness on a grand scale because self-assessment offered ways to defend against being marked as a degenerate or deviant. Heterosexuals learned to experience heterosexuality—to think about themselves as "being" and "feeling" heterosexual, to believe that there is a difference between "being heterosexual" and "being homosexual"—because they needed, in newly official ways, to know what they *weren't*.

Sexual irregularity was no longer really a matter for the Church. It had become, as Krafft-Ebing's introduction to *Psychopathia Sexualis* made clear, a problem for lawmakers, cities, and states. Anyone and everyone could be a sinner. By definition, in fact, everyone *was*. Sin was lamentable, but it was understandable, even expected. What was not understandable or expected, and certainly not excusable, were deviance and degeneracy. Nor were the stakes at all the same. This is where the concept and experience of this thing called "sexual orientation" come from. It does not stem from relatively small numbers of people wanting to signal to others like them the ways in which they were sexually outside the mainstream. It stems from enormous numbers of people being very anxious about the possibility of seeing a degenerate in the mirror.

DEFINING "HETEROSEXUAL"

"Heterosexual" does not have a single standard scientific definition. Different disciplines, and indeed even different researchers within single disciplines, use the word to mean different things. This is more than merely incidental sloppiness. Scientific method and scientific authority depend in part on clear and consistent definitions that are supported by careful observation. Yet when heterosexuality is the subject, scientists all too often behave like Lewis Carroll's Humpty Dumpty:

> "When *I* use a word," Humpty Dumpty said in rather a scornful tone, "it means just what I choose it to mean—neither more nor less."
>
> "The question is," said Alice, "whether you *can* make words mean so many different things."
>
> "The question is," said Humpty Dumpty, "which is to be master—that's all."[7]

This is not merely a vocabulary problem or even an attitude problem. It is a scientific problem. In biological, physical, and social sciences, the lack of standardized definitions creates inconsistency and lack of clarity in research, and introduces serious problems to the process of interpreting data.

The potential meanings of "heterosexual" run a wide and problematic gamut. "Heterosexual" may simply be an adjective describing different-sexed individuals, specifically male and female, engaging in some sort of shared behavior. The behavior could be sexual or reproductive, but it need not be. "Heterosexual" pairs of monkeys might groom one another or fight over food. This doesn't necessarily tell us anything about whether the monkeys had any sort of sexual relationship, or whether there were or weren't particular social bonds between them. It just means that pairs of monkeys, each consisting of a male and a female monkey, engaged in particular social behaviors.

This is sometimes what "heterosexual" means even when the context of the study does have to do with mating or reproduction. Researchers Ralph Greenspan and Jean-Francois Ferveur, for instance, discussed heterosexual courtship in *Drosophila* in a *Review of Genetics* article.[8] Here again, "heterosexual" means merely "different-sex" or "male/female." It does not imply anything about what motivates the observed behavior, let alone anything about the subjective experience of the fruit flies under consideration. It certainly doesn't imply that there are also homosexual *Drosophila* who come out to their parents or hang out in itty-bitty fruit fly gay bars. "Heterosexual," in the context of this article, just characterizes the biological sexes of creatures that happen to be engaging in a behavior related to sexual reproduction. It does not imply that these creatures are "heterosexuals" in the same way that humans might be.

So far, so good. But what happens to these simple, straightforward uses of "heterosexual" when what scientists actually *observe* in nature is not what they expected to find? What happens to "heterosexual" when the relationship between biological sex and sexual behavior does not conform to our expectations? In the 1970s, for example, endocrinologists conducted studies on rats treated with heavy doses of sex hormones that upended their normal hormone profiles. In rats, sufficiently high doses of sex hormones can override an animal's usual sexual behavior instincts, so that biologically male rats given heaping doses of estrogens will present their rear ends in the female-typical mating posture known as lordosis, while biologically female rats similarly treated with testosterone will mount them in the manner typical of male rats.

Scientists remarking on this research pointed out that these rats could be accurately described as behaving either heterosexually, in that they were engaging in sexual behavior with a rat of a different biological sex, or homosexually, in that the rats were engaging sexual behaviors that were identical to those that their different-sex partners would normally exhibit, female rats behaving as males toward males, male rats behaving as females toward females. Or the rats could be described as behaving *simultaneously* heterosexually and homosexually. It depended on which variable—the biological sexes of the participants, or the behaviors they engaged in—was seen as the one that counted more.[9] If "heterosexual" mating activity could, strictly speaking, encompass behavior completely unlike what is colloquially understood by "heterosexual mating activity," critics asked, how scientifically meaningful was the term "heterosexual"?[10]

Such ambiguities are compounded when "heterosexual" is used in regard to human beings. Does the researcher mean one of the types of "heterosexual" outlined above? Or is he instead referring to the variable and dynamic mixture of cultural identity, emotional response, sexual desire, physiological arousal, economic and social role playing, erotic activity, and reproductive potential that we mean when we use "heterosexual" in conversation? It is rather, as Mark Twain might've put it, like the difference between "lightning bug" and "lightning."

We also must consider who does the labeling. Does the research in question rely on having subjects self-identify their sexual orientation? We know all too well that not everyone does this in the same way or with the same criteria. Or has the researcher assigned the "heterosexual" (or "homosexual") label to his subjects, and if so, on what basis? Researchers often identify subjects as heterosexuals merely because they are not identified otherwise, a sort of "innocent until proven guilty" approach. Or they may diagnose subjects' sexual orientations based on criteria that might or might not be linked to heterosexuality, for instance, assuming that any woman who has given birth to a child must be heterosexual. In his 1991 research into sexual difference in the region of the brain called the hypothalamus, neuroanatomist Simon LeVay classified his subjects' sexuality based on their cause of death. Subjects who had died of AIDS-related causes were counted as "homosexual" while the other subjects were assumed to be heterosexual. Numerous scientific critics slammed LeVay for "compiling inadequate sexual histories," a professional way of saying that LeVay was assigning sexual orientation to subjects based on evidence that could not prove what he claimed it did.[11] But these well-justified criticisms did not make it into the mainstream media, where news of LeVay's "discovery" of "gay brains"—solidly refuted since, it should be noted—was making headlines, and LeVay's career.

Without a rock-solid standard definition, or at least a strict protocol for articulating definitions with respect to any particular research project or study, we do not actually know what lies under the hood of a scientific "heterosexual." This makes it very difficult, if not impossible, to draw any scientifically meaningful conclusions from study to study.

Furthermore, as Dr. LeVay's example shows, an awful lot of doxa can hide in the assumptions that are made in the setting-up and conducting of scientific research. This does not mean that physical science is not a useful tool, or that it has nothing to tell us about "heterosexual." What it does mean is that we have a long way to go before physical science is even sure what it's talking about when it talks about "heterosexual," let alone before it has anything definitive to teach us about what that might be.

KNOWING SEX, KNOWING DOXA

Material and biological sciences simultaneously know a great deal about sex . . . and not very much about it at all. Material science is good at describing objects and phenomena that can be observed and measured. Biology is brilliant at documenting and describing physical actions that take place, and reasonably acute at figuring out the functions performed by those actions. This is why there is so much excellent scientific work about the biology, physiology, and anatomy of sex. Bodies and their workings are material objects, subject to consistent natural laws. Physical actions are interactions with the material world, with observable and documentable consequences.

What material and biological sciences are not so good at doing— for the very simple reason that it is not what they are set up to do—is documenting and explaining things that are not physically tangible. The physical and biological sciences can, for instance, explain how penises become erect. They can explain how vasodilation takes place and blood flow to the penis increases, how the spongy bodies in the penis fill with blood, what physics and hydraulics are involved in making the penis stiffen, and how blood is temporarily kept inside the penis so that the penis can remain erect. But no scientist can tell you whether that erect penis is gay or straight. An erection might be caused by a heterosexual desire or a homosexual desire or, for that matter, by the action of a drug. These things do not affect how erections happen or how they function. From the standpoint of the physical and biological sciences, one erect human penis is more or less interchangeable with the next.

This is something we often have a difficult time accepting when it comes to human beings and human sexuality. Lurking deep in our doxa, and possibly quite a bit deeper than that, is the notion that aspects of who we are and what we have experienced will inevitably manifest themselves physically in the body. It is a conceit we are reared on: how many children's stories have evil characters who are hideous or deformed and good ones who are beautiful? We stigmatize the disabled, the deformed, and the just plain funny-looking on the basis of their bodies, assuming them to be stupid or incompetent.

We do this where sex is concerned, too. Even now, despite there being no proof for it whatsoever, many people are still profoundly attached to the idea that having penetrative sex for the first time permanently changes a woman's body, that you can tell that a woman is no longer a virgin by the width of her hips or the way she walks.[12]

But we non-scientific laypeople are not the only ones guilty of assuming that when it comes to who we are or what we have experienced sexually, the body will out. Physical and biological scientists who look for evidence of distinctive "gay" bodies—whether in terms of genes or hormones or brains or gross anatomical features like fingers or genitals—are working from the same principle. In order to look for evidence of a physically or biologically distinctive "gay" body, an additional assumption is necessary: that there is also a distinctive "non-gay" body from which to draw comparisons.

This line of thinking has an exceptionally long history. Both the ancient Romans and nineteenth-century Italian neurologist Paolo Montegazza, apparently independently of one another, proposed that "true" homosexual males (men who took on the receptive role with other men) could be explained by "an anatomical anomaly that sometimes leads the final branches of the [genital] nerves to the rectum; therefore its stimulation causes for the passives that genital excitement that in ordinary cases can be caused only through the genitals."[13] No such bodily anomaly has ever been documented. But the claim that "normal" men's nervous systems arranged themselves properly in the penis, while abnormal men's nerves arranged themselves in such a way that the anus became like the vagina—built to be penetrated, as it were—had a tempting psychological logic. The possibility that the sensory nerves normally present in the anus, rectum, and the prostate might be capable of transmitting pleasurable sensation apparently did not occur to Montegazza. Along similar lines, historian of homosexuality Gert Hekma has found early nineteenth-century reports by Dutch physicians claiming that men who engaged in anal intercourse had anuses that bordered on the vaginal, funnel-shaped and bordered by delicate, hairless, skin analogous to the labia minora in women. Heterosexual men, on the other hand, were said to have "normal" anuses.

Such comparison tactics have not been limited to the territory below the belt. Pioneering Berlin sexologist and homosexual rights defender Magnus Hirschfeld, eager to prove a biological basis to homosexuality in the hopes that it could be used to create a legal defense, surveyed features like voice, musculature, height, weight, and so on in hundreds of subjects to try to find evidence of biological differences between male homosexual and heterosexual bodies. The physical traits Hirschfeld and his followers recorded, however, were not assessed in terms of ounces, megahertz, degrees of inclination, or thickness of dermal fold, but on "direct impressionistic observations," meaning whatever sort of impression the researcher had of the subject upon observing him directly. The angles at which subjects carried their arms, the distribution of fat on their bodies, the pitches of their voices, and many other characteristics were assessed and labeled not as a series of measurements in degrees or inches or megahertz, which would have been good scientific practice, but according to whether they struck the researcher's sensibilities as being masculine or feminine.[14] Hirschfield's researchers were not the only ones to attempt this sort of research. Nor were they the only ones to find that their data, even with the bias they introduced to it themselves, did not support clear conclusions. Inevitably such studies produced nothing in more copious quantity than evidence that there were homosexuals with "masculine" characteristics and heterosexuals with "feminine" ones. This was variously ignored, massaged out of the statistics, or simply declared irrelevant.

This is the sort of thing that happens when doxa meets science. There is nothing inherently unscientific about the intersection of doxa—our beliefs about the world—and science. Indeed, the scientific process provides a genuinely useful and exceptionally sensible method for testing doxa and determining whether what we believe to be true about the observable and quantifiable world is indeed so. There is nothing unscientific about designing experiments to test the doxic belief that if a person is sexually unorthodox or different, this difference will also exist in the person's physical body. What is unscientific is doing such experimentation and then being unwilling to accept results that did not turn out the way you thought they would . . . or wanted them to. If you set out to test the doxa that human behavioral variation manifests itself in the physical body, two of the possible outcomes of such testing are that it does not at all, or that it does not do so predictably or reliably. In science, a negative result is just as scientific, and just as meaningful, as a positive result.

The tendency for scientists to use physical and biological science to test principles derived from doxa or belief is, again, not inherently unscientific. The tricky bit lies in how aware scientists are of the doxa that influences their work. For instance, ideally Magnus Hirschfeld would have been aware that he was assuming that heterosexual bodies manifested a distinctive set of gendered characteristics (to which the gendered characteristics of homosexual bodies could be compared). He would have realized that this was not an assumption he could simply make, as a scientist, because it made intuitive sense to him as a human being. Without actual observation and measurement of the characteristics of heterosexual bodies, he could not actually say whether they *did* manifest a distinctive set of gendered traits. Scientifically speaking, Hirschfeld failed to adequately characterize his control because doxa led him to believe that he already knew everything he needed to know. As it turned out, he did not, and what his experiments proved without a shadow of a doubt as a result is that in the absence of an adequately characterized control, it is difficult if not impossible to make meaningful comparisons.

———

As much depends on whether the tools the scientists choose to use are appropriate for and capable of testing the things the scientists want to test. Returning to Hirschfeld, we have already noted that he chose to use "direct impressionistic observations" rather than various standardized units of measurement. This, in large and unambiguous form, is doxa showing up again: another way of saying "direct impression-istic observation" is *I know it when I see it*. One of the reasons that scientists generally choose to use instruments rather than their own senses, and standardized units of measurement rather than descrip-tive characterizations, is to eliminate this inbuilt potential for human biases to prejudice data.

The last piece of the puzzle is whether the data scientists are ca-pable of gathering is actually adequate to answer the questions the scientists are trying to ask. Because doxa is in many ways a short-hand that we use for making sense of how the world works, it often blinds us to how complicated some things really are. We are accus-tomed to an "everyone knows" ideology of sexuality that is obvious and clear-cut: male or female, straight or gay, kinky or vanilla, sick or healthy. We are similarly used to an "everyone knows" thinking about bodies as being essentially mechanical collections of individual, well-understood components starting with DNA. The temptation is to as-sume that the relationship between the body and sexuality must be straightforward and uncomplicated. After all, it doesn't *feel* compli-cated when we experience it. This, as we shall see, has proven to be a particularly problematic assumption, sending us deeper and deeper into ever more specialized and detailed aspects of the body to try to tease out how—and indeed whether—the physical, material body is connected to the behaviors and experiences of sexuality.

THE ESSENTIAL INVERT

There are few better demonstrations of the tensions between sex doxa and sex science than the biomedical approach to homosexuality known as "sexual inversion." For most of human history, little distinc-tion has been made between biological sex and gender. The idea of a sex "essence," some mysterious aspect of biological sex that creates the gendered persona, remains common. Karl Ulrichs's theory of "inver-sion" is the basis of this concept's modern incarnation: his contention was that homosexual men were, in a sense, hermaphrodites; biologi-cal males with a female "essence," a psyche or soul that was inherently feminine. In various ways and to various degrees, this idea that homo-sexuality and bisexuality are caused by an "inversion" of a gendered "essence" that is either psychological or biological remains pervasive, and at the center of much current research into sexual orientation.

This is important to a history of heterosexuality because heterosexuality is just as implicated in the idea of sexual inversion as homosexuality. If sexuality is in fact a matter of whether all the inherent sexed aspects or qualities of a human being are properly matched according to type, then this is just as relevant in terms of what makes someone a heterosexual as it is in terms of what makes someone not a heterosexual.

The hypothesis is straightforward. For over a hundred years now, scientists have looked for biological evidence of sexual inversion on multiple fronts and have found no conclusive evidence that it exists.

The easiest, and hence both the earliest and commonest, way to search for proof of sexual inversion has involved that fine old Victorian hobby, hunting for evidence of mismatches between biology and gender. Feminized maleness, historically, created the most pressing sense of crisis.[15] The word "feminism," in fact, originated not to describe a pro-female sociopolitical movement but as a quasimedical term meaning "feminization." It shows up in French sources from the 1870s in which neurasthenia and homosexuality are cited as consequences of a man's unfortunate *féminisme*. Homosexual men have been stereotyped as both physically and mentally feminine, limp-wristed, "pretty," and prone to girly displays of high emotion and interest in the decorative arts, possibly simultaneously. As recently as 1995, British psychiatrist and sexologist Richard Green, in discussing the links he believes to exist between gender identity and homosexuality, famously quipped, "Barbie doll at five, sex with men at twenty-five."[16]

This all fits in nicely with the doxa of the sex and gender binary we inherited from our Enlightenment and Victorian ancestors, but what is actually demonstrated by the current state of play in scientific research is not so cut and dried.

Science seems to be of two minds about whether biology is likely to hold evidence of orientational destiny. On the one hand, no reputable scientist today will argue, for instance, that heterosexual men are more virile and hairier than their gay brothers, or that lesbian women are by nature more muscular and sexually aggressive than straight women, although at one point both these notions were accepted as true. Researchers freely acknowledge that there is an extensive laundry list of physical and behavioral traits that were once believed to be linked to sexual orientation but that have been proven not to be. At the same time, they continue to seek evidence for a distinctive "homosexual body" that deviates somehow from the "normal" body that heterosexuals are still presumed, yet still not in fact proven, to possess. Within just the last ten years, genes, brains, hormones, and even bits like fingers, ears, and hair have all come under the scrutiny of scientists searching for some sort of bodily telltale of sexual orientation.

This search for distinctive evidence of sexual orientation in the body itself has followed a telling—and scientifically sensible—pattern. Whenever one part of the body or aspect of physical function fails to provide a telltale diagnostic, the scientists look someplace else. When appearance, gross external anatomy, and characteristics like voices failed to produce the desired evidence, as they did quite early on, scientists began to turn their gaze inward. Aided by advances in chemistry, microscopy, surgery, and ever more specialized tools and technologies, biomedical scientists have proceeded to look at ever smaller and ever more deeply internal parts of the body.

Whether or not this will succeed in revealing any differences between gay bodies and straight bodies remains to be seen. One thing it definitely does succeed at doing, however, is making it much more difficult for laypeople to evaluate the validity of scientific claims made about the relationship between the body and sexuality. How many people who aren't neurologists are sufficiently aware of what a hypothalamus even is to be able to guess whether someone who tells us that there is a distinctively "gay" hypothalamus is likely to be right or wrong? We certainly do not have any sense of our own hypothalamus, or any conscious awareness of it; its influences upon us are silent and unseen, and essentially irrelevant to our workaday sense of self. As scientists have taken the search for the distinctively gay body to these tiny, unfamiliar, and inaccessible arenas, the public has had little choice but to trust these very privileged and frankly esoteric viewpoints. We have sufficient experience as body experts to be able to question whether a scientist who claims that all lesbians have excessive facial hair is making an accurate statement. When it comes to the interior of the brain, or the genome, or the endocrine system, on the other hand, we are much more likely to trust what we are told. We simply don't have the experience to argue.

The history of biomedical research into sexual orientation suggests strongly that regardless of our lack of experience, we would do well to be very stingy and very skeptical with our trust. As a research paradigm, the search for biological markers of sexual orientation has yet to produce any sturdy positive results. Most of the results that have been produced in this search have been negative: given what we know so far, sexual orientation does *not* appear to be directly or causally connected to the physical body. The processes by which we have learned this have, however, not been benign.

In the early twentieth century, the newly discovered biochemicals called hormones and the endocrine glands that produced them were exciting new subjects for research. It was known that hormones, and particularly sex hormones, had a great influence on the body, and many doctors were experimenting with "glandular extracts," sometimes taken from pigs and monkeys, as therapy for everything from impotence to aging. Austrian pathologist Eugen Steinach jumped aboard the hormone-therapy wagon with the contention that homosexuality was due to a sort of intersexual condition in which homosexuals had sex-hormone glands that were the "opposite" of what was biologically typical.

If Steinach had been correct about this, it would have been nothing short of revolutionary, because it would have meant that heterosexuality was created by a fairly straightforward organic mechanism. By extension, it would also suggest that homosexuality could be fairly simply converted into heterosexuality. Steinach and his followers tested their theory on humans, transplanting "normal-sexual" testicles into "invert" men. Clearly enamored of his own seductive theory, Steinach pronounced the procedures a success. Only later would he admit that the surgeries had been pointless, and that the transplants hadn't changed a thing.

This did not deter other researchers from pursuing the same line of research. Sex hormones can, after all, strongly influence and even alter patterns of sexual behavior in some, but not all, animals. Hormone therapy was a particularly popular line of inquiry during the Nazi regime, whose interest in eradicating homosexuality is well known. Danish physician Carl Vaernet, working for Heinrich Himmler, conducted hormone-pellet implantation studies on homosexual men imprisoned at Buchenwald, hoping to transform them into heterosexuals. Like Steinach's surgeries, Vaernet's did not work, and for the same reason: there was nothing that his technique could fix. Hormonally speaking, men who desire men are no different from men who desire women. More importantly, human sexuality cannot be led by the hormonal nose. It is easy enough to make a male rat display female-typical mating behaviors by fiddling with its sex hormones, or a female rat display male-typical ones, but human sexuality, surprisingly enough, is more complex than a rat's. Not that it would necessarily tell us anything about the origins of homosexuality if one *could* substantially alter human sexual behavior via hormones. Just because a behavior can be compelled hormonally does not mean the same behavior might not exist for other reasons, without the hormonal trigger, as well.

Yet endocrinologists still have not stopped looking for a hormonal "inversion" explanation for homosexuality. The search has simply gotten narrower and more esoteric. Having gotten nowhere with adult hormone levels or gonad function, research now often focuses on potential links between prenatal hormone exposure and adult sexual orientation. Much of the physical and physiological sex differentiation that occurs when a fetus is developing happens as a result of its being exposed to hormones in the womb. Endocrinology researchers have postulated that homosexual men might become homosexual as a result of being exposed, as fetuses, either to particularly high levels of "female" hormones or else to conditions that compromise their bodies' ability to respond normally to "male" hormones. (In actuality there are no such things as "male" or "female" hormones. Hormones have no sex of their own, and all types of sex hormones are present in all human beings in varying amounts.) This hypothesis relies on the same old inversion paradigm: a gay male is gay because he is in some way(s) not male.

Anatomical research has similarly shrunk its scope and retreated into ever smaller and harder-to-see arenas. The currently popular body part in which to hunt for a biological token of gayness is the brain. Like endocrine research, brain research too has a grim history in terms of experimental "treatment" based on unproven scientific conjecture. In the early 1970s, surgeons proceeding on the basis of theories espoused by leading German researcher Günter Dörner attempted to cure homosexuality in several men by burning out the alleged "sexual center" of the central hypothalamus. The surgeries caused severe personality disturbances, and were only halted because other leading researchers, like sexologist Volkmar Sigusch, publicly criticized their inhumanity. To the biomedical world's credit, such human experimentation is on the wane, but has not completely vanished.

There are many reasons that it can be difficult to trust, let alone defend, the ongoing search for a biology of sexual orientation. Perhaps the hardest pill to swallow, however, is that even if we did suddenly find ourselves with indisputable positive evidence of a link between the physical body and sexual orientation, it is likely that we would still lack the science to make sense of it. The leap from biology to behavior is a big one, and we simply do not know very much about how it works. If we found a "straight gene" tomorrow, we still wouldn't be able to explain how we get from the creation of specific proteins—which is all that DNA is capable of instructing the body to do—to a complicated, highly variable complex of behaviors like heterosexuality. At this stage, our science cannot even figure out what causes some people to be left-handed while others are right-handed, a much simpler characteristic than sexual orientation by far. Our hubris in thinking that we would be able to make sense of a physical telltale of sexual orientation if one were found is every bit as entrenched as our certainty that there must be such a thing as sexual orientation in the first place. This is, I submit, no coincidence.

LIFE SCIENCE

Why do researchers continue, despite so much negative evidence, to hunt for proof that sexual orientation has a material or physical component? For that matter, why do material and biological science continue to assert that heterosexuality and homosexuality are even subjects that are suited to being explored in material and bioscientific ways? One answer is *life*.

The anthropic principle, one of science's foundational philosophical conceits, is the underlying theme that unifies the way science approaches heterosexuality and the subject of sexual orientation in general. In a nutshell, the anthropic principle maintains that since we are alive and able to observe the natural universe, the natural universe must therefore be set up so that life can exist. This may seem to be just a casual tautology, but it also packs a strong hit of teleology: it implies that life is the purpose of the universe. If this is our starting point, in terms of studying the natural world, then whatever exists that does not appear to contribute directly to the existence or continuation of life requires some sort of explanation.

This plays out in science in any number of ways. We look, for example, for life-affirming rationales to justify the existence of things that seem hostile or dangerous. Nettles have stingers because it protects them from being eaten so they can live out their life cycles, forest fires help certain species of plants to propagate their seeds, and naturally occurring minerals that are lethal to us in quantity, like selenium or even common table salt, are also things our bodies require in tiny quantities or we become sick and die. In each case, we can find an anthropic rationale, and in each case we can reassure ourselves that these unpleasant and harmful things—nettle stings, forest fires, toxic minerals—are redeemed by having life-promoting qualities.

When Darwin's theories of natural and sexual selection exploded into the mid-nineteenth century, they intensified and lent justification to this feeling that life itself is, and indeed in a sense should be, the prime motivator behind nature's workings. *On The Origin of Species*, published in 1852, snapped the anthropic principle into a distinctively biological focus:

> Owing to this struggle for life, any variation, however slight and from whatever cause proceeding, if it be in any degree profitable to an individual of any species, in its infinitely complex relations to other organic beings and to external nature, will tend to the preservation of that individual, and will generally be inherited by its offspring. The offspring, also, will thus have a better chance of surviving, for, of the many individuals of any species which are periodically born, but a small number can survive. I have called this principle, by which each slight variation, if useful, is preserved, by the term of Natural Selection, in order to mark its relation to man's power of selection.[17]

At a stroke, any variance between one creature and its neighbor became something that could spell success or failure in the all-important struggle. Darwin was careful to point out that evolution happened at the level of populations, not at the level of individuals, but the message the public took away was that individual traits and individual variation were directly, immediately responsible for the future of society.

Arriving at a time when Western culture was struggling hard with order and hierarchy, Darwinian ideas offered a psychological, emotional, and political compass with which to navigate the threateningly anarchic nineteenth century. Industrialism, urbanization, global expansion, and colonization all threatened to unseat the priorities of the status quo, and the rise of empirical science as an authority had undermined the notion of the Great Chain of Being. In its place, however, thinking men and women could place their trust in the anthropic principle and the Darwinian ascent of man: the goal of Creation was life, and the goal of life was to continually improve its survival and success.

In this brave new evolutionary world, anatomy, physiology, anthropology, and many other disciplines indulged in shameless social Darwinism. The darkest-skinned, least technological peoples were proposed as evolutionary "missing links." African women's pelvises were compared, by anatomists, to those of gorillas and other apes.[18] Leading surgeon and early anthropologist Paul Broca not only claimed that black-skinned, wooly-haired people had never "spontaneously arrived at civilization" but warned that back home in the civilized world, women calling for more equal treatment should be carefully monitored, since disruption in the social order "necessarily induces a perturbation in the evolution of races." [19] James Hunt, founder of the Anthropological Society of London, openly intended the work of his society to show "that human equality is one of the most unwarrantable assumptions ever invented by man." Success in the Darwinian struggle, these authorities were quite clear, meant the bourgeois white Anglo-European status quo.

Heterosexuality was part of this status quo. Not only was it socially normative; it was biologically critical. Sexual activity between male and female partners is perhaps the easiest possible thing to explain by the lights of the anthropic principle. It has the potential to create life. This, in turn, is the process by which evolution is enabled, and thus its importance is self-explanatory. It is no wonder that when a term came along that seemed to contain the whole dynamic process—"heterosexual"—it was accepted quickly, quietly, and completely. And it is even less of a wonder that, until very recently indeed, there seemed to be no reason to study the everyday couplings of men and women at all: their purpose was self-evident.

It was homosexuality, with its apparent disregard of the anthropic principle, that demanded scientific attention. How could it serve the continuance of life to have members of a species who are, as our culture asserts is true of homosexuals, generally disinclined to engage in potentially procreative sex? Even if we assume that homosexuals are the only humans who are inclined to engage in nonprocreative sex—a brash assumption!—this is a problematic question. Heterosexuality is not equal to conception; conception is not equal to life. Reproductively speaking, things fail to happen at least as often as they succeed. But the anthropic principle is powerful doxa and powerful dogma: life is *sacred*. Science, religion, and our own animal existence combine to encourage us to believe that life itself is its own raison d'être. Little wonder that we have customarily excused heterosexuality from its turn beneath the microscope.

The truth is that we still don't know whether "sexual orientation" and its subtypes can actually be said to exist from the perspective of science. As Wendell Ricketts wrote, "No one knows exactly why heterosexuals and homosexuals ought to be different, and the blatant tautology of the hypotheses appears to have escaped careful attention: heterosexuals and homosexuals are considered different because they can be divided into two groups on the basis of the belief that they can be divided into two groups."[20]

If we want to know why natural science has not told us more about heterosexuality, we need to ask whether natural science is actually capable of doing so. What scientific evidence we have been able to gather in regard to sexual orientation suggests that "heterosexual" and "homosexual" may simply not be qualities that exist in the realm of material phenomena occurring spontaneously in nature. This does not mean they don't exist. It just means that they may not exist as what are called "natural kinds," the groups of things that equally and identically share particular physical attributes, and equally and identically are affected by natural laws and are thus appropriate subjects for physical science: electrons, diamonds, quadrupeds, anaerobic bacteria, amputees.

People of differing sexual orientations, on the other hand, do not seem to have physical attributes that differ in ways that map to their sexual orientations, and thus do not seem to be differently affected by natural laws on that basis either. Sexual orientations seem to be a lot more like what philosopher of science Edward Stein calls "social human kinds."[21] Social human kinds are groupings of human beings based on common social factors: Democrats, vegetarians, Frenchmen, athletes, Catholics. What this suggests is that the social sciences may have more meaningful things to tell us about the organizing principle we call sexual orientation than the physical and biomedical sciences can. Sociology, anthropology, political science, and economics should all be very useful in helping us understand more about heterosexuality and how it works. Leaving the study of heterosexuality, and of sexual orientation generally, to the social sciences may be difficult for a culture whose doxa still holds that only the natural sciences possess truly impartial authority. It may, however, not only prove to be the most intellectually honest path, but the most scientifically rigorous as well.

CHAPTER FOUR

The Marrying Type

Single women, decreed the anonymous author of the vicious and popular 1713 *Satyr Upon Old Maids,* were "the Devil's Dish," "nasty, rank, rammy, filthy Sluts." So grotesque were these spinsters, *Satyr* continued, that they ought to hurl themselves into matrimony with whoever they could find to take them, even idiots, lechers, or lepers, so that they could avoid being "piss'd on with Contempt" for their unseemly, unwomanly, inappropriate singleness.[1]

By 1962, well before the so-called "sexual revolution" or even the feminist slogan "a woman without a man is like a fish without a bicycle," Helen Gurley Brown could write in *Sex and the Single Girl,* "I think marriage is insurance for the *worst* years of your life. During your best years you don't need a husband. You do need a man of course every step of the way, but they are often cheaper emotionally and a lot more fun by the dozen."

Clearly, something major changed between 1713 and 1962. But it wasn't just a shift in attitudes about single women. The transformation of the unmarried woman, from repellent, ridiculous freak to savvy, sophisticated bachelorette, could be more accurately viewed as an indicator of far larger and deeper changes in how people of all sexes thought about and experienced heterosexuality. One way to understand what was going on is to look at marriage, the defining issue for both *Satyr* and *Sex and the Single Girl,* which, as social conservatives never tire of reminding us, has historically been the canonical, form-conferring relationship type of heterosexuality.

How, indeed, did we get from *Satyr* to Helen Gurley Brown, or for that matter, to even less economically and socially hetero-normative non-marrying role models like Oprah Winfrey? Once, marriage was so central to expectations of the life trajectory that those who failed to marry (and it seems consistently that around 10 percent did not, typically for reasons beyond their control) could be openly mocked, harassed, and perhaps even arrested and imprisoned.[2] Now, not only do both men and women regard marriage as part of a strategy of personal fulfillment, just as Helen Gurley Brown counseled all those years ago, but they can consider it separately from other sources of personal fulfillment like sexual activity, making a living, or having children. The forms we expect intimate personal relationships between men and women to take, the roles we expect them to fulfill, and what we've expected them to do for us have changed dramatically. This has occurred thanks to three major arenas of cultural change, all essentially issues of individual (and especially female) autonomy in terms of subjective desire, civic identity, and reproduction.

TO MARRY ACCORDING TO YOUR DESIRE

Desire, as any teenager can tell you, is a wild and variegated ride. Our desires can be reasoned or impulsive, fleeting or steadfast, and for things or people, sensations or possessions, experiences or emotions. Desire is also, as Buddhism reminds us in one way and consumerism in another, a constant of the human condition.

Contemporary Western culture is a culture steeped in and driven by individual desires. It has come to seem utterly logical that marriage, foremost of all our human relationships, be based in desire, specifically in emotional and sexual desire. But this has not always been the case. For most of human history, desire and marriage have not had much to do with one another. Marriage was an obligation. Wanting to marry, and even wanting to marry a particular person, had little or nothing to do with it.

Erotic desire in particular was not seen as truly relevant to marriage until the twentieth century. Historically, it simply does not seem to have been viewed as a particularly big concern, especially for women. It was taken for granted that men and women would be capable of fulfilling their reproductive duties in marriage. Beyond that, there seems to have been much more concern about making sure that sexual behavior was not excessive or sinful than there was any worry about whether it was of a sufficiently high quality. We don't have any way of knowing how most married men and women felt about one another sexually. It seems reasonable to assume that the range of sentiments ran the complete human gamut, from enthusiastic love and passion to boredom and alienation, and inevitably in some cases to fear and trauma. But very few people left any sort of record of their sexual lives at all. In most cases all we know is that most married couples managed to get it on, and we only know this because they had children. They were only doing what they had to: not for nothing was spousal sex, particularly insofar as it called for the wife to submit to the husband's sexual needs, called "paying the marriage debt."

If we are to talk about marriage in the West prior to the past few centuries, we can assume that sexual activity was included, but lust, desire, pleasure, and a sense of the erotic were not necessarily part of the picture. Nor did marriage imply romantic love. Prior to the modern era, marriage was a social, an economic, and frequently also a religious obligation, but whether or not it would or should be anything else in addition was not an issue on which everyone could agree. Should a spouse be capable of fulfilling one's wants for friendship, warmth, sympathy, and affection, or were these things unnecessary to the serious business of marriage? Did it matter whether a betrothed person actually liked his or her spouse-to-be, found him or her to be charming or sympathetic or amusing? Should you actually *desire* the person to whom you were betrothed? These were serious and divisive questions.

For much of human history, the process of acquiring a spouse was much more like what we'd experience today in making a new hire. It was a choice made by committee, for one thing. The potential new spouse usually got a vote, but she or he did not always have a veto. Candidates were usually selected by parents, near relatives, and various neighbors and friends, not so much on the basis of personal qualities or looks—it was assumed that any reasonable person could fill the

bill, just as we assume with regard to new coworkers—but on the so-
lidity of their qualifications. For the elites this meant lineage and title,
expectations of inheritance, and land. For the rank and file, qualifications were less glamorous: a man needed skills or a trade, perhaps
access to a family farm or workshop. A woman likewise would not be
a good catch unless she too was known to be hard-working, skilled,
healthy, and capable of cooking, gardening, caring for animals, milk-
ing, sewing, and innumerable other responsibilities. Just as we don't
want new coworkers who have to have their hands held through every
new job responsibility, our ancestors didn't want spouses who couldn't
hit the ground running. Character and good standing in the community counted for a lot, too, although men and women were held to
different standards. Ideally a new spouse would also bring good con-
nections. Perhaps a new bride's family had grazing rights that the husband's family would now be entitled to share. Maybe a new husband's
family owned a shipping barge, meaning expansion possibilities for
the bride's family business.

All these things were important in a spouse. Love was not. Our
foremothers and forefathers didn't expect to be in love, or even to fall
in love, with their spouses any more than we expect to find an instant
best friend in a new coworker. A wife was not a man's best friend, let
alone his lover. All the way up to the turn of the twentieth century it
was typically considered shameful to treat one's wife "as one would
a mistress." Spouses had a purpose, but the purpose was primarily pragmatic. Colonial American preacher John Cotton was plainspoken about the utility of the marital relationship: "Women are
Creatures without which there is no comfortable Living for man . . . it
is true of them what is wont to be said of governments, *that bad ones
are better than none.*" Yet Cotton did not regard wives themselves as
a utility to be taken for granted. "They are a sort of Blasphemers then
who despise and decry them and call them *a necessary Evil,*" he continued, "for they are *a necessary Good;* such as it was not good that
man should be without."[3] Men needed wives; women needed husbands. The relationship was reciprocal, interdependent, and mutual.
As teammates, they could expect to grow to know one another well
and, with some luck, become fond of one another. But their primary
job was not to be affectionate. Their job was to start, run, maintain,
and support a new branch of the family.

But of course coworkers do sometimes fall for one another, and some married couples did too. The evidence for this is not always crystal clear. Praise for a spouse engraved on a tombstone, for instance, might or might not reflect the existence of an affectionate relationship between spouses while both were alive. It does seem, however, that at least some married men and women experienced the kind of emotional and erotic combination platter we refer to when we talk, these days, about "being in love." But they were not necessarily in the majority, and neither was passionate emotion for a spouse always seen as a good thing. Plutarch, the great chronicler of the late Roman republic, repeatedly ridiculed the legendary military leader Pompey for his "effeminate" public displays of affection for his fourth wife (and Julius Caesar's daughter), Julia. This wasn't merely Roman machismo talking, but a demonstration of an ideal that persisted for well over fifteen hundred years. Historian Marilyn Yalom describes the ideal of marital affection throughout most of Western history as being "affection in harmony with duty and reason." As the *Lady's Magazine* lectured its English readership in 1774, "The intent of matrimony is not for man and his wife to be always taken up with each other, but jointly to discharge the duties of civil society, to govern their families with prudence, and educate their children with discretion." Even in the eighteenth century, as the idea that affection and even passionate love might have a role to play in marriage was coming into a general if often grudging acceptance, such things were understood to be acceptable only within limits.

As difficult as it may be for us to believe today, particularly if we have had the seemingly involuntary, overwhelming experience of "falling in love," anthropological and historical evidence both suggest that falling in love is not actually something human beings are hardwired to do but a behavior pattern that is learned. In cultures where there is no significant cultural pattern of experiencing romantic love, most people do not. Such a pattern did ultimately develop in the West, but for most of our history it was not part of the everyday experience of the average person.

It should not, therefore, be surprising that the question of whether love should have any meaningful role in people's lives, and particularly in their marriages, could be hotly controversial. *Romeo and Juliet*, as we moderns sometimes must be reminded, is a *tragedy*. Early feminist

Mary Wollstonecraft was not alone in her sentiments when she wrote, in her 1792 *A Vindication of the Rights of Woman,* "Love is, in a great degree, an arbitrary passion, and will reign like some other stalking mischiefs, by its own authority, without deigning to reason. . . . In the choice of a husband [women] should not be led astray by the qualities of a lover—for a lover the husband, even supposing him to be wise and virtuous, cannot long remain." Not for nothing did phrases like "he who marries for love has good nights and bad days" and insults like "cunt-struck," the eighteenth-century equivalent of saying that someone was thinking with his dick, survive into the Victorian age.

Romantic passion, in other words, was not always, and certainly not automatically, considered a reasonable basis on which to base a marriage. But in order for romantic love to even be an option as a requirement for marriage, another door had to be opened first: unmarried people had to be routinely permitted to choose their own marriage partners for their own reasons.

This seemingly elementary step, so basic to the way we think about marriage today, radically transformed the institution. Anthropologists and historians refer to this as the shift from "traditional"— marriages arranged primarily for social and economic reasons—to "companionate" marriages. "Companionate" marriages are based on companionship between partners, including the idea that both members of a married pair should be at least emotionally well-disposed toward one another.

Companionate marriage arguably grew out of the Protestant Reformation. Martin Luther, himself a former Augustinian monk, thoroughly dismissed the elemental Catholic contention that virginity and celibacy counted for more in terms of holiness and virtue than the married state. He also believed that marriage was good for more than just what traditional Catholic theology claimed for it, namely the production of legitimate children and the avoidance of fornication. Protestants, very much including Martin Luther, argued that marriage was a holy state in and of itself. Using the example of Adam and Eve, he argued that marriage was part of God's intention for humankind.

The idea caught on. In 1549, Archbishop Thomas Cranmer, architect of Henry VIII's many marriages as well as the split between the Catholic Church and the Church of England, wrote this essentially

Protestant point of view into the first Anglican Book of Common Prayer. To the traditional two marriage goods the Catholic Church acknowledged, Cranmer added a third. Marriage, he wrote, ought to provide spouses with "mutual society, help and comfort, that the one ought to have of the other, both in prosperity and in adversity." This did not merely allow but mandated that the subjective responses of spouses to one another be a consideration in marriage. Spouses were to be more than just boss and underling in the business of marriage and children. They were also to be friends, sympathizers, supporters, and providers of affection. Spouses didn't have to be in love by any means, and Cranmer probably would've found the idea distressing. But they did have to be in some kind of like.

It would be impossible to imagine either contemporary marriage or contemporary heterosexuality without this. The core assumption that individual desires and personal connection are what drive people to seek out one another for emotional and sexual relationships is an integral part of how we conceive not just our own experiences with romantic and sexual relationships. They are also a fundamental part of our doxa of what relationships are and how they work.[4] If men and women mated automatically and inevitably, as many animals do when they go into estrus and rut, then what individuals wanted emotionally or erotically wouldn't really make much difference. In the traditional marriage model, this is the underlying assumption: mating is the point of the exercise, and how one feels about it is of less importance than getting the job done. But if relationships between men and women legitimately included expectations of mutual, pleasant, sociable engagement; practical support; and emotional reassurance—or "society, help, and comfort"—then suddenly, the actual or prospective partners became fit judges of whether or not these criteria were met. Whether a spouse, or a marriage, was satisfactory was no longer a decision that could adequately be made solely by the consensus of parents and relatives. The feelings of the potential spouses started to matter.

Marriage criteria did not change overnight. Although over time, a potential spouse's prospects and social standing mattered less, wealth and status still counted for quite a bit. As Jane Austen telegraphed so efficiently in the famous opening line of *Pride and Prejudice*: "It is a truth universally acknowledged, that a single man in possession of a good fortune must be in want of a wife." But they were no longer *all* that mattered. Emotions now mattered too. Our expectations of what marriage and male-female relationships in general were supposed to be have never gone back.

The change took hold not so much because it was so much more dramatically fulfilling to individual married people—it could hardly have been uniformly so, given that it isn't even today. But it offered the *promise* of personal fulfillment, and in so doing it reflected and personalized potent political and philosophical movements of the time. Not only did it reflect Protestantism's emphasis on the importance and worth of marriage (a sentiment that even some leading Catholics, like Erasmus, heartily agreed with), but this concentration on happiness and the satisfaction of individual desire was also perfectly in line with emerging notions of individualism and the idea of personal happiness as an ethical and civic good. This nascent ideology had many sources across the sixteenth and seventeenth centuries: Jeremy Bentham's (and, later, John Stuart Mill's) utilitarianism, John Locke's theory of property, Adam Smith's early ideals of a self-regulating capitalism based on the individual desire for profit. In America, the précis of this philosophy with which we are most familiar is Thomas Jefferson's bold statement in the Declaration of Independence of the three inalienable rights of man as "life, liberty, and the pursuit of happiness."[5] Whether in politics, citizenship, or one's personal life, happiness is nothing if not subjective.

At least as much as the Enlightenment's obsession with science and empiricism, this new focus on happiness—personal and subjective fulfillment—helped erode older, generally religious notions of how thoughts and actions should be calibrated and judged. As historian Roy Porter put it, "Formerly a sin, self-centeredness was being transformed into the *raison d'être,* the pride and glory, of the modern psyche; thanks to the 'cunning of history,' Christian self-denial was thus giving way to the urge—even the 'right'—to self-expression."[6] It would soon seem inevitable and logical that people would marry whom they desired, and that the notion of arranged marriage would seem old-fashioned, presumptive, and invasive. Before long, extremely self-expressive practices of romantic love and sexual pleasure would not only emerge from the shadows but leap aggressively to the top of the list of marital and relationship priorities.

On the basis of the new precept that individual emotional fulfillment was a proper part of marriage, individual and intensely subjective reactions and emotions first challenged, then dominated the earlier consensus criteria for choosing a partner. Relationships with the other sex could become, as Gurley Brown put it, "more fun by the dozen," because the fulfillment of personal desires had become a legitimate motivation to enter into relationships in the first place.

TO BE ONE'S OWN MASTER

"If absolute sovereignty be not necessary in a state, how comes it to be so in a family?" asked English writer Mary Astell in 1700. "Or if in a family, why not in a state; since no reason can be alleg'd for the one that will not hold more strongly for the other?"[7] It was a good question. The rising sense that the individual had a right to certain kinds of sovereignty in life prompted many enlightenment writers to wonder just who had the right to hold authority over others, and why.

Rebellion against established authority was a constant motif of the age. From Cromwell's bloody legacy to the storming of the Bastille, the coronation of William and Mary to the Philadelphia Convention, the Enlightenment was bookended by political and philosophical revolution. Underpinning it all lay the distinctly humanist spirit of reform that had fueled the Reformation.[8]

Questions of rights, liberties, and ethical authority were central to the Enlightenment. But so was the question of who was to have these rights and liberties and why. New practices based on ideals of civil rights, universal citizenship, representative government, and egalitarianism began to be served up out of the uneasy cauldrons of revolution, but portions were by no means ladled out equally. Old habits die hard; even after the French and American revolutions and the triumph of parliamentarianism in England, even after de Condorcet and "all men shall be created equal," most people's positions in the social pecking order did not change much. Women, children, the poor, and ethnic minorities remained at the bottom of the heap. It was almost business as usual, but there was one crucial difference: baseless inequality was no longer so easy to defend as it once had been. Mary Astell and many others like her took up the cause of applying Enlightenment egalitarianism as equally as its philosophies implied.

Over the course of the eighteenth and nineteenth centuries, this reformist mood manifested in multiple philosophical, moral, and political agendas. The massive and ultimately triumphant abolition movement grew out of the combination of revolutionary politics and the strongly antiauthoritarian evangelical Protestantism of groups like the Quakers. What is now considered the "first wave" of Western feminism arose from the same fertile ground. Not only overtly feminist women like Mary Wollstonecraft but popular novelists like Daniel Defoe openly and graphically compared women's lot in marriage to slavery. Our friend Mary Astell held forth on the issue with typically vehement clarity: "*If all Men are born free,* how is it that all Women are born slaves? As they must be if the being subjected to the *inconstant, uncertain, unknown, arbitrary Will of Men, be the perfect Condition of Slavery?*"

. The Enlightenment was, in other words, aware of its own sexism. But there was nothing like universal agreement that this sexism was a problem. Many, in fact, enthusiastically defended it. Lord Halifax's best-selling *Advice to a Daughter,* first published in 1668 and enjoying its seventeenth edition in 1791, was quick to remind readers that, in marriage and in life, women and men were nowhere near equal and should not expect to be: "You must first lay it down for a foundation in general, that there is inequality in the sexes, and that for the better economy of the world, the men, who were to be the law-givers, had the larger share of reason bestowed upon them, by which means your sex is the better prepared for the compliance that is necessary for the better performance of those duties which seem to be most properly assigned to it."

To be sure, this was precisely the attitude to male and female roles in marriage that was enshrined by law and custom throughout the West. The legal convention throughout Europe, Britain, and in the New World was that of *coverture,* a principle meaning, in essence, that when a woman married, her legal and civil personhood was "covered" by her husband. In practice this meant that women had no rights or liberties unless their husbands permitted them . . . and a husband's permissions could be revoked at any time. Outside of special legal circumstances, which were rare, husbands controlled all property and earnings in their households, regardless of who had earned or brought them into the family. Men had sole, binding authority over what happened to family resources and were entitled to make executive decisions regarding children and other dependents without necessarily having to consult their wives. If a husband wanted to sell the family's house and sell the children into indentured servitude in a faraway city, there was little a wife could do except beg and plead. Coverture created some liabilities for men. They could, for instance, be held liable for crimes committed by their *femmes couverts,* because the law presumed that whatever wives did was done under a husband's direction. But on the whole, coverture offered men almost complete ownership of their wives. Even rape was not recognized within marriage. A husband and wife were "one person" under the law, thus any wife who refused to pay the marriage debt was depriving him of access to something he already owned. How could it be wrong for him to seize what was already his?

There were sometimes exceptions to coverture. Unmarried or widowed women were *femmes soles,* solitary women, technically (but usually not practically) legally equivalent to men. But they were rare, and often other laws existed that replaced coverture with an array of other restrictions on where they could live, work, and socialize. In various towns in late medieval Germany, women's wages were limited by law. Single women might be forbidden to wear silk or satin even if it was given them as a gift, or be punished for discussing religion in public. Laws in numerous places restricted the unmarried or widowed woman to a single, low-status, low-paying occupation: that of spinster, a person who spins fiber into yarn or thread. Unmarried women and widows were also often under the practical, if not necessarily the legal, control of their fathers, uncles, brothers, or (male) employers.

In some ways it did not matter much whether or not a woman was married. She could not escape being on the losing side of a gender hierarchy where the men held all the power. But where *femmes soles* had the possibility of a little leeway, in marriage the power differential was set in stone. This is not to say that every marriage was miserable. Under coverture, as under slavery, some husbands, like some slave owners, were humane, caring, and altogether reasonable toward the people over whom they held so much power. But some were not.

The deeper problem, in both slavery and marriage, was that those who were disempowered and subjugated had little recourse. Under Catholicism, divorce was unknown and annulments permitted only under extraordinary circumstances.[9] Informal separations were more common, but separated couples could not remarry or take other partners, and women particularly suffered economically for it. Protestants were scarcely more permissive. (Judaism and Islam have always permitted divorce, but their traditions have had little to no influence on mainstream Western law and custom.) The party line throughout the West was Matthew 19:6: "What God has joined together, let no man separate."

Conditions, even within marriages that were considered quite good, could be grim for women. Men could punish their wives in a number of ways, including physical beatings, for faults real or imagined. Only if beatings were considered "excessive" was anyone likely to intervene. And of course the sexual double standard applied. Husbands had the right to expect submission and service from their wives both personally and sexually, and to hold them to a strict standard of monogamy. Women, on the other hand, were commonly encouraged to take their husbands' philandering in stride, lest "indecent complaint," as Lord Halifax put it, reflect poorly on the wife. Women, in short, were stuck with the very short end of the stick.

This was the system that feminists and humanists began to question during the Enlightenment, questions that ultimately found their most effective form in a legislative crusade. This too was a hallmark of the age. The rule of reason and justice through law, rather than the potentially arbitrary divine right of kings or churches, was one of the major motifs of political change during the Enlightenment. The critical legal idea at the heart of marriage reform was the notion of the civil contract as a bi- or multilateral document that creates and defines obligations between two or more parties, and provides a basis for redress for any party if those obligations are not met. Historically, Christian marriage involved a binding agreement, but these agreements did not include many of the other elements we recognize as essential to a legal contract, particularly the option for seeking redress.[10]

The creation of civil marriage contracts was part of a long, slow pattern of increasing state involvement in marriage. For many centuries, weddings could be astonishingly informal and sometimes arbitrary affairs that might or might not be formally witnessed, officiated, or written down. Even a promise of marriage or an act of sexual intercourse could be considered a binding marriage agreement. This had predictably chaotic consequences. Fraudulent, bigamous, or otherwise problematic "secret marriages" were common. Yet it was not until the Counterreformation, in 1566, that the Catholic Church instituted a policy that all marriages had to be announced in advance (the reading of banns) and conducted by a priest in the presence of witnesses, theoretically creating at least two points at which objections to a marriage could be raised. French theologian John Calvin wanted to take things a step further, proposing that all marriages be recorded by civil authorities, not merely religious ones. It was an idea whose time would come.

In 1753, England's Parliament declared its formal interest in controlling marriages in the form of what was known as Lord Hardwicke's Marriage Act. The Marriage Act required that for a marriage to be valid under English law, it had to be performed in an official ceremony by the clergy of a religion recognized by the state. All other marriages were considered invalid, and any children born from an invalid marriage were considered illegitimate. (Famously, a historical loophole meant that the Marriage Act did not apply in Scotland, which quickly became a travel destination for eloping English. Las Vegas's wedding-chapel Elvis impersonators have nothing on the blacksmiths of Gretna Green.) The state had officially started to take over the regulation of marriage—France would follow in 1792—and with it, marriage began to become a civil agreement, bound by civil law. What this meant for women was that the door had been opened, if only a crack at first, to the possibility that the law could be used to make marriage better. Before long, two areas of legal activism, divorce law and property rights, emerged as the linchpins not just of marriage reform but of a fundamental revision of the role of women in society.

Legal reforms involving marriage were eternally controversial and never uniform. Divorce proceedings became a civil matter in England as early as 1857, but double standards (both there and in other countries, including the United States) made divorce a much simpler matter for men than women until well into the twentieth century. No-fault divorce did not become a legal reality in most of the West until the late twentieth century.[11] Before that, those who wished to divorce a spouse had not only to allege fault but to produce proof, and women's reputations, as ever, were much more susceptible to damage than men's. Even women who desperately wanted to be rid of their marriages struggled to avoid being dragged through the mud of a lawsuit and the social disapproval that was attached to divorce. It took many years before women were able, more or less, to freely take advantage of what was technically accessible.

The problem was, of course, not entirely social. Just as marriage was and still is, divorce was, and remains, an economic issue. Even today, women who divorce are likely to find their standard of living declines, while that of divorced men goes up. This cuts even deeper because women generally retain responsibility for any children. In an era before it was possible for many women to own property or hold down paying jobs, what good would a divorce do a woman if her husband's rights to marital property meant that she would have to leave it with the clothes on her back and little prospect of more? The establishment of women's property rights that let women control their earnings and inheritances, own or rent property, make wills and trusts, and otherwise take responsibility for their own financial existence went hand in hand with divorce law in altering the way marriage worked. In the United States, states began to give wives the right to control their own property as early as 1839—uncharacteristically, the first to make this progressive move was Mississippi—but it took the rest of the century and then some for the same privilege to be extended to all American women. Some states, seeking to retain some aspects of the legal jointure provided by coverture, developed community-property laws instead. England's Married Women's Property Acts, in 1870 and 1882, firmly established married women's rights over all types of property. By giving women the legal ability to earn wages; write independent wills; inherit, keep, buy, and sell property by themselves, and so on, these laws gave married women meaningful legal personhood.

This was not universally seen as a good thing. The female free agent had always been viewed with suspicion, and on that front little had changed. Women's access to property was often qualified with trusts and other encumbrances. It was not until 1975 that it was finally made illegal in the United States for a married woman to be required to get her husband's written permission to take out a loan or open a line of credit. Perhaps the most telling legal example of society's deep ambivalence toward egalitarian male-female relationships, though, were "head and master" laws. In some American states, wives were given the ability to control their own money and property by one set of laws, while at the same time those laws were superseded and undermined by a second set of laws that gave their husbands complete legal authority over household decisions and jointly owned property. Husbands could, and sometimes did, make unilateral decisions about major property issues, such as the sale of a family home, without wives' knowledge or consent. Only in 1981 did the Supreme Court—in a ruling on a sordid case in which Louisianan Joan Feenstra's husband, Harold, awaiting trial on charges of having sexually molested their daughter, mortgaged the family home (for which Joan had paid) without Joan's knowledge or consent in order to pay his lawyer—finally determine that such laws were unconstitutional violations of the Equal Protection Clause of the Fourteenth Amendment.[12]

For all the flaws and continued bias in the legal system, though, the emergence of women as full legal beings who participate in marriage on an equal contractual basis with men changed the tone of heterosexuality. When "heterosexual" was coined in the mid-nineteenth century, women were still at a marked disadvantage to men in marriage and in society in general. They might have had more say about whom they would or wouldn't marry, and their feelings about their marriages and their husbands might have been more influential, but a woman's identity and her agency were still ordinarily subsumed by that of her father or her husband. Legal personhood changed this, making both expectations and experiences of heterosexuality more egalitarian, a dynamic in which both partners' desires and responses were crucial to the success of the enterprise.

Heterosexuality also changed in response to the increasing numbers of women entering paid labor and higher education. Women had always worked, and had always contributed in material, economic ways to the welfare of their households and families. But as more women went into industrial-age wage-labor jobs, at a time when their earnings were increasingly determined to be their own to control, the marital power picture dramatically changed. Women earned less than men (a state of affairs that still pertains on the whole), but their economic contribution to the household was no longer viewed so much as something to which a husband was automatically entitled. Women's greater flexibility with regard to earned income also made it slightly less difficult for women to go it alone, not an insignificant thing in terms of helping to lessen the stigma of divorce.

Women's increasing access to education further leveled the sexist playing field. Men, feeling threatened on their own turf and unsettled by what seemed like a wild upsetting of sexual roles, launched a vocal backlash. "The one thing men do not like is the man-woman," Montagu Burrows, the Chichele Professor of Modern History at Oxford, wrote in 1869. "For the young ladies who cannot obtain 'a higher education' through their parents, brothers, friends, and books at home, or by means of Lectures in cities, let a refuge be provided with the training governesses; but for heaven's sake, do not let us establish the 'University-woman' as the modern type."[13] Educated women were commonly spoken of as "degenerate" and "unsexed," their bodies described as hairy and masculine with small, unwomanly breasts. The selfish bluestocking's refusal to content herself with domesticity and children, and her unseemly insistence on cramming learning into a smaller, softer brain that wasn't made for such things, made her an enemy of the God-fearing, normal family.

Behind this hyperbolic fear of the educated woman was a grain of marriage-resisting reality. As larger numbers of women entered colleges in the second half of the 1800s, there was a noticeable dip in the numbers who married. "From the 1870s to the 1920s," writes Carroll Smith-Rosenberg, "between 40 and 60% of women college graduates did not marry, at a time when only 10% of all American women did not."[14] The reasons college women were so much less likely to marry, however, are not entirely clear. Some men surely balked at the idea of marrying an educated woman. But some of the resistance originated with the women themselves, and surely the fact that women generally had to forgo marriage in order to put their hard-won educations to professional use had something to do with it.

For those college women who did marry, getting an education

meant that they typically married later than they would have otherwise. But college women were not the only ones postponing (or refusing) marriage. As the labor market grew, and more women moved in to fill at least the lower-paying ranks of industrial workers, average ages of marriage rose to almost the levels they are at today: women marrying for the first time in their late twenties, and men a few years later.

We are, of course, used to all these things now. But if you, like most people who will read this book, have never lived in a culture where these things are not considered standard, it can be difficult to imagine just how massive the impact of women's legal personhood, economic autonomy, and education really was. Steven Seidman documents that between 1880 and 1920, the female workforce in America increased by 50 percent. By the post–World War II boom, the demand for workers had grown so much—at the same time that the age of marriage dropped—that laws and employer policies changed en masse to permit more married women to work. Over the course of the 1950s, there was a 400 percent increase in the number of mothers in the workforce.

Today, working women, whether single or married, parenting or not, are the norm, not the exception. As of 2008, according to the US Department of Labor, women accounted for 46.5 percent of the labor force.[15] This is on par with the 46.7 percent of the global labor force that is made up of women, according to the United Nations.[16] The business of the world, quite literally, could not continue without women workers, and this has also changed the faces of both marriage and heterosexuality. The more women have been able to afford to back up their demands for better marriages—legally, economically, and socially—the more egalitarian and less mandatory marriage has become, and the more heterosexuality has had to accommodate women's demands in addition to men's.

Autonomy is the key to all of it. In a way that simply was not true for the Victorians, who invented the concept of the heterosexual, we care deeply about agency and, in particular, about women's ability to speak for themselves. It's not enough, for most of us, to say that "obviously" God or Nature intended for men and women to have relationships. We require that the men and women *want* to be in those relationships, and that they have the option not to be in them if they so choose. There is a huge difference between perceiving sexual attractions and acts as automatic or inevitable, and perceiving them as volitional acts and rational choices. It is now rare, in the West, for people to view different-sex relationships as inevitable or as a matter of duty. Autonomy of the individual has taken our relationships, as historian Stephanie Coontz puts it, from "public institution with private consequences" to "private agreement with public consequences."

Heterosexuality today is for the most part understood as being a matter of individual subjectivities and preferences among peers. Men and women do not tend to consider one another automatically as superiors and inferiors, and neither men nor women are statutorily entitled to hold power over one another or obligated to submit. We tend today to view the objects of our desire as being only superficially different from ourselves. Sexism, racism, and other prejudices surely linger, but we also profoundly believe in the legacy of Enlightenment egalitarianism: that when push comes to shove, we are all of a single human kind. Without this nonhierarchical vision of humanity, in which every person is his or her own master, a heterosexuality that rests in the fulfillment of mutual personal desires could never have come to be.

TO BREED OR NOT TO BREED?

For a very long time, babies were egalitarian marriage's Waterloo. For most of human history, babies have been an inevitable part of sexual activity between men and women, and the most fundamental purpose of marriage. The profound importance of children to marriage shows itself in the infertility miracles of the Bible, all the stories of Abraham and Sarah, Isaac and Rebecca, Hannah, and others that revolve around miraculous reversals of barrenness. It is also evident in the Roman legal codes, which permitted barren couples to adopt so they could avoid dying without heirs, and in the fact that in the medieval era, impotence and nonconsummation of marriage were two of the very few grounds on which the Catholic Church would annul a marriage. The "goods of marriage" in both Catholicism and Protestantism, as we have seen, included the generation of children.

Having babies remained an essential aspect of marriage, and one of the main issues in any male/female sexual relationship, until late in the twentieth century. It should come as no surprise that our Victorian ancestors who pioneered the concept of the heterosexual tended to think not just of women's sexual desire but of femaleness itself as manifestations of an irrepressible natural desire to bear children. As gynecologist W. Balls-Headley wrote in 1894, the "sex instinct" was the "*raison d'être* of woman's form, the expression of the cause of her existence as a woman; it is the evidence of . . . the instinctive necessity that the female reproductive cell must meet the male fecundating cell; the object is the propagation of the race."[17] Even plainspoken sexologist reformers like Havelock Ellis waxed rhapsodic about "the mystery of pregnancy," a realm of human experience "where our highest intelligence can only lead us to adoration."[18] Pregnancy was, for most couples, the inevitable result of routine sexual intercourse and, as such, the inevitable result of marriage. Even radicals like Bertrand Russell believed in a sort of default link between marriage and children, arguing in his 1929 *Marriage and Morals* that "children, rather than sexual intercourse, are the true purpose of marriage."[19]

Children are still a common part of marriage. But on the whole our views on them are rather different. The same changes in social ideals and expectations that gave would-be spouses a voice regarding whom they would marry, and provided women an autonomous social and civil existence, also dramatically changed our attitudes toward reproduction.

Today in the West, it is considered something of a default setting that pregnancies and childbirths will be, or at least ought to be, planned. "Accidents happen," as the saying goes, but when it comes to reproduction, an accident is considered irresponsible, possibly shameful. Bearing as many children as come one's way, without family planning of any kind, is so unusual now that we view it as nothing short of a freak show: witness the several iterations of reality television shows about the Jim Bob and Michelle Duggar family, whose nineteen children have made them the poster family for the controversial, fundamentalist Christian "Quiverfull" movement.[20] Parents of large families, particularly if they are poor (and especially if they receive government assistance) are often demonized as selfish and lacking restraint. Alternately it may be assumed that they are the unquestioning

dupes of authoritarian religion. In either case, the marriage that centers around raising many children is presumed to be old-fashioned
and frumpy.

It wasn't always like this, of course. For most of human history,
women had no real option other than to cope, one way or another,
with however many pregnancies happened to them. It was common
for women to bear many more than the two children that women in
most of the West average today, although not all of those children
were likely to survive. Families were often large, and a fairly constant
round of pregnancies was a standard feature of many women's lives.
The gulf between that approach to marriage and childbearing and today's is the result of a fortuitous merging of technology and culture,
the science of reliable conception plus the various forces that contributed to its social legitimacy.

The desire to control fertility is nothing new. Since time imme-
morial, women (and some men) have tried virtually anything to limit
the likelihood of conception. Ancient Egyptians used acacia pessa-
ries; Europeans from the ancient Romans to the nineteenth century
ingested herbs like Queen Anne's lace and pennyroyal. Across history,
women desperate not to bear a child did whatever they could think
of—throwing themselves down stairs, lifting heavy weights, leaping
from heights, sitting over boiling pots of water, drinking turpentine
or gin mixed with iron filings, stewing themselves in hot baths, and
much more besides—if they thought it could help them avoid it. The
desperation of some of these methods speaks with great clarity to
the fact that these were no mere attempts to create a situation where
women could enjoy more sex and more sexual pleasure without paying the proverbial piper. While the "women just want to have con-
sequence-free sex" anti-contraceptive argument is often trotted out
by latter-day social conservatives, such a view is a cruel and misogynist oversimplification. A more realistic assessment of the struggle for
effective contraception would be to see it as the struggle to achieve
some level of control over the single most dangerous, resource-
intensive, and biologically crucial activity in which human beings
regularly engage.

Conception, of course, is unpredictable. Even today we have no
really good way of knowing whether or not any individual act of in-

tercourse might result in a conception. It was not until 1927 that we could reliably test to see whether conception *had* taken place. Prior to that, early pregnancy could only be guessed at based on whether or not a woman's menses arrived on time. Historically there were many would-be contraceptives available, from coitus interruptus and herbal brews to improvised condoms. But access was unreliable, some methods were toxic, others difficult or inconvenient, and even the best historical contraceptives were not particularly dependable. Given that even the timing of ovulation in the context of the menstrual cycle was not well understood until 1924, penis-in-vagina intercourse, for most of human history, was nothing more and nothing less than a game of chance.

The chance of a pregnancy, in turn, meant the assumption of frankly terrifying risks, to say nothing of responsibilities. Pregnancy has always been a fraught time, gradually interfering with women's physical function even when it doesn't bring serious discomforts or complications. It has always meant the prospect of another mouth to feed. What we often forget, from our first-world perch with its hospital births, antibiotics, and antiseptic procedures, is that until the twentieth century, childbirth was also deadly.

Prior to the twentieth century, maternal mortality never fell much below 7 percent.[21] However, Lawrence Stone notes, in a sobering statistic, that from the sixteenth to the nineteenth century, three out of every four marriages among the aristocracy that ended before the tenth anniversary did so because of the death of the wife.[22] Nor was early childhood any safer, with an infant mortality rate that ranged from 15 percent to 25 percent, a rate that today is found only in the poorest of third world nations. Angola's 2009 infant mortality rate, for example, was around 18 percent, and Afghanistan's around 15 percent, according to the *CIA World Factbook*. Compare that to less than 1 percent for the United States, United Kingdom, and the European Union countries.

To us in the West today, these numbers describe an alien world. It is so unusual for a woman or an infant not to survive a pregnancy today that we regard it as a tragedy when it happens. For our ancestors, it was a sad commonplace. So too was the awareness that repeated childbearing tended to sap women's strength and leave them (and frequently their children as well) vulnerable to illness and injury. Little wonder that many of our foremothers openly feared and avoided sex. Theirs was not a world where there could be any sense of balance between sexual pleasure and the perils of pregnancy and childbirth.

Maternal health and welfare were not the only motivations in the struggle for reliable contraception. In fact, thanks to the advent of antiseptic practices, maternal mortality was already on the wane by the time Margaret Sanger went to work as a visiting nurse in the immigrant tenements of New York City in 1912. But Sanger, whose own mother had died miserably at fifty after bearing eleven children, was deeply aware of just how much further there was to go before pregnancy and childbirth could become a net positive in women's lives. She was not the first to consider contraception essential to solving this problem. Since the nineteenth century, reformers like Eliza Duffy had been arguing against "enforced childbearing" for the sake of women themselves, as well as the sakes of their children. In the early twentieth century, as women solidified their legal and economic independence and governments increasingly took on the responsibility of assuring public health, maternal and child health began to become more compelling civic issues. But feminist appeals on the subject—then as now—met with only limited success. Socioeconomics provided a far more convincing argument for contraception than women's welfare had.

The early nineteenth-century's Reverend Thomas Malthus had correctly identified fertility and population growth as crucial economic and political issues, both at the level of the individual household and of the nation: if population outstripped resources, he argued, disaster would result. These ideas proved central to early contraceptives campaigns, and are still used today by groups like Population Connection (formerly known as Zero Population Growth). The language employed to decry the "overproduction" of children was a useful, clinical-sounding counter to the moral indignation levied against contraceptive practices. People long accustomed to the notion that pregnancies represented God's will could be induced—through the high-status language of industrial success and failure—to agree that perhaps it was not so bad for human ingenuity to intervene in the Divine plan, now and then, in the name of common profit.

Malthusian arguments also fit in well with the social Darwinist worries of the age. On a relatively benign level, these manifested in the familiar concern that children should not be brought into the world unless their parents were prepared to give them a "proper," meaning middle-class, upbringing. The ability to provide "respectable" education, clothing, nutrition, and the like to children was seen not just as the admirable goal it had been earlier, but was now a standard by which readiness for parenthood could be measured. There was a growing expectation that the well-prepared parent would provide for children in very specific and often costly ways, including the use of myriad new specialized products often touted as "scientific": commercial baby foods, purpose-built toilet-training equipment, specially designed children's clothes, nutritional supplements.[23] All these new inventions were touted as necessary because, as the editorial tagline for *Parents Magazine* read, from its founding in the 1920s until it was changed in 1951, "The future of the race marches forward on the feet of little children."

With the "future of the race" at stake, fears about inappropriate childbearing also assumed more sinister forms. An increasingly widespread fear that the "unfit" and "unsuitable" were breeding at such a rate that their numbers would overtake those of the "fit" and "worthy" slotted in neatly beside common paranoia about the poor, the nonwhite, the slum-dweller, and their even more terrifying cousins, the addict, the prostitute, the indigent, and the disabled. That such sorry specimens might theoretically outbreed the upright, respectable middle classes intensified the nineteenth-century tendency to panic about "race suicide" and national failure. Such fears continued unabated into the twentieth century, when they eventually received a red-scare makeover. As politically influential Dixie Cup magnate Hugh Moore put it in a widely circulated 1956 letter, "We're not primarily interested in the sociological or humanitarian aspects of birth control. We *are* interested in the use . . . which the Communists make of hungry people in their drive to conquer the earth."[24]

The solution to both increasing birth among the worthy and minimizing it among the unworthy, at least in theory, was relatively simple. The fit and worthy were to be encouraged to have more children. They would be supported in the effort to boost the middle-class population through government-sponsored maternal benefits, classes for new parents, and child welfare programs, all of which sprang up in quantity throughout the West during the interwar years. As part of this overall effort, the phrase "family planning" came into being in the 1940s, its reassuring overtones promising an appealing brand of domestic security. If having a family could be planned, in the same way one might plan the building of a house, doing it systematically seemed to make the task much less daunting.

Then there were those who were not to be given the option of parenthood, whether planned or not. Compulsory sterilizations in small numbers were performed in the United States on "undesirables" beginning in 1907. The practice was adopted in Scandinavia in the interwar years. An attempt to establish sterilization as a state policy in Britain in 1913 failed, but, in 1933, Germany passed a Eugenic Sterilization Law, modeled on the Model Sterilization Law developed by the Eugenics Record Office of the United States. The Eugenic Sterilization Law, in turn, swiftly became an infamous tool of the Third Reich.

One might think that considering the extremes to which governments were willing to go to stop the wrong people from having babies, garden-variety contraception would have been, as it were, a simple pill to swallow. But anxiety that the right people would procreate, combined with centuries of moral opposition to contraception (not least that of the Catholic Church), meant that this was hardly the case. In many jurisdictions, contraception was either illegal or of dubious legal status. In virtually all, it was officially taboo.

What governments or religious authorities dictated, and what the average Joe and Jane did in their private lives, however, were often two different things. After all, economic, medical, and social motivations for family planning are hardly limited to governments. The nineteenth century appears to have been an era of widespread do-it-yourself family planning. Researchers including Karl Ittmann and Daniel Scott Smith have found ample evidence that even among the poor working classes in the turn-of-the-century United States and UK, enough people were deliberately limiting family size for it to be demographically apparent in statistical retrospect.[25] Imperfect as the available methods were (withdrawal was the favorite), Victorians' dedication to their contraceptive practices must have been impressively consistent. Birthrates among American white women declined from 7 babies per woman in 1800 to around 3.5 in 1900, a sort of drop that simply does not happen without some sort of intentional brake on fertility. This was precisely the sort of decline in birthrate among the "right" people that provoked so much paranoid "race suicide" speculation.

By the start of the twentieth century, it was becoming obvious that intentional fertility limitation was not just a superficial trend but increasingly a part of standard middle-class experience. Faced with a fait accompli, religious authorities and then major secular governments began to grant their grudging approval to contraception. The Church of England was first, permitting it as of 1930 for married couples who felt a "moral obligation" to limit parenthood. The influential Council of Churches of Christ, representing about 22 million American Protestants, followed with a similar pronouncement in 1931. It was not until much later that major Western governments got on board. In 1965, *Griswold v. Connecticut* established that contraception was constitutional in the United States on privacy grounds, while Britain's National Health Service Amendment (Family Planning) Act of 1967 established that contraceptive devices could be distributed freely under the auspices of the National Health Service.

What finally tipped the scales of government acceptance was the contraceptive pill, a technology born of equal parts scientific innovation and feminist daring. Legal, moral, economic, and societal obstacles made contraceptives activism and research difficult at best. Fearing reprisal, universities, major medical researchers, and pharmaceutical companies refused to get involved. This was largely a social fear. Corporations were well aware of just how lucrative the contraception market was: Goodyear Rubber made $150 million in the condoms market in 1958, while simultaneously refusing to acknowledge that it manufactured them.[26] It was clear that if the job of developing a contraceptive pill was going to get done, it would have to be done privately. It was ultimately funded and directed by two formidable women. Margaret Sanger coordinated the effort, and philanthropist Katherine Dexter McCormick provided the capital.

Even before it became available, though, the Pill was a topic of intense, even desperate, interest. When news that it was in development hit the media, the researchers received a flood of desperate letters:

> I am about 30 years old have 6 children, oldest little over 7,
> youngest a few days. My health don't seem to make it possible
> to go on this way. We have tried to be careful and tried this
> and that, but I get pregnant anyway. When I read this article
> [*Science Digest,* September 1957] I couldn't help but cry, for I
> thought here is my ray of hope.[27]

Many went so far as to offer themselves as research subjects, even though they knew virtually nothing about the drug or its possible side effects—it was worth almost anything to find a solution to the problem of unplannable, unstoppable pregnancies.

No one who had been involved with the development of the Pill was surprised by the eagerness and devotion with which women began to take it when it became available in 1960. The culture at large and the media, however, were flabbergasted, and sometimes horrified, that within five years more than six million women in the United States were taking it. But soon it was apparent that the Pill had ushered in a brave new world. By 1970, more than half of all adult women, married or unmarried, were using some form of contraception or had been voluntarily sterilized. Our relationship to marriage and childbearing was transformed.

Birthrates, already on the decline, dropped still further as more women availed themselves of the new technology. In England, a woman who married between 1851 and 1860 was likely to bear six children; an Englishwoman in 2007 would, according to the British Office for National Statistics, average 1.9.[28] In the United States, the story has been much the same. Even the supposedly extraordinarily fecund post–World War II "baby boom" American families averaged only around three children. By 2007, according to the Centers for Disease Control, the American fertility rate had dropped to around the 2.1 births per woman average that is considered a baseline replacement rate for the existing population.[29] In both the US and UK cases, these very low fertility rates actually represent an increase over the all-time lows recorded in the early 1970s, shortly after both countries made contraception legally accessible to all women.

Such decreased fertility has meant, among other things, that women spend much more of their reproductive lives doing things other than having and rearing children. It has also changed what happens to women's lives when, and indeed if, they marry. Marriage, in the early twenty-first century, is by no means a relationship to which children are presumed necessary, let alone all but inevitable as they were in the past. For a woman to go through life without ever bearing a child is no longer considered a startling anomaly. Married or unmarried, around 15 to 20 percent of American women aged forty to forty-four, at this point, have never had a child. It may be that the decreased emphasis on having children is also part of the decrease in the numbers of women who choose to marry. In 2002, it was about 79 percent likely that an American woman would get married, according to the National Center for Health Statistics, and in 2008, the British media engaged in a bout of handwringing over the revelation that the marriage rate there had fallen to its lowest since 1862.[30]

The simple fact is that children are no longer presumed necessary to marriage. Marriage, likewise, is no longer presumed inevitable because of the demand that one procreate. And should one wish to have a child, one need only do it: marriage is increasingly optional. In both the United States and the UK, approximately 40 percent of babies are now born to unmarried parents; in Iceland, Sweden, and Norway, the percentage ranges to 50 to 65 percent. So much for the vilified "stinking Sluts" of eighteenth-century satire: unmarried women and men can now opt to live out their lives unmarried and still be happy, healthy, productive, mostly unremarkable members of society. They may be mothers. They may well even be partnered. Cohabitation without marriage has grown dramatically throughout the West, and people, not least celebrities like Angelina Jolie, openly and happily choose both unmarried partnership and unwed parenthood.

What all this means for marriage is that its nature and purpose are fundamentally different now than at any time in history. While the old meanings and functions still exist, economically and socially, they do not dominate in the way they once did, and indeed are open both to public debate and deliberate reconfiguration. This is nowhere so true as it is with regard to fertility. Contraception, not to put too fine a point on it, has enabled companionate marriage to become focused almost entirely on that companionship. Financially, emotionally, and physically, spouses need not share their resources with children unless they choose to, and then, in most cases, only with the number of children they desire. There is no longer a sense that marriage means the near-inevitable arrival of a tiny, squalling roadblock to putting one another first.

This expectation has spilled over into all heterosexual relations. Our optimal version of heterosexuality has become one where the entire gamut of conception, pregnancy, childbirth, and childrearing not only can be but normally is cordoned off, a separate realm from sexuality altogether. Our contemporary heterosexuals are not compelled, willy-nilly, by biology or family pressure or religious dogma or government mandate, to pair up and make babies Just Because. They are free agents whose liberty to pursue sexual, emotional, and reproductive happiness with the partner of their choice has effectively become, no matter how social conservatives squawk, another human right.

CHAPTER FIVE

What's Love Got to Do with It?

"Nearly everybody gets twitterpated in the springtime," Friend Owl explains in Walt Disney's classic animated film *Bambi* (1942). "You're walking along, minding your own business," Owl continues, "you're looking neither to the left nor to the right, when all of a sudden you run smack into a pretty face. Woo woo! You begin to get weak in the knees. Your head's in a whirl. And then you feel light as a feather, and before you know it, you're walking on air. And then you know what? You're knocked for a loop, and you completely lose your head!"

Sweet and superficial, this sort of step-by-step instruction in the emotional practice of heterosexuality is everywhere in Disney films. It always has been, from the very first of their animated fairy tales, *Snow White and the Seven Dwarfs,* which taught its 1937 audiences that if a pure-hearted young woman fervently believed "Someday My Prince Will Come," he inevitably would.[1]

With their vaguely medieval fairytale settings of princesses and princes, witches and fairy godmothers, Disney's classic films have an appealingly timeless, magical feel. Their plots, many borrowed from the fairy-tale collections of European writer-collectors like Charles Perrault, Hans Christian Andersen, and the Brothers Grimm, are familiar, for all that they've been brightened, lightened, and defanged. With the darker themes of traditional myth pushed into the background, narratives of romantic heterosexual love are inserted where necessary and blown up to superhuman size. Even in latter-day Disney films, like 1998's *Mulan,* whose plot and characters have clearly been influenced by feminist criticisms of Disney's tradition of hapless but plucky heroines in need of gallant male rescue, male-female attraction and romance are still central to the narrative.

Heterosexual romance, in most of the Disney oeuvre, is necessary to the happy ending. And the happy ending, in the Disney universe, is also the moral of the story: *And they all lived happily ever after.* The Disney corporation has a long tradition of selling this fantasy of heterosexual romantic bliss to every conceivable audience, starting virtually in the cradle. Disney's online store offers an entire division devoted to "Disney Princess" merchandise, including *Cinderella's Fairy-Tale Wedding Book,* aimed at girls ages four and up. And when little Disney Princesses grow up and want a real wedding, they can turn to Disney's Fairy Tale Weddings division, which since 1991 has offered services for every aspect of a Disney wedding, from gown to honeymoon, at an average price of $20,000 per ceremony.[2]

Surely there is nothing particularly novel in the annals of human history in looking for a happily ever after, a life that is secure and pleasant and easy. Expecting it to be the result primarily of romantic love, on the other hand, is a fairly recent historical trend. Even more modern is the oddly naïve insistence—particularly in otherwise sophisticated men and women—that somewhere out there, Prince Charming or a perfect princess is waiting for them, the only thing standing between them and a perfect life. For good reason, my circle of friends refers to this kind of overinflated, codependent fantasy of romantic love as "Disney damage."

A NOVEL ROMANCE

It isn't all Disney's fault, of course. Disney is just the most iconic recent manifestation of a sort of cultural propaganda that had its beginnings in the Renaissance, around the same time of the many other cultural changes—the Counterreformation, the rise of humanism, the birth of companionate marriage—that have transformed heterosexual experience. The Protestant emphasis on marriage over celibacy, a new focus on individualism, and of course the notion that there should be an affectionate element in marriage all provided a congenial climate in which the tropes of the romantic love story could take root and grow. And grow they did: as early as 1670, the Catholic bishop and scholar Pierre-Daniel Huet could declare of the earliest prose novels or "romances" that "we esteem nothing to be properly Romance but Fictions of love Adventures, disposed into an Elegant Style in Prose, for the Delight and Instruction of the Reader."[3]

Huet's insight that novels are instructive is instructive itself. His was an age in which literacy was still limited primarily to the elites, and a long connection between reading and religious study meant that the mere activity of reading tended to be viewed as automatically educational in nature. But as Huet pointed out, the stories were teaching tools of a specific kind. These "love Adventures" taught the reader about the battle between virtue and vice and the struggle to avoid disgrace in a very specific context, that of relationships between women and men. This was important, Huet explained, because enthusiasm for love and love stories was apparently universal. They appealed to the intellectually sophisticated and the frivolous, the man of letters and the lady of leisure. Romances easily captivated the imagination and the attention, the passions "agreeably provoked and appeased."[4] Much, Huet explained, could be effectively conveyed straight to the hearts and minds of readers through these "Dumb Tutors, which succeed those of the College, and teach us how to Live and Speak by a more Persuasive and Instructive method than theirs."[5] The question, which has been asked again and again over the centuries, was not whether novels (or films, or video games, or pop songs) were influential, but whether their influence was a good one. Huet was a moderate on the subject, his views summed up with a liberal shrug: "I know what they are accused for: They exhaust our Devotion, and inspire us with Irregular Passions, and corrupt our Manner. All this may be, and sometimes does happen. But what can't Evil and Degenerated Minds make an Ill Use of?"[6]

Novels did not just promote the ideal of companionate marriage but also the notion that it should be arrived at through an experience of passionate romance. Fictional examples encouraged ever larger numbers of readers to accept the possibility, and perhaps even the desirability, that the roles of lover and spouse might ideally be filled by the same person. Some of these books became well known, like

Fanny Burney's 1778 *Evelina,* still taught today and popular enough that Jane Austen referred to it by name in her own 1817 *Northanger Abbey.* Other titles of less lasting reputation but nearly identical attitudes toward romance numbered in the thousands, including those of the almost ridiculously prolific Eliza Haywood, more or less the Nora Roberts of her day. Haywood published more than thirty-five novels with titles like *The Distressed Orphan; or, Love in a Madhouse* and *The Fatal Fondness,* each one a testament to the pressure on writers to produce a happy-ending love narrative the public could find irresistible. Even Charles Dickens succumbed, rewriting, with a bit of prodding from colleague Edward Bulwer Lytton, the very ending of *Great Expectations* to suggest the possibility that Pip would find a happily-ever-after with Estella and thus, he hoped, boost the novel's acceptance. (If you found the ending unconvincing, now you know why.)

To be sure, the romantic-love novel had its loyal opposition. Mary Wollstonecraft and Samuel Johnson tended to be of the opinion that romantic love was, as Lawrence Stone puts it, "no more than a purely artificial emotion invented by novelists and adopted by men as a cover for sexual desire."[7] Wollstonecraft's unfinished final novel *Maria, or the Wrongs of Woman* (1792), in fact, depicts the disaster of what the titular heroine believed to be a love-match marriage. Maria's husband, George, turns out to be a libertine, gambler, and general wastrel who put up a gentlemanly and loving front while courting Maria in order to secure her large dowry. Maria's attempts to salvage her life, marriage, and fortunes result in her husband committing her to an insane asylum. It is a grim story that seems all the bleaker by contrast with the wildly popular cult of the happily-ever-after. Yet it too explores a part of the reality of what romantic love brought to the practice and experience of heterosexuality.

As time went on, Romantic-era novelists would come to focus on the potentially catastrophic fallout of love. The theme fuels some of the era's greatest works, including Goethe's *The Sorrows of Young Werther* and Flaubert's *Madame Bovary.* But even such dramatic critiques of the romantic-love dynamic could not counterbalance the overwhelming number of stories that pursued their romantic storylines to an ending that could be summed up in the same way that the last chapter of *Jane Eyre* (also a Romantic-era novel) begins, "Reader, I married him."

Some readers were aware that the novels they loved amounted to a propaganda campaign, that the love stories had a particular agenda that might or might not have anything at all to do with reality. But then as now, being a canny and independent-minded consumer of popular media did not bar one from also enjoying being manipulated by it. Thomas Carlyle's wife, the astute woman of letters Jane Welsh Carlyle, was surprisingly fond of some truly trashy novels, including Dinah Craik's 1849 potboiler *The Ogilvies*.[8] Of this turgid tome, complete with love triangles, rumors, and a meddling benefactress, Carlyle said, "It quite reminds one of one's own love's young dream."[9] Carlyle's comment not only shows that she was quite aware of the distance between fiction and reality, but also reveals that her enjoyment of the book depended on her own experience of idealizing and fantasizing romantic love. Where did Carlyle's "own love's young dream" come from? Most likely at least some of it came in turn from an earlier reading of novels, different in their style but nevertheless dependable in terms of providing the stories Huet so aptly characterized as "amorous adventures."

Young and poor people's access to romantic novels was seen as a serious issue indeed. Moralists typically presumed that readers, particularly young women readers, had no critical faculties whatsoever and would passively internalize the unrealistic expectations of novelistic romance with dismal results. The family resemblance between the eighteenth- and nineteenth-century novel and the films of Walt Disney is thus not just about content. It is also about popularity, accessibility, and reception.

As early as the 1680s, Boston booksellers' records show that sales of books in the category "romances, etc." came second only to that of Bibles and religious works.[10] In 1785, novelist and literary critic Clara Reeve attacked the institution of the circulating library because, with its affordable subscription rates and voluminous shelves, it made the voracious reading of novels so easy. She was, it must be said, standing in at least a partially glass house when she threw that stone in the pages of her *The Progress of Romance* (1785): her literary reputation at the time rested primarily upon her Gothic novels, including *The Old English Baron* (1777). Reeve would have been more horrified still by the nineteenth- and twentieth-century proliferation of railway book stalls, book clubs, "penny dreadfuls" and dime novels, and especially the explosion of periodicals whose publication of fiction—often in serial form, as in the case of many of Dickens's novels—in cheap, mass-produced form made them accessible not just to the educated middle classes, but to the increasingly literate working classes as well. It is probably just as well that Reeve didn't live long enough to experience American-style public library systems, which made all kinds of books, including the hugely popular romantic novels, available to even the poorest of the poor for no charge.

The "love adventure" may have had its finest literary moments as a middle-class phenomenon, but the urban masses of the industrial age enjoyed the love story just as much as anyone else. Romance fiction became a staple of mass media and mass culture, training not just the well-off and educated but also the working-class and poor to expect a very particular—and historically peculiar—version of relations between men and women. This is still true today. The romance market is consistently the top-performing category on the *New York Times,* *USA Today,* and *Publishers Weekly* best-seller lists, according to the trade association Romance Writers of America, and the US romance fiction market grosses about $1.35 billion yearly. Yet it is considered a literary "ghetto," associated with the pink-collar working class, and generally not regarded as literature by the mainstream middle-class press.

Clearly, a greater tolerance of and even enthusiasm for romantic love was already in the air when the popularity of the novel began to spread. Even had the novel not become the massive force of cultural propaganda and instruction that it did, we might still suffer the same romantic effects. But as it happened, the growth of the culture of romantic love in the West was inextricable from the growth of the novel. Our culture of heterosexuality runs, in a very real way, on the repeated inscription of a fantasy of romance between men and women that gets replayed a thousand times a day with every clunk of the printing press, every whir of the film reel, and every iconic photo of Disneyland's Sleeping Beauty Castle.

"ENCIRKLED IN THOSE BLESSED ARMS"

Heaven, preached seventeenth-century Calvinist Thomas Shepard, was a "Celestial Bride Chamber and Bed of Love." Unlike in earthly life, where even the saints could only occasionally catch a glimpse of

God or steal a kiss from Him, in Heaven, he claimed, "there shall be that intimacy that there is between the most loving husband and most beloved wife, and transcendently greater . . . they will not be interrupted Caresses which they shall have from him. . . . There will be no more Coyness on their parts, nor Anger on his, but the delights which they shall enjoy, shall be both full and uninterrupted . . . the reciprocal ardors of Affection between him and us, shall break over all Banks and Bounds, and we shall be entirely satisfied, both in Soul and Body. Then shall we come to our Rest."[11] Just as literature was learning to detail the twists and turns of the "love adventure," religion was also learning the language of love.

Even in the seventeenth century there was, of course, nothing particularly new about love imagery in religion, particularly in Christianity. The Song of Songs had, after all, been around for a good long time. Since the Reformation, Christian iconography also included a heavy dose of Christ as the Bridegroom, come to join metaphorically with the believer, who took on the role of the vulnerable, eager Bride. What was new to seventeenth-century Protestantism, particularly as it was practiced in North America, however, was the notion that individual Christians might, and perhaps even should, have personal experiences along the same ardently emotional lines.

Some American Protestants, like minister Cotton Mather, drew a distinct line between vivid metaphor and appropriate Christian practice. But others, particularly as the eighteenth century wore on, did not make such a clear separation. The evangelical approach to Christianity did not view God's grace as something that worked primarily through reason and learning, as earlier Protestants and Catholics had, but as something one experienced directly with the emotions. Evangelicals came to see emotional experiences as one of the ways in which God worked on humans, appealing directly to their soft hearts instead of struggling to get through their hard heads. This approach to faith had many manifestations: revival meetings, the ecstatic dancing of the Shakers, "speaking in tongues," swooning or trembling during worship, and even the relatively sedate Quaker practice of "waiting on the Lord." The idea that a Christian's proper relationship to God was internal, emotional, and profoundly personal became increasingly commonplace.

Along with this came a slow but seismic shift in the ideology of emotions. Difficult to control, maddeningly changeable, and suspiciously close to the unruly agendas of the animal self, strong spontaneous emotion was redeemed by the fact that it could also be a conduit for God. Particularly in North America, where evangelical approaches to religion were common (and in some places dominant), the experience and expression of emotion became elevated and spiritualized. For many, the more intense the emotional experience, the more intense the spiritual experience. Metaphors of love, passion, and ecstasy were not just metaphors; they were the best language these Christians, who so carefully cultivated their emotional relationships to God, had to describe their experiences. When believers described feeling "ravished" by God, or "melting" into a state of spiritual "rapture," it both was and wasn't just a figure of speech.

In time Christians began to attribute a similar spiritual meaning to those emotions when they felt them in regard to other human beings. As historian Zsuzsa Berend argues, evangelical Christian emotional practices provided a way to legitimize the potentially anarchic force of romantic love between human beings. "Attraction became the sign of a God-ordained union, oneness a spiritual ideal deemphasizing sensual and sexual implications, and self-forgetfulness the epitome of selflessness," Berend writes.[12] "True love," the epitome of an emotional and erotic romantic love, was redeemed from suspicions of sensuality by Christian interpretations of spontaneous passionate emotion as pure, noble, moral, and (paradoxically enough) selfless. If a man and a woman felt such powerful internal stirrings for one another, it was interpreted as a sign from above. God approved, that was why they felt so strongly.

God's love reconciled romance, and even "romantic adventure," to middle-class society. The most private emotions and spontaneous surges of feeling could now be interpreted as being eminently respectable. Especially if they led to formal courtship and marriage, there was no gap between passionate love and responsible participation in all the obligations of adulthood. But the spiritualization of romantic love created new obligations, too. As the nineteenth century progressed, it became apparent that it was no longer enough to find a partner for whom one could feel affection and sympathy, or even enough to find a partner one could love. One had to find a very specific and demanding kind of love. This love had to have a core of spontaneous passionate emotion but also encompass "true unity," a perfect and scrupulously mutual balance of the emotional, the erotic, and the spiritual. As Mrs. John Farrar wrote in her 1837 *The Young Lady's Friend*, "[T]he great end of existence, preparation for eternity, may be equally attained in married or single life; and that no union but the most perfect one is at all desirable."[13]

Finding such a perfect union was not easy. Indeed, for some, taking the task too seriously meant that they could never assure themselves that they had truly found the "one who could be all things to the heart," and they ended up without any union at all. To be sure, this may have come as a welcome escape for some men and women who had no interest in marriage and possibly no interest in the other sex. But for others, like pioneering physician Elizabeth Blackwell, it was a self-imposed prison sentence. For her, the extraordinary steps of attending medical school and pursuing a life of singlehood and service were her way of coping with an attraction to a man whom she felt could not measure up to the standard of perfect union. Medicine was a productive place to channel the feelings she "could not wisely yield to, but could not otherwise stifle."

The process of getting to a perfect—or at least perfect enough—union could be complex. Men typically made the first move by declaring their interest. Whether the woman would respond in kind was by no means assured. Women often played their cards very close to their chests, frequently going so far as to test their suitors' sentiments in various ways, because once a woman reciprocated a man's interest it was assumed that she would most likely agree to marry him. Men often appealed to the families of the women they hoped to court in advance of talking to the women themselves, an illuminating practical example of how the shift from traditional to companionate marriage manifested in everyday life. Men sometimes even wrote their love letters not *to* the women they hoped would become their sweethearts, but *about* those women to their siblings, parents, and other relatives who might be able to influence the young lady's opinion.[14] Courtship proper began when a woman reciprocated a man's interest. Across the eighteenth and nineteenth centuries, middle-class courtships became increasingly verbose affairs, replete with confessional and philosophical explorations of emotion. In face-to-face conversation as well as in the pages of voluminous letters, courting couples scoured their histories and their consciences for the sake of ascertaining whether theirs was, or could be, a perfect love.

In doing so, they forged paths through tricky and sometimes treacherous realms of sexuality. In the letters shared by historian and novelist Charles Kingsley and his intended, Fanny Grenfell, Kingsley in particular became deeply involved with the question of how physical desire and a spiritualized love could best be reconciled. "Our animal enjoyments must be religious ceremonies," Kingsley wrote to his bride-to-be, setting the bar quite high from the start. Drawing a sharp and profoundly religious distinction between sensuality and true love, the vocally libidinous Kingsley went so far, in his correspondence with Fanny, as to propose that since he wished "to shew you & my God that I have gained purity & self-control—that intense as my love is for your body, I do not love it but as the expression & type of your spirit—and therefore when we are married, will you consent to remain for the first month in my arms a virgin bride, a sister only."[15] The proposition was extreme, but not too far out of keeping with the priorities of the era. Self-control and the strict management of sexual activity were crucial to the ability to spiritualize romantic love. Sexual activity was acceptable as an expression of that spiritual love, but the desire for it could not by any means be allowed to gain the upper hand. Negotiating this was central to Kingsley's ongoing conversation with the woman he loved. Finding the right way to have a sexual relationship, he hoped, would "give us more perfect delight when we lie naked in each other's arms, clasped together toying with each other's limbs buried in each other's bodies, struggling, panting, dying for a moment. Shall we not feel then, even then, that there is more in store for us, that those thrilling writhings are but dim shadows of a union which shall be perfect?"[16] That a husband-to-be would write with such frank expectations of joint emotional and physical ecstasy shows just how far the idea of mutually companionate marriage had come.

The 1838 correspondence between the American abolitionists Angelina Grimke and Theodore Weld was similarly revealing of the priorities of the era. Lasting only three months, their courtship letter-writing was deeply influenced not just by shared Christianity and abolitionist principles but by Grimke's fiery feminism. In Grimke's essay "Letters to Catherine Beecher," she blasted the contemporary culture of masculinity, calling it "a charter for the exercise of tyranny and selfishness, pride and arrogance, lust and brutal violence," and pilloried conventional expectations of femininity as robbing women of their essential humanity and rights. Weld was sympathetic to these views, and agreed with his beloved's assertion that "when human beings are regarded as moral beings, sex, instead of being enthroned upon the summit . . . sinks into insignificance and nothingness."[17]

In the course of their courtship, Grimke and Weld's shared feminism, and Grimke's keen and critical awareness of gender, brought them to the point of questioning heterosexuality altogether. They did not call heterosexuality by that name, of course; the word did not yet exist. Yet in the midst of their whirlwind correspondence, Grimke wondered aloud, "Why does not the love of my own dear sister and of my faithful Jane [Smith, Grimke's dearest female friend] satisfy, if as a human being I must have *human love?* Why do I feel in my inmost soul that you, *you* only, can fill up the deep void that is there?"[18] It was a good question. Grimke and Weld certainly do seem to have experienced their love for one another as spiritual, so much so that they both worried they might unintentionally be engaging in idolatry. They also believed that the spirit had no sex or gender but was transcendent and universal. If love was spiritual and the spirit had no sex or gender, then why indeed did it seem to matter so much exactly *whose* love existed in their lives? Why should they both long to be together physically? Why, as Grimke asked Weld, was it true that "those of our own sex *cannot* fill the void in human hearts?" Weld, who confessed that it had never before occurred to him to wonder why this was so, fell back on religious explanations. Maleness and femaleness were part of God's plan, and the apparent inevitability of their mutual attraction was, too. Yet at the same time, neither he nor Grimke was willing even to theoretically root their love in something as base, as potentially sinful, or as fraught with power imbalance as biological sex.

Just as Charles Kingsley worked to find a way to reconcile lust and spiritualized love for his fiancée and himself, Angelina Grimke and Theodore Weld battled together to hammer out the terms of a marriage that could provide them with emotional, political, and spiritual unity. Romantic love did not "come naturally" for these nineteenth-century couples. It was much too important for that. This demanding, complicated model of love swiftly became seen as such a vital part of marriage that, as of the 1860s, even the law began explicitly to accommodate it. As Harvard-trained lawyer and law professor Robert C. Brown put it in 1934, "[T]he most important legal action given for the purpose of protecting marital relations from unjustifiable interference by outsiders is what is known as the action for alienation of affections."[19] Love was not love, as Shakespeare put it, that bent with the remover to remove. Love was serious, mutual, obligatory business. Popularized in literature, spiritualized and made equal in practice, by the end of the nineteenth century romantic love between men and women had become a defining component of heterosexuality all its own, a newly standard destination in the itinerary of an average life.

DATING AND RATING

Around 1914, it became possible to go out on a date.[20] As the Victorian era drew to a close, and the cult of true love trickled down from the middle classes to the working class and the poor, a new style of courtship emerged. Dating arose as an urban alternative to the more rural and suburban custom of "calling," a courtship practice where young men would hopefully await an invitation from a young woman's family (usually the mother) to "call on" a young lady and visit her at her family's home. By contrast, dating literally removed the courting couple from the domestic realm. In the "calling" system, courtship was not necessarily heavily policed—historians including Ellen Rothman have documented how many families went out of their way to give courting couples privacy and time alone—but it did mean that courting still took place in the context of a woman's family and neighbors.[21] In the "dating" system, a young woman's home may have been where a date began and ended, but the date itself had the city as its stage.

The two systems were worlds apart. Courtships carried out in cafes and restaurants, parks and theatres were simultaneously less supervised but more public than calling. They were less challenging to arrange, since a man could simply ask a woman for a date rather than having to wait and hope for an invitation to call on her at home. But they were much more expensive, requiring men to pay for food, entertainment, and transportation rather than taking advantage of the home comforts that were already there. Dating had far less in the way of safety nets or quality control for women, since a woman's family had no real ability to vet who might ask their daughter out on a date, nor were family members likely to be in the next room when the date was in progress. On the other hand, this meant a great deal more personal choice for both men and women in terms of whom they might court and how they might behave in the process of doing so.

Dating was also suited to urban life's opportunities for meeting people. Although most dates still happened among people who shared social circles—among coworkers or friends of friends—it was also quite possible for a man to approach a woman who was a complete stranger. Dating, like marriage, was to remain mostly segregated along ethnic, religious, and socioeconomic lines for many decades (it is largely so today), but the relative spontaneity with which a date could be arranged broadened the range of what was possible and, indeed, what might be considered permissible. Particularly in North America, the end of the nineteenth and early twentieth centuries were a time when many ethnically diverse Northern European immigrants "became white," assimilating to an American ideology of race in which all white-skinned people were more alike than they were different because all whites were contrasted to all blacks. Dating between white ethnic groups was part of this process, and led in many cases to the motley national ancestries so common among those who appear today to be simply "white North Americans."[22]

Economically, dating was tailor-made for the urban worker. With factory-based industry well established, many turn-of-the-century urban workers could reach their peak earning level quite early in life. Even if not, most could at least find a reasonably regular wage. Not yet responsible for wives and families, young urbanites tended to have money to spend on streetcars and cab rides, dances, restaurants, and the occasional corsage. Such spending patterns only became more commonplace as the rituals of dating spread both up and down the socioeconomic ladder. Dating, like marriage, was an overtly economic transaction, and was at least superficially organized along what had become traditional male-provider lines. Men paid for the opportunity to date women, just as they expected to be responsible for the economics of the marital household and the support of their wives. Paying for dates was both a symbolic demonstration of the male-breadwinner paradigm and a pragmatic reflection of the superior earning power men had in comparison to women.

But women also had an economic role to play in dating, one that proved critical to the development of modern consumer culture. Men paid for the dates themselves, but women paid to become attractive enough to be considered hot dating property. In the less family- and community-centric world of dating, an attractive appearance was instrumental not only to an individual man's subjective response to her; it also determined how she and her beau were perceived when they were out together in public, and how much status he would acquire from being seen dating her. Female beauty became the coin of the realm. But beauty was also naturalized and spiritualized. Just as one would not freely admit that a suitor's money had a role to play in one's decision to marry, one would not say that one dated a woman only for her looks. Neither could women just come out and say that cold cream was the secret to their "naturally" radiant complexions or confess to the hours spent with their hair tied up in rags in order to achieve those darling caps of nonchalant curls.[23] Because of the mythology that held a woman's beauty to be both "natural" and an outward reflection of her inner virtues, all the hours, effort, and money she spent on her appearance had to be, by general agreement, invisible.

Because "the right look" was simultaneously hidden and highly public, the rise of dating was paralleled by an almost unbelievable rise in the production and advertisement of consumer products relating to personal appearance. Many of the modern cosmetics types and brand names we still recognize—tube lipsticks, mascara, Max Factor, Estee Lauder—had their origins in the early twentieth century. The ready-to-wear clothing industry also took off during this time, and periodicals of the era show a sudden explosion of ads for everything from skin creams to stylish shoes. Dating provided a big incentive to buy into a consumer-friendly paradigm of personal attractiveness that just required the right supplies. Ideally effortless and genuine, beauty was supposed to come from within, but at the same time there was a belief that any woman could become attractive "if she tried." All it took was the right attitude and the right products. The culture of dating was not the only factor that fueled the rise of the consumer fashion and beauty industries, but it was certainly a strong component in a world where women were constantly told that they could "put him in the mood for matrimony" with Pond's face cream.

This may sound superficial, but looks were nothing if not important to dating culture. The fact that dating was carried out in public spaces meant simultaneously that dating offered a species of lost-in-the-crowd anonymity, and that anyone and everyone could be the audience for a date. Cities offered numerous public venues like theatres and parks that gave considerable privacy. They also offered community in the form of various convenient places—dance halls, cafes, ice-cream parlors, and so on—that would be adopted by particular groups of friends, coworkers, or neighbors.[24] As with the case of the longstanding European tradition of leisurely promenades taken as a see-and-be-seen sort of ritual for the whole community, American dating was an opportunity to scope out the options and the competition while simultaneously showing yourself off. It was not just women who stood to gain status and attention if their appearance attracted high-quality dates. Men wanted dates whose appearance reflected well on them when they were seen together.

Particularly prior to World War II, the public nature of dating created a culture of competition that came to characterize the whole proceeding. As historian Beth Bailey writes in her revealing history of twentieth-century dating, *From Front Porch to Back Seat,* "You competed to become popular, and being popular allowed you to continue to compete. *Competition* was the key term in the formula."[25] A particularly blatant system known as "rating and dating" existed on college campuses from the mid-1920s until World War II changed the mood and removed enormous numbers of men from universities. Potential dates were quite literally graded on their worth in the dating scene. A group of University of Michigan women rated men from A for "smooth" to D for "semigoon" and E for "spook."[26] Women were rated every bit as harshly by men, making many women feel desperate to prove that they "rated."

In all these ways, dating culture was not so much the death knell of traditional mate-finding practices as it was the coroner's report. Courtships no longer mandated larger family involvement, as men and women physically, economically, and emotionally removed their pursuit of love relationships from the family's reach. Vestiges of the older system lingered, of course. Parents might have protracted fights with children over their children's tastes in date material, emphasizing just how far out of the mate-selection picture parents and extended family had been pushed. Indeed, parents might not meet their children's romantic partners until a relationship was well established. Meeting a date's parents for the first time is still a rite of passage that continues to underscore just how likely it is that a dating couple might come from sufficiently different social circles that they would not already be casually acquainted with one another's families.

As dating became more and more popular, romantic love became something most people at least hoped they would personally experience. Rising industrial affluence and an abundance of employment meant economic survival was not as directly dependent on marriage. Men and women both could increasingly afford to prolong courtship, turning dating into a phase of life that lasted years. Courtship became less serious, at least up to a point, insofar as calling off a dating relationship was nothing like breaking an engagement. Marriage was still the very palpable goal of dating. But the goal was distant and could be approached at leisure. There were plenty of detours where romantic love could be experienced for its own sake, without necessarily ending in marriage.

Critics worried about the popularity of these new romantic dalliances. Would the expectation or the experience of falling in love lead to the development of unrealistic ideas about marriage? Would these crash courses in emotional excitement ruin young people, particularly young women, for the more complex love of a proper marriage? "These nomads of the affections give and take so little as they pass from hand to hand," Maude Royden wrote in 1922, "that they become cheap and have little left to give at last; nor do they really get what they would take. Men and women claim the right to 'experience,' but experience of what?"[27]

The experience that worried Royden was, of course, sexual experience. Although it had been the Victorians, not their children, who had been responsible for what Ellen Rothman has characterized as "the invention of petting,"[28] it seems that these Victorian parents, like many since, were terrified at the thought that their children might experiment sexually in the same ways they had themselves. On cursory examination it seems that the older generation might not have had too much to worry about: the few surveys of sexual behavior that exist from the early decades of the twentieth century indicate that actual sexual intercourse before marriage remained a rarity. But on the other hand, the dating system had considerably changed the picture of premarital sexuality. Young people had many more opportunities for the kinds of noncoital sexual play commonly included under the heading of "necking and petting," and with more partners. Possibilities for casual, noncoital promiscuity were thick on the ground.

These sexual opportunities had a distinctive economic side. Because of the nature of the date and the need to "go out," companionship had a price tag. It was not entirely unlike the dynamics of prostitution, and men who paid for dates felt justified in expecting "thrills" in return for their investment. They frequently got them. As Beth Bailey puts it, "What men were buying in the dating system was not just female companionship, not just entertainment—but power. Money purchased obligation; money purchased inequality; money purchased control."[29]

If dating seemed more perilous than earlier modes of courtship, it was because in many ways it was. There was more privacy, more autonomy, and more danger. Many more women of a much wider range of socioeconomic classes were subject to sexual commoditization and exploitation on the a la carte basis of the date than had previously been the case. But there was more to the picture for women than just danger and exploitation. Sex could be a source of power, pleasure, and profit for them, too. So-called "charity girls" were likened to prostitutes who provided charity service because they gave sexual favors (possibly but not necessarily including intercourse) in exchange for the various things that a date might buy, including meals, entertainment, and gifts. And of course such "irregular relations" might be based in mutual respect and affection as well. Women's greater sexual latitude could even be viewed as a feminist victory. "Ethically it is better than prostitution," Alison Neilans wrote in 1936, "because such relations, though they may be temporary, are not necessarily promiscuous on either side, and are often based on some friendship and liking and on mutual interests. To some intelligent feminists this new approach to a single standard of morals represents the final triumph of the equality movement; to them this is, at last, freedom."[30]

TEENAGERS IN LOVE

At about the speed of the automobile, which swiftly became an all-but-indispensable accessory to a date, dating spread out of the cities and into the suburbs and countryside. At first a primarily American phenomenon, it also began to spread elsewhere in the West. Wherever it went, it took with it a new universal: teenagers in love.

Dating had become much more than just a path to marriage. By the time of the Second World War, dating had become a phase of life, a period between childhood and settled, married adulthood. One could speak of a young person who was "old enough to be dating" but still "too young to get married." This phase of life coincided, more or less, with a period commonly called "youth" but also increasingly "adolescence," a term popularized by American psychologist Granville Stanley Hall.

Adolescence was a realm of emotion. To an extent that was not, Hall claimed, true either for children or adults, adolescents were the subjects of "storm and stress," an intense and reactive emotionality all its own.[31] One of adolescence's hallmarks was the awakening of a conscious interest in sex and love. Adolescents, Hall believed, were "psychologically in the condition of Adam and Eve when they first knew they were naked."[32] This vulnerable stage had to be managed carefully, lest "premature or excessive experience in Venusberg" forever bar them from being able to achieve ideal adult relationships.[33] Hall and others like him strongly encouraged parents and educators to keep their hand on the rudder of the dating habits of the young and to actively educate them about love, so that love could be "less haphazard and less purely sentimental" and they would not fall prey to sexual promiscuity.[34]

Dating, in this context, could be a form of education, a way of wading experimentally along the shores of the great sea of adult, married sexuality. Part of what made it acceptable was that before World War II, dating was not generally expected to involve exclusivity or emotional depth. "Playing the field," at least in theory, was safer for the young and offered the opportunity to meet and get to know a variety of potential mates.

Then things changed. In what could be characterized as a desperate end-run around the harsh prewar world of dating-and-rating competition, couples began to take a different approach. Serial monogamy, in the form of "going steady," became the norm for dating.[35] At the same time, the age of marriage plummeted, due to a combination of factors that included relief at the end of a long and brutal war plus enormous postwar economic activity. People were marrying earlier, and their marriages came as the culmination of a very different type of dating, one whose expectations of monogamy, exclusivity, and emotional intensity could much more accurately be described as "playing marriage."

Prior to World War II, "going steady" had been the stage at which dating became courtship, where the popularity-oriented antics of dating and rating turned to a more serious dynamic that at least implied eventual marriage. By the early 1950s, playing the field had virtually vanished, and couples went steady from the outset. Dating couples were "boyfriend" and "girlfriend" to one another rather than just "dates," complete with all the accompanying connotations of romantic love and monogamy.

As the age of marriage dropped, so did the age at which both adolescence and dating were slated to begin. In 1961, a professor of family relations at Pennsylvania State University, Carlfred B. Broderick, studied children in a nearby school district and found that about 40 percent of the fifth graders were already dating.[36] This lengthy education in male-female coupledom did not necessarily have much to do with finding a mate. Dates didn't merely focus on *attending* entertainments like movies; dating *was* an entertainment. It was a hobby, a challenge, and something to do on a Saturday night. One went out on dates not only because one hoped eventually to marry or because not dating was a social faux pas. One did it because it was—at least in theory—fun. The ups and downs, but particularly the neurochemical highs of infatuation and the swoons of romancing, became the obsessive subject of literally thousands of pop songs, teen-focused movies, and a dizzying array of periodicals.

Emotional pleasure for its own sake was becoming part of the ethos of heterosexuality. As critic Margaret Kornitzer wrote in 1932, "The fluffy-headed are persuaded that having a good time is not merely risky amusement, but is, in fact, the way to get the most out of life. . . . The serious are intellectually assured that self-gratification is a kind of sacred mission connected with their rights."[37] This "fun morality," as Stephanie Coontz characterizes it, made it permissible to judge dates not on how well suited they were as potential mates but simply on the basis of whether or not they were a good time.

But not all pleasure was the same. Which kinds of pleasure were permissible or important, and whose pleasures should set the priorities of dating, were difficult questions. Whether or not the unmarried would engage in sexual activity became a more fraught and intense decision as dating turned into "going steady," in large part because it centered around a stylized version of romantic love. "Making out" was a fairly standard part of dating. But declarations of romantic love might up the ante. Each symbolic move in the direction of marriage—whether or not it was sincere, and whether or not the relationship ever got there—was more likely than the last to open the gates to actual intercourse.[38]

It had been some time since love was expected to emerge postmaritally out of a diligently conducted and prudently chosen partnership. Now it was also coming to seem quaint to expect love to be the result of the heaven-sent meeting and intertwining of selfless, kindred adult souls. As a drama of pleasure and power, romance was coming to be seen as an inherent part of the adolescent Sturm und Drang. But it was also, and simultaneously, a form of emotional entertainment reflected in thousands of song lyrics and movie plots, a goal to be obsessively striven for, and an experience that meant emotional authenticity and social success. The 1959 plaint of Dion and the Belmonts, "Why must I be a teenager in love?" was purely a rhetorical question. What else, indeed, could any midcentury American adolescent have aspired to be?

LOVE IS A BATTLEFIELD

"The only position for women in the movement is prone," civil rights leader Stokely Carmichael said, faced with Ruby Doris Smith Robinson's 1964 critique of the sexism faced by women in the Student Nonviolent Coordinating Committee (SNCC). Throughout the West and especially in North America, the 1960s were bringing in a culture-rattling tide of political and social criticism, struggle, and change. Activists and rabble-rousers were smashing idols and questioning almost every realm of society except, it seemed, for relations between men and women.

The men of the 1960s Left, born and raised in the strictly gendered culture of post–World War II America, tended to view women as support staff and sexual outlets, just as their Atomic Age upbringings taught them to do. This view was compounded by emerging attitudes toward women's sexuality that centered around progressive politics and the Pill. "Free love" was fast becoming synonymous with throwing off Establishment shackles and getting rid of "hang-ups." The Pill made pregnancy worries a thing of the past. All known sexually transmitted diseases were curable with antibiotics. Much of the reason that the "sexual revolution" happened when it did was that medical science had rendered two of the main barriers to unfettered sexual activity fairly easy to overcome. But women had not had enough social and economic autonomy for a long enough time to have developed many effective ways of refusing to be shunted into the role of staff to men. They also had few workable ways of saying no to sex with them. Perhaps unsurprisingly, few men, even on the far Left, evinced much problem with this.

Women, on the other hand, got fed up with being saddled with the day-to-day "shitwork" of political action and the emotional care and sexual servicing of politically active men. Large numbers of women abandoned the male-dominated New Left to concentrate on feminism. Like the "first wave" feminists of the nineteenth and early twentieth centuries, this "second wave" of feminists banded together because, although it was a time of generally greater social and political sensitivity and struggle for change, women's specific concerns about sex, gender, and the power imbalance often still went unheard.

First-wave women had dominated campaigns for property- and marriage-law reform and women's right to the vote. Second-wave women wanted something even more sweeping: an end to discrimination and unequal treatment based on sex in all realms of public and private life. It was a tall order. But there was an oddly sticky obstacle: love.

The desire for love spurred women to conform to cultural expectations that they would shape themselves socially, behaviorally, and physically in order to attract men. Once they did find love with men, they looked to marriage, wifedom, and motherhood as the ways to make love last. Romantic heterosexual love, it was claimed, shaped women's entire lives in one way or another. It was seen as the force that opened the door to a woman's participation in a whole system of male power and female subservience.

Not unreasonably, feminists questioned this. They had done so before. Many second-wave feminists, indeed, echoed Cicely Hamilton's 1909 plaint: "[U]nder present conditions, it is not easy for [a] self-respecting woman to find a mate with whom she can live on the terms demanded by her self-respect."[39] Radical feminists like Ti-Grace Atkinson described love as the "psychological pivot" of women's oppression and complained that "perhaps the most damning characteristic of women is that, in the face of horrifying evidence of their situation, they stubbornly claim that, in spite of everything, they 'love' their Oppressor."[40]

Some feminists insisted that the solution was to refuse love with men. Martha Shelley, a member of the feminist group the Radicalesbians, wrote that "[i]n order to throw off the oppression of the male caste, women must unite—we must learn to love ourselves and each other, we must grow strong and independent of men so that we can deal with them from a position of strength." She went on, protesting that women are "told to be weak, dependent, and loving. That kind of love is masochism. Love can only exist between equals, not between the oppressed and the oppressor."[41] Shulamith Firestone likewise recommended that because women were so often defined by love relationships with men, the best course of action was to do without them. Such scathing indictments and harsh demands were far from popular. Even other feminists found them hard to swallow.[42] But at the same time, such uncompromising critiques did pierce the extremely durable armor of the doxa of romantic love.

Second-wave feminism, particularly its radical wing, helped expose a central problem with the conceit that heterosexuality and all its trappings were all of a natural, seamless, perhaps even God-given piece. Before the Victorians, little thought was given to the nature of attractions and emotions between women and men. It was simply the way things were, God's or Nature's way of taking care of business. Victorian culture had looked a bit closer and parsed out more individual bits, yet still the argument that the status quo was "natural" or "God-given" underlay most understandings of the relations between men and women. Women's erotic desire was often conflated with the desire for motherhood, women's love of men with the love of being mastered by them. Freud and Havelock Ellis dwelt at length on innate female masochism and the role it played in creating a gender-normative, male-dominant hierarchy in love, marriage, and society. Certainly the coining of "heterosexual" did not help to tease out fine distinctions, putting a falsely unifying stamp on a vast, complex topography of male/female interaction. The feminists of the second wave dismantled and denied such essentialist "biology is destiny" messages, replacing them with "the personal is political."

At the same time an increasing number of women, feminist-identified and not, began to treat heterosexuality as a buffet from which they could pick and choose. Vastly wider options for economic, legal, and reproductive autonomy, many the result of explicitly feminist effort, meant that women had more ability to decide which, if any, parts of the heterosexual system they wanted to partake of. Women who loved men could do so with or without marriage, if not necessarily without controversy. Marriage gradually became less of a requirement for forming a household, having and raising a child, and being part of a family. At the same time and for the same reasons, it also became easier for women to express their love of other women. Gay and lesbian rights organizations emerged out of similar ferment, seeking acceptance, liberty, and ideological and cultural change. Love was still important. It still carried a lot of expectations. But the horse and carriage of love and marriage had been uncoupled. Love roamed more freely without the bulky carriage in tow.

What *was* love, then? How did it work? What did it mean? Was it voluntary or involuntary, strategic or spontaneous? Was it universal, paying no heed to silly things like gender and sex, or was it somehow rooted in biology? Did it obligate certain behaviors—like marriage or having children—or was it complete in and of itself? It was harder than ever to imagine love as being simple and inevitable, as God's imprimatur on a union between a man and a woman, or as evidence of a natural "magnetism" between opposites in a biological binary. There was simply no logic by which one could pin the whole apparatus of behavior, belief, and culture we like to call "heterosexuality" on something as variable, as mercurial, and as vexingly resistant to analysis as love.

We continue to wrestle with these questions. Our Disney Damage—or romantic novel damage, if you prefer—with its deep-seated longing to believe in love's transformational, life-perfecting magic, clashes with medical science that reveals love's euphoria to be the result of dopamine and norepinephrine, two chemicals produced by the brain when we fall in love or use drugs like cocaine. Our hopeful faith that shared love between women and men can be a foundation for egalitarian partnerships has to contend with our awareness that love is exploited on a daily basis when it is used to tether people to abusive and violent relationships. We spend billions yearly on the diets, gyms, clothes, cosmetics, and other accessories we use to make ourselves loveable, sexy, and attractive, and we spend millions of dollars and hours on therapy and rehab centers and meetings of Sex and Love Addicts Anonymous, desperate to shed our feelings of dependence and helplessness in the face of love.

As a culture, we are fairly sure that heterosexuality is natural, normal, and desirable, and that heterosexual love is among life's most validating and positive experiences. We organize heterosexuality around the principle of love now more than we have at any time in the past—the experience of romantic love is what legitimizes not only marriage, but separately legitimizes sexual activity and the having of children as well. Yet this love experience, this inherent part of heterosexual existence, it seems, can also be as anarchic, as fleeting, and as prone to slip out of our control as our ancestors warned us it would be. Perhaps this, as much as anything, explains the enduring fantasy allure of the happily-ever-afters of the Wonderful World of Disney, the moody sparkly-vampire love and angst of the blockbuster *Twilight* novels, and the shelves upon shelves of romance novels in every bookstore. Only in fiction and fantasy is the heterosexual "love adventure" something we can genuinely control, and therefore trust, regardless of how hard we try to make our real-life heterosexuality in its image.

CHAPTER SIX

The Pleasure Principle

It was a stupendous thing, and at fifty pounds a night, in the late eighteenth century, it better have been. James Graham's Grand State Celestial Bed surrounded its occupants with "celestial and electrical fire," serenaded them with music, tantalized them with "stimulating vapours," and dazzled their eyes with a veritable forest of gleaming glass columns and a romantic canopy of flowers and caged turtle doves, all the better to spur them on to the very heights of love. The Celestial Bed was novel, but not new. There has always been an array of things—oysters, champagne, Spanish fly, heart-shaped hot tubs—that are supposed to goad us to the heights of sexual ecstasy. Technically speaking, there is no such thing as an aphrodisiac, a substance that incites sexual desire from nothing. But there is definitely such a thing as the placebo effect. The word "placebo," Latin for "I shall please," has been in medical use since the eighteenth century. Hope springs eternal in the human breast, and elsewhere in the anatomy too.

In the end, though, as the spendthrift Graham was rudely reminded when he went bust in 1784 and had to sell most of his belongings, a bed was only a bed. And indeed, today's ED ("erectile dysfunction") drugs are only vasodilators. For many, their documentable effects are about the same as Graham's tilting, chiming, perfume-emitting temple to sexual intercourse: they work about as well as you believe they will. Research indicates that Viagra and its relatives in the class of drugs called PDE5 inhibitors are effective at improving erections only among men who actually have pre-existing problems with blood flow to the penis.[1] Contrary to what many believe, PDE5 drugs cannot give healthy men harder or quicker erections than they would have otherwise, prolong orgasm, or intensify sexual sensation. Yet thousands of men every day shell out five dollars or more per dose for PDE5 drugs, with Pfizer alone making $466 million in Viagra sales in 2009. Weightlifters take them to try to mask the infamous dick-limpening side effects of steroid use, and men who take Prozac and other libido-dampening antidepressants sometimes resort to Father's Little Helpers. The CIA has even used Viagra to bribe Afghani warlords.[2] Since Viagra first became available in 1998, over 25 million men around the world have taken the aggressively marketed, aggressively priced, erection-promoting drug therapeutically, recreationally, and as a security blanket.[3] The drugs are perhaps the most frequently illegally marketed prescription pharmaceuticals in the world (as I wrote this paragraph, a spam e-mail arrived in my in-box, exhorting me to buy Viagra from a shady Internet pharmacy so I could "Be her CEO in Love Making!"). But for vast swathes of the men who take them, PDE5 drugs are—just like every other substance touted as an aphrodisiac since the dawn of time—objectively doing nothing much.

Viagra and its relatives are admittedly more pharmaceutically complicated than, say, oysters or champagne. But the majority of men who consume PDE5 drugs do not actually have the cardiovascular conditions that it alleviates, or suffer from vascular-related impotence. Even when they do, this isn't the main focus for someone who takes a PDE5 drug. These drugs are sold and taken as pleasure drugs. Pharmaceutical companies acknowledge this. Their ad campaigns for PDE5 drugs depict snuggling couples, suburban wives being swept off their feet, and, in the 2007 "Viva Viagra!" campaign, graying dude-bros in a lamentably funk-free garage band, jamming about the joys of chemically enhanced sex. My favorite Viagra ad, a Spanish-language print ad I saw some years ago, simply shows an image of the distinctive blue pill with the text "Un divorcio menos. Gracias, Pfizer." ("One less divorce. Thanks, Pfizer.") The subtext, that a lack of husbandly erections meant a lack of pleasurable sex for the wife, and in turn a looming divorce, speaks volumes about the place of a particular version of sexual pleasure in our current version of heterosexuality.

Viagra might not seem to have a lot to do with sexual orientation. A drug is a drug, and works the same way on those who take it regardless of their sexual preferences or partners. But the model of pleasure that Viagra is marketed to serve has a great deal to do with sexual orientation. Viagra has only one major clinical use, which first appeared as a side effect when sildenafil was still in development: to create erections, the irreducible bona fide of male-identified sexual performance since before the first Paleolithic cave painter scrawled a phallus on a rock wall.[4] What they are marketing as generating and what they do in actuality generate—in the users for whom they are capable of generating anything at all—is the ability to perform a particular kind of sexual act. An erect penis can penetrate any orifice. But Viagra ads make it clear that Viagra-fueled erections are intended for vaginal penetration, the one distinctive act of "heterosexual sex" and the only fully legitimate source of sexual pleasure for most of Western history.

UNGUILTY PLEASURES

In a very real way, the hard penis *is* heterosexual sexual activity. In virtually every era, in virtually every culture we know, to be a sexually active male is to penetrate with the penis, and to be a sexually active female is to be penetrated by one. Not for nothing are lesbians sometimes raped by those who think it will convert them to a "correct" heterosexual appreciation for the penetrating penis. The medieval English take on it was that in sex, there are two partners, "the man that doeth and the woman that suffereth."[5] This did not mean that the woman suffered pain or was made miserable by sex. It meant that the man, not the woman, engaged in sexual activity—he penetrated— while the woman merely permitted it to be done.

For most of Western history the penetration of the vagina by the penis was not merely the only sanctioned form of sexual activity between men and women; it also seems to have actually been the form of virtually all sexual activity between men and women. Prior to the eighteenth century we have only scant evidence of other types of sex acts taking place at all, and most of the evidence we have comes from medical or legal accounts in which nonintercourse acts are being framed as problematic, sinful, or illegal. This does not mean that none of our forebears experimented with, let's say, performing oral sex on one another. Undoubtedly some of them did. But the evidence suggests that they probably didn't do so in great numbers or with great frequency.

We know very little, actually, about what kinds of sex most of our ancestors had, how they felt about it, or whether they had any intellectual concept of why they enjoyed the things they did. They did not, as a rule, spend a great deal of time woolgathering about the whys and wherefores of their own sexual experience. What we do know, from the law books, medical tomes, and religious texts that have survived, is that penis-in-vagina intercourse is the only source of sexual pleasure that has never, so far as we can tell from the historical record, been challenged.

No other specific sex act enjoys, or has ever enjoyed, universal approbation. No other source of sexual pleasure is as uniformly accepted, or has ever been. The fortunes of all other sex acts and all other sources of sexual pleasure have varied widely. Sex between males might've been acceptable to the ancient Greek elite, and is increasingly acceptable in much of the West today, but has certainly not always been seen as a permissible form of sex or a legitimate source of pleasure. Masturbation and mutual masturbation, anal penetration, and fellatio have been accepted at some times and in some places and not in others, even when performed by a different-sex couple. Cunnilingus, for reasons probably having to do with its lack of focus on the male's direct pleasure, has until quite recently indeed been considered at least déclassé and perhaps even a disturbing, feminizing perversion. But penetrating a woman's vagina with an erect penis and taking pleasure in that experience have never been perceived as anything other than understandable, natural, and indeed inevitable.

Even the Catholic Church fathers, despite their profound resentment of the body and its appetites, could not bring themselves to call for the outright abolition of penis-in-vagina intercourse. Because of its apparent compliance with God's reproductive will, it was the sole sexual act of which they could bring themselves to approve. The Christian party line on what sex was for, as Augustine phrased it, was "*proles, fides, sacramentum*"—children, faithfulness, and the sacrament of marriage. Pleasure did not officially enter into it. Church fathers like St. Clement recommended a cool, distant approach to sexual activity, engaging in sex out of reason, not out of desire. Pleasure might distract the believer, or even tempt him into prioritizing the pursuit of sex over the pursuit of holiness. Ideally, a good Christian would think of sexual pleasure as merely a side effect of doing God's bidding to "be fruitful and multiply." As the Church grew and its doctrine solidified, so did its attitude that sexual pleasure, even in sanctified, penetrative vaginal sex between the duly married, could be tolerated but not celebrated. And there the matter rested.

Or did it? In practice, Church influence and a healthy appreciation for the joy of sex existed side by side. People were no less complicated then than they are now, and our ancestors were more than capable of simultaneously believing in the Church's priorities and being enthusiastically interested in their own sexual pleasure. The perennial existence of prostitutes testifies to this, as do the reports we see of male same-sex activity. In fact, even though rulers were technically as strictly obligated to canon law as anyone else, governments occasionally used sexual pleasure as a carrot to motivate the public when the stick of legal action and religious condemnation had failed. Ruth Mazo Karras cites the example of Florence, Italy, which in 1403 commissioned an Ufficiali dell'Onesta, or Office of Honesty, to open an official municipal whorehouse.[6] Florentine officials of the time perceived the city as suffering from a sodomy epidemic. Their hope was that by offering Florentine men the option of the more legitimate pleasure of sex with women (even if they weren't married to them), they might give up the scandalously illegitimate pleasures of sex with men.

Medieval literature likewise testifies that sexual pleasure was much on people's minds. In Chaucer's "Miller's Tale," a young and sexually vital wife named Alisoun, married to an old gullible carpenter, becomes a lust object for both the student Nicholas and the young clerk Absalom, whose machinations in trying to bed her drive the story. Drinking songs, poems, and other texts likewise show us that sex between women and men was valued as pleasure, above and beyond its reproductive potential or its role in marriage. In the famous collection of eleventh- and twelfth-century student songs and poems called the *Carmina Burana* is this little rhyme, famously set to music by Carl Orff:

Si puer cum puellula	If a boy and a girl
moraretur in cellula,	linger in a little room,
felix coniunctio.	they make a happy union.
Amore succrescente,	Love increases,
pariter e medio	both find that boredom
propulso procul taedio,	is driven far away,
fit ludus ineffabilis	and an ineffable game is played
membris, lacertis, labiis.	With legs, arms, lips.

In a sense, there were two worlds when it came to sexual activity. In the idealized world of the Church, sexual activity was to be avoided whenever possible and even the most correct penis-in-vagina intercourse was to be as dispassionate as possible. In the messy and necessarily pragmatic world of everyday men and women, on the other hand, few were able to live up to the religious standard and few seem to have tried. Medieval and Renaissance people, indeed, believed that women were if anything more lustful than men, and that they took great pleasure in penetrative sex. But just as there were strict limits on what sexual pleasures were legitimate, doxa was also firm about what women were supposed to find pleasurable in having sex with men.

A GIRL'S BEST FRIEND?

"They [women] receive pleasure from the motion of the seed that is in them," tenth-century Muslim physician Ibn Sina (also known as Avicenna) wrote in a text that, in Latin translation, was a standard of Western medicine for centuries. "They receive pleasure from the motion of the man's seed in the mouth of the womb, descending from the womb." Thirteenth-century Albertus Magnus claimed that women had more pleasure from sex than men, because women not only emitted their own semen but received the man's emission, while men merely got to discharge. Some also believed, after the classic opinions of Galen, that semen itself induced the urge for penetrative sex, "a serous, irritating humor that produces a most demanding itch in precisely that part of the body contrived by Nature to be hypersensitive to it."[7]

It could be argued, as indeed it has been, that male physicians described women as getting sexual pleasure from exactly what men wanted them to enjoy. Certainly Ibn Sina's assertions didn't hurt the cause of male penetration any. But there was more to them than just self-service. Ibn Sina was, in some degree, merely telling the truth. Some women do enjoy, physically or psychologically or both, having a male partner ejaculate inside their vaginas. According to the humoral models of the era, it made perfect medical sense that they would. Semen, defined according to Aristotle and his colleagues, was literally the essence of life, a distilled form of the *pneuma* or breath. This made ejaculation both the most important part of any sexual act and the most potentially risky: *pneuma,* like blood, was a finite resource, and a man could suffer terribly if he lost too much. Being masculine, and composed of breath, semen had the qualities of heat and dryness, traits that the cool, dense, and wet female body tended to lack. The masculine body, being more "perfected" than the feminine, did not require infusions of these feminine characteristics, but feminine bodies benefited enormously from perfecting doses of masculine heat. Women derived pleasure from ejaculation because it literally put a good humor into them.

This proved a surprisingly long-lived idea. As late as 1928, British sex educator Marie Stopes made an only slightly modernized version of the same claim. She updated her imagery from a humoral system to a chemical one, but left the nature of the interaction conveniently vague when she claimed that female "hunger for nourishment in sex union is a true physiological hunger to be satisfied only by the supplying of the actual molecular substances lacked by her system."[8] Again—still—on some semimystical, semibiological level, semen satisfied women.

Penile penetration and the ejaculation of semen into the vagina were therefore legitimate pleasures both for women and for men. But they could also be dangerous. Women who developed an unrestrained appetite for such pleasure could, it was believed, debilitate or even kill their men, draining them with relentless demand. "Of woman's unnatural, insatiable lust," complained Richard Burton in the 1621 *Anatomy of Melancholy,* "what country, what village doth not complain?" The fantasy of the insatiable destructive woman— femmes fatales, sirens, and "black widows" are all descended from this idea—got the better of the cultural imagination.[9] There is no evidence that any community ever actually has found itself plagued by sex-mad women, and in any event there is also no evidence that repeated ejaculation does anything worse to men than to make them temporarily a bit dehydrated and tired. But facts were never the point of the specter of the draining, deadly, hypersexed woman. Even today, the image of the monstrous, devouring woman is brandished as a cautionary tale in movies and television and sometimes in real life: these are the voracious antiheroines of films like *Fatal Attraction* and find real-life echoes in the actions of murderers like Aileen Wuornos or Carolyn Warmus. In the hollows and hills of rural Appalachia, people still speak of "white-livered widows," women whose "high nature" has killed several (usually younger) husbands, drained of their life force by the woman's inveterate hunger for sex.[10]

The mix of approval, fear, and distaste are telling. Vaginal penetration and ejaculation were, as they still are, seen as good, legitimate acts in which both men and women take pleasure. But even when women desire what they're supposed to desire, and take their pleasure from male orgasm achieved through vaginal penetration, it is made very clear that too much desire is wrong, damaging, perhaps literally deadly. The underlying message that women and men alike are meant to take from these proclamations about women, pleasure, and semen is that women are supposed to want and like men's ejaculations and semen, but never more than the men do.

A NEED-TO-KNOW BASIS

As the middle class emerged, so did its own particular version of the rules of legitimate sex and pleasure centered on the married household, the nuclear family, and the generation of a limited number of well-bred, carefully educated children. It idealized marital sex simultaneously as a response to true love and as a solemn, quasicivic responsibility. Intercourse between married couples was to be deliberate, not spontaneous, a perfectly orchestrated joint undertaking of heads, hearts, and reproductive organs. Physician John Cowan, author of *Science of a New Life* (1897), earned the endorsement of leading feminists like Elizabeth Cady Stanton for his recommendation that couples enjoy a single, transcendently beautiful, extremely intentional sex act per carefully planned and much-wanted pregnancy. This was surely a bit extreme, to say nothing of impractical—conception is not quite so predictable and reliable as all that. But virtually all middle-class sex writers of the nineteenth century counseled some version of this restrained, deeply domesticated, extremely purposeful sex life. Sex once or twice a week was considered quite enough. More frequent sex risked both the evils of sensuality and the disorder of bodily depletion.

For all its painstaking moderation, though, this domesticated sex life was also expected to provide pleasure, albeit not so much spontaneously shared as jointly curated. Properly reared women of the nineteenth-century middle classes were expected to have little in the way of spontaneous lust of their own, their sexual capacity theoretically laying dormant until marriage. At that point, it was up to the husband to educate his bride in the pleasures of the flesh; in an idealistic spirit, the novelist Balzac wrote in his 1826 *Physiologie du marriage,* "The husband's self-interest, at least as much as his honor, prescribes that he never permit himself a pleasure which he has not the talent to make his wife desire." Women were, if anything, more obligated than men. Writing in 1889, the doctor Henry G. Hanchett informed the wife that it was her "duty to her husband, her children and herself, to heartily enjoy with her husband sexual intercourse, and to keep herself in such condition that she may enjoy it."[11] Middle-class sex between men and women was supposed to be simultaneously mutual and also a thing that "the man doeth and the woman suffereth."

For those who followed these guidelines, they were simultaneously a way of demonstrating class identity, a way to help shape society, and a way of defending themselves and their families against the deviance that seemed to threaten from all sides. Nobility and the extremely wealthy were viewed as poisonously decadent and self-indulgent, while the working classes were commonly stereotyped as cheap sensualists who lacked either refinement or self-restraint. The poor were brutes and primitives who could do no better and often did much worse. In the United States particularly, there was an additional racial element to these distinctions. African Americans were stereotyped as not merely lacking middle-class sexual restraint and the habit of experiencing refined emotions, but as being incapable of them. The carefully regulated sexual lives of the white middle classes were part of their careful buffer against the terrifying prospect of social and racial disorder.

Science was to be their ally in this effort. The nineteenth-century boom in academic, scientific, and popular commentary on sex was something genuinely new. To the early Enlightenment, sexual urges had been considered hardly different from the needs to urinate, defecate, or eat. But the world had changed, and so had the perception of the sexual instinct. In the nineteenth century it had become an all-powerful force, "a most powerful influence," as Dr. Frederick Hollick put it in 1885, "upon both individual action and upon the destinies of nations."[12]

SHARED PLEASURES

This "most powerful influence" required a substantial anchor for safety's sake, and that anchor was the middle-class family. In the second half of the nineteenth century, one of the forms this took was the dramatic expansion of the literature on sex intended for the nonspecialist, nonmedical audience. Although there were exceptions, like the famous *Aristotles Master Piece*, which appeared first in 1684 and ran to some twenty-seven editions by the 1830s, sex manuals intended for a general readership were few and far between prior to the nineteenth-century explosion of both print and literacy. The increasing role of print in daily life in the later nineteenth century, however, met the new desire for sex information and education head on, with the result that dozens of physicians and other biomedical experts—a group that admittedly incorporated some we might not include today, like phrenologist Orson Fowler—leapt into print with books that aimed to teach the middle classes how to conduct a "scientific" and proper sex life.

Increasingly these doctors and others acknowledged, as influential Philadelphia physician and author George Napheys did in his 1871 *The Physical Life of Woman*, that most women had sexual feelings. These were, they emphasized, entirely compatible with propriety, dignity, and, if channeled through the legitimizing conduits of true love and marriage, even with spiritual and social respectability. The jewel in the crown of a companionate marriage, these late Victorians preached, was mutually crafted, mutually satisfying sexual pleasure.

This represented something of a sea change for the Western approach to marriage. The official acceptance of eroticism for its own sake was, in the face of thousands of years of procreation-focused copulation, fairly radical. So was the idea that the quality of marital sex for both spouses actually mattered to the marriage itself. As attitudes shifted, good sex started to signify better marriages, healthier offspring, greater longevity, and a better quality of life. But what exactly was "good sex"? And more to the point, how did one go about having it?

These were, as was immediately apparent, questions primarily about women. Male sexuality was viewed as transparent. Even Havelock Ellis, that inexhaustible chronicler of all things sexual, dismissed the male sex drive in a single sentence in his 1904 *Studies in the Psychology of Sex: Analysis of the Sexual Impulse*: "[T]o deal with it broadly as a whole seems unnecessary, if only because it is predominantly open and aggressive."[13] Although impotence occasionally became an issue for men, their sexual functioning and pleasure were an otherwise foregone conclusion. Men did not have a problem attaining sexual pleasure; they only had a problem resisting the impulses to have too much of it or get it in illicit ways. It was women whose bodies, impulses, and responses were the part of the picture of "good sex" that was changing.

This, however, changed sex for men: there was, formally and officially, more on their plates than just looking after their own pleasure. With the acknowledgment that women felt sexual desire and pleasure came the assertion that they should be feeling more of it. But women could not be expected to know how to do this all by themselves. Their husbands were to be their teachers in the school of love, and this was not necessarily easy. "To gain real possession of a woman's soul and body," Havelock Ellis wrote, required "the whole of a man's best skill and insight."[14]

The situation was not made much easier by the fact that while the "repeal of reticence" allowed more open discussion about ideals of pleasurable marital sex, it didn't permit much more in the way of detailing actual technique. Sexologists and sex advisors waxed rapturous about the shared joys and benefits of properly conducted intercourse, and the destination of mutual orgasm—simultaneous mutual orgasm if it could be managed—was clear. But the map by which one was to get there was vague. Even after the turn of the century had yielded to the notorious permissiveness of the Jazz Age, instructional descriptions rarely got much more graphic than this excerpt from Dr. Walter Robie's 1922 *Sex Histories:* "A long sequence of endearments and gentle caresses, and final specific manipulation of nipples and clitoris, and perhaps adjacent structures, to produce the overwhelming erotic feelings and the free flow of precoital mucus which are necessary to make coitus mutually pleasurable and simultaneously climactic, both of which are necessary if it is to be scientifically correct."[15]

The idea that mutual orgasm was "scientifically correct" was the window-dressing that made sexual technique discussable even in such broad outline as this. Just as the spiritualization of love had made the introduction of romance to marriage acceptable, making sex scientific helped to establish sexual technique as a topic fit at least for discreet, duly married inquiry.

As expectations of mutual orgasm and of wives' willing and desirous participation in marital sex became more widespread, so did the anxiety of those who had not achieved what writers euphemistically called "true marriage" or "the completed sex act," namely mutual orgasm. Sex advisors received hundreds of anguished letters—Marie Stopes's well-preserved correspondence includes approximately five thousand—from people with a wide array of sexual fears, faults, and complaints. Long-married women who had "never felt anything" during intercourse wanted to know what was wrong with them; men who ejaculated too quickly to provide the ten to twenty minutes of intercourse some writers recommended for proper female satisfaction wanted to know how to do better. Men about to be married wrote of their panic that they might inadvertently, as sex advisors claimed was so often the case, permanently ruin their wives through clumsy overeagerness on the wedding night. Huge numbers of women pleaded for help with contraception, saying that what really stood between them and sexual enjoyment wasn't a lack of interest but a fear of pregnancy. Forlorn husbands wondered whether it was inevitable that wives would simply never let themselves be seen in the nude.

Declaring the standard of a "good sex life," it seemed, opened a Pandora's box of previously unutterable and seemingly ubiquitous dissatisfaction. Some of the causes of unhappiness were things no sex advisor, no matter how well meaning, could help with, and a sizeable portion of the causes existed mostly due to concerns the sex advisors themselves had helped to create. Men, facing new vistas of performance anxiety, could not rest easily or happily in their wives' arms out of fear that they might not be doing the "job" of sex well enough.

Women, of course, were also under pressure to perform. Even before the heyday of Freud's "vaginal orgasm" (about which more presently), Havelock Ellis contended, the woman who had not learned to want and enjoy sexual intercourse had "not acquired an erotic personality, she has not mastered the art of love, with the result that her whole nature remains ill-developed and unharmonised, and that she is incapable of bringing her personality—having indeed no achieved personality to bring—to bear effectively on the problems of society and the world around her."[16]

This stood at serious odds with the doxa with which most middle-class people had been raised in regard to female sexuality. Open acknowledgement of female desire and pleasure had for centuries been deemed excessive, sinful, and destructive; synonymous with promiscuity and prostitution. It is no wonder that people felt confused, anguished, and frustrated. No matter how willing women and men were to try to achieve the new goal of an eroticized marriage, they could not necessarily change their beliefs and emotions about women's desire and pleasure overnight.

Nor could people instantly reverse deeply rooted beliefs about the morality of sexual acts other than intercourse. Sex authorities were increasingly willing to consider an array of other types of stimulation as legitimate foreplay, so long as penis-in-vagina intercourse and accompanying orgasms were the ultimate result. This approach would eventually provide men and women many welcome liberties. But to people raised with the Victorian abhorrence of masturbation, encouragement to manually stimulate a wife's clitoris might seem suspect, to say the least. Although Walter Robie's correspondence features a letter from a woman who exulted in "husband's hands—that they give a perfectly legitimate joy!," Marie Stopes's correspondence includes letters from women who were terribly upset by achieving orgasm through such "unnatural" means.[17] Although there were those—like gynecologist Alice Bunker Stockham, who advocated approaches to mutual pleasure less procreatively oriented even than this—they were considered far out on the fringes.[18] Early sex surveys, such as Katherine Bement Davis's 1929 *Factors in the Sex Lives of 2200 Women,* hint that more people were at least considering erotic pleasure as one of the goods of marriage, independent of the potential for reproduction. But most people, and indeed most sex authorities, operated on the same age-old assumption that the Freudian "vaginal orgasm" contingent would shortly reinforce: that pleasure in sex should be derived from penis-in-vagina intercourse, if it was to be derived at all.

By the eve of the Second World War, mutual sexual satisfaction was held to be not just *a* crucial ingredient of successful marriage but probably *the* crucial ingredient. Even the conservative Central YMCA College in Chicago could state, in its 1932 handbook, *The Hygiene of Marriage,* that "reproduction is neither the sole nor the chief purpose of marriage," but rather "the desire for sexual communion and companionship." Although it seems fairly plain that many relatively happy and functional marriages must have coexisted with sex lives that did not live up to the high standards of the sex manuals, the intense emphasis on a sexually compelling marriage changed how people thought and behaved. Sexual desire and sexual pleasure were newly and openly on the table as marriageability issues, and in time they would be qualifications for premarital relationships as well. In ways that had never before been true, sex appeal and the promise of sexual competence became important criteria in the selection of a boyfriend, a girlfriend, or a spouse. Sex was no longer only, or even primarily, the ultimate physical manifestation of the spiritual union of true romantic love that it had been for earlier Victorians. Erotic pleasure, albeit by a particular and mannered approach, was a newly official standard for heterosexual relationships.

COPULATION ON THE COUCH

This brings us back to Freud, whose bourgeois Viennese upbringing, education, and social standing gave him the useful vantage point of being able to probe the most difficult questions of sexuality's origins, development, and influences among the very population most concerned about them. Among the many beliefs Freud shared with his generally well-off bourgeois peers was a deep, nearly mystical belief in the importance of penis-in-vagina copulation.

Additionally, Freud accepted from Krafft-Ebing the idea that there was a human attribute called "heterosexuality." Krafft-Ebing had used the word more or less as a synonym for an ultimately reproductive drive toward male/female penetrative sex. Freud expanded on this in novel ways. For Freud, as Jonathan Ned Katz points out, "heterosexual" is not merely a noun but frequently an adjective, describing a "drive," a "love," an "instinct," and a "desire," as well as a sexual activity and a type of person.[19] In Freud's thinking, "heterosexual" was a quality that encompassed not just behaviors but perceptions, emotions, even something that could almost be called a sensibility or aesthetic. This made it possible, for the first time, to speak of heterosexual *feeling,* whether or not heterosexual behavior was involved. When combined with the Freudian notion of the libido, "heterosexual" became part and parcel of a politics of healthy versus unhealthy pleasures.

In Freudian thought, the libido is more than just the sexual impulse. It is the formless, insistent, and universal part of the psyche that desires. The libido itself does not have any productive intent; it just wants what it wants and what it wants is its own satisfaction. Freud's libido, with its goal of subjective satisfaction regardless of the source, stood in stark contrast to Krafft-Ebing's sex instinct, so firmly anchored in the reproductive urge.

This presented a vexing problem: why should choosing a sexual object for the libido seem, in theory, like something that should involve so much freedom, yet in practice involve so little? The process of learning to channel the libido toward proper and healthy sexual objects, Freud claimed, was not just a central part of human socialization but something that revealed a great deal about a person's psyche and mental health, for it was the central drama of the development of personhood.

To explain it, Freud invented an elaborate theory of psychosexual development, first articulated in *Three Essays on the Theory of Sexuality,* in 1905. Adult sexual preferences, Freud asserted, were what resulted after the child's unformed and malleable libido was put through a forge of primal psychological drama. For males this was relatively straightforward, aggressive, and uncomplicated. During the "phallic" or "genital" phase, a phase lasting from approximately ages three to five, the child would experience the desire to have the mother as a mate. For boy children, Freud claimed, this included the desire to kill his rival, the father, resulting in castration anxiety and emotional ambivalence toward other men. This was the moment at which the male sexual nature coalesced.

Things were different for girls. Girls began like boys, madly in love with their mothers. But this desire to possess the mother, Freud claimed, would inevitably meet with frustration as the child realized that she did not possess the penis necessary to take her father's place. Freud explained that at this point, the female child would back down from wanting the mother and instead learn to want to *be* her. In emulating her mother, a girl would develop an appropriate feminine identification. As part of this, on a subtle, subconscious level, the girl would lose her interest in her clitoris, the genital part with which she associated her desires during that early genital phase. By the time she finished puberty, she would have somehow, in a semimystical process of transference, switched her erotic focus from her clitoris to her vagina, the better to take the mother and wife position with her own eventual husband.

Freud never adequately explained why this should happen in exactly this way, but he was sure it did. On this basis, he claimed that women who continued to derive sexual pleasure from the clitoris as adults were immature, their sexual development halted somewhere in early childhood. They were also neurotic, possibly hysterical, likely to be hostile toward men, overly masculine, and aggressive. Stuck as they were at the stage of the little mother-desiring girl, they might well be sexually attracted to other women.

For a woman to derive pleasure from the vagina, on the other hand, was mature, appropriate, and fully heterosexual. Freud by no means invented the idea that women's sexual desires and pleasures should focus on being penetrated vaginally with a penis. But he did invent a radical—and, to many, convincing—new explanation of why this should be so. These ideas seemed a tailor-made rallying point for social conservatives appalled at the seeming gender anarchy of feminists, suffragists, New Women, and flappers. By the 1930s, thanks to Freud's students and followers who carried on his work both before and after Freud's death in 1939, the idea that "vaginal orgasm" was the only valid heterosexual orgasm for women had gathered an extraordinary amount of steam.

Some proponents of the vaginal orgasm, like Helene Deutsch, one of Freud's favorite students, were optimists who took what could be called a "pro-vagina" stance. In her *Psychology of Women* (1944), Deutsch theorized that healthy women's sex drive was literally rooted in the vagina. In fine Victorian style, the "silent" vagina was to be awoken by a skilled, patient penis. Deutsch compared the process to the awakening of Sleeping Beauty, echoing Havelock Ellis's similar statements, a few decades prior, about male responsibility to awaken female sexuality, including his assertion that a girl "must be kissed into a woman." A woman might experience a first penetration as a violent invasion, Deutsch allowed, but the pleasure she would experience from having her vagina penetrated would transform those perceptions. Intercourse would become a mystical merger of sensual, reproductive, and gender-role fulfillment. Deutsch claimed that during intercourse a woman would experience herself as a helpless child, in relation to her adult and in-control partner, and simultaneously imagine herself as the child that she fantasized about conceiving as a result of the intercourse. The vagina, therefore, was not just a reproductive organ; it was also, if you will, the organ by which the true heterosexual woman gave birth to herself.

Other Freudians didn't love the vagina so much as they detested the clitoris. Eduard Hitschmann and Edmund Bergler claimed that the clitoris was destructive, masculinizing, even subversive. Women's failure to transfer erotic focus from the clitoris to the vagina was what made women refuse their role as "normal" wives and mothers, they argued. It could turn them into feminists. Most of all, it made them "frigid."

For Hitschmann and Bergler, "frigidity" had a single criterion: "absence of the vaginal orgasm." The standard was unqualified and absolute. A woman who did not enjoy intercourse: frigid. Women who derived sexual pleasure from acts other than intercourse were frigid too. Nothing else mattered, only whether a woman had an orgasm because a man's penis was inside her vagina. Sexually aggressive women were labeled "frigid" because of the association between masculinity and aggressiveness. Womanhood that was not passive was not properly womanly. "Frigidity," as Jane Gerhardt points out, "thus became a label and a diagnosis that defined how much sexual desire a woman must have and in what kinds of sexual behavior she must engage to be 'healthy.'"[20]

"Healthy" and "normal" female heterosexual performance and pleasure began to seem so exacting that it was a wonder anyone qualified. Freudian-leaning sex educators, like the best-selling Marynia Farnham and Ferdinand Lundberg, in their *Modern Woman: The Lost Sex* (1947), wanted readers to believe that "well-adjusted" women were an endangered species. Farnham and Lundberg correctly calculated that, in a United States that was desperately trying to get back to business as usual following the upheavals of global war, many men and women would find the authoritatively "sciency"-sounding prescriptions of Freudian sex reassuringly conservative and strict. Their book, and others like it, taught the mainstream that women's sexual pleasure had only one proper source, the vagina, and that women would only be able to take pleasure from the vagina if they had correctly "adjusted" to their proper, heterosexual gender roles. As for women who could not manage to have vaginal orgasms? Perhaps they could find a way to overcome their neuroses, given enough time on the Freudian couch.

COIN OF THE REALM

There is no official international unit for measuring sexuality, but if there were, it would be the orgasm. This is Alfred Kinsey's fault. Unlike his predecessors in the field of sexology, Kinsey chose to base his research, as much as possible, on measurable, distinct physical experiences and biological phenomena. The most prominent of these, used for counting and classifying sex acts, was orgasm. Part of the shock that *Sexual Behavior in the Human Male* produced when it was published in 1948 was due to Kinsey's conclusive evidence that far more men were experiencing orgasms far more often, and as a result of far more kinds of sexual activity, than polite society willingly imagined, and each orgasm represented a fait accompli. And when, for example, it turned out that only about half the orgasms Kinsey's several thousand male respondents reported had occurred in the course of vaginal intercourse with their respective wives, it was not a welcome revelation.

Orgasm-counting delivered another wallop to traditional expectations about sex when *Sexual Behavior in the Human Female* was released, in 1953. While the ubiquity of masturbation and the 37 percent of men who had experienced sex with other men had been the shocking revelations of the male Kinsey report, the mindblowers of the female version were women's pre- and extramarital sexual activity and the diversity of their orgasmic experience. Nearly half of Kinsey's women subjects had engaged in intercourse before they married, a figure that American society pretended to find appalling despite the fact that it was obviously commonplace and took place, for the most part, as Kinsey demonstrated, with fiancés whom the women went on to marry. Worse still was the approximately one-quarter of married women (26 percent in Kinsey's figures) who had engaged in extramarital sex.[21] Furthermore, Kinsey's women, including the adulterous ones, tended to enjoy sex. His sample ran the full gamut of histories of sexual response, from the 10 percent of women who had been married at least fifteen years but had never experienced an orgasm and the 14 percent who were frequently multiply orgasmic, to the approximately 50 percent of the women who reported having orgasms almost every time they had sex.

Kinsey's orgasm-counting made him a sex-doxa whistleblower. The difference between what people believed the average sex life was like and what it seemed to genuinely be was staggering. But the way Kinsey measured the difference was just as influential as his research. By using orgasms as the beads on his sexological abacus, Kinsey effectively declared that reproduction no longer counted as the baseline of sex between men and women, pleasure did. This had been increasingly true for at least half a century in practice. After Kinsey, it was also true in sexological and biomedical theory.

Kinsey's orgasm-counting also turned the focus of sex theorizing and research firmly away from moralizing. Statistics and demographics, both nineteenth-century inventions, had been making their influence felt in sexological circles for some time. In fact survey-based sex research had been going on longer than anyone really suspected, as was later proven in 1974, when historian Carl Degler uncovered the surveys Dr. Clelia Mosher had conducted of her women patients' sex lives beginning in the 1890s.[22] But by relying on physical events for his metrics, Kinsey added a bench-science attitude to the mix, the attitude that one could observe human sexual behavior and response with the same value-neutral detachment that would be used in documenting the vital statistics of, say, gall wasps. Wasps, indeed, represented Kinsey's major contribution to science prior to his sexological work. Of the 18 million insects in the collection of the American Museum of Natural History, around 5 million are the mindboggling and painstaking collection of gall wasps and galls assembled by Alfred Kinsey.

This bioscientific approach permitted, even encouraged, a new focus on mechanical processes and physiological events, centering around the most dramatic and easily observed: orgasm. Chapter 15 of Kinsey's *Sexual Behavior in the Human Female,* "Physiology of Sexual Response and Orgasm," became an instant touchstone, for no one had previously approached the subject in such a methodical and comprehensive fashion. Shortly thereafter, when William Masters began his research on sex in 1954, he immediately concentrated on the mechanics, techniques, and phenomena of sexual arousal and climax. By the time Masters, by then working in partnership with Virginia Johnson (whom he would later marry), published *Human Sexual Response* in 1966, the research team had observed 382 women and 312 men in what they estimated had been approximately ten thousand "complete cycles of sexual response" that included both penis-in-vagina intercourse and, radically, masturbation. Technology was a major factor in their work, including miniaturized cameras mounted inside plastic phalluses that let them document, for instance, what took place inside the vagina during orgasm. Masters and Johnson's research led to a complete overhaul of the biomedical understanding of what happened physiologically during sex, and to a ground-up reevaluation of female orgasm in particular.

Kinsey had asserted—although it was well buried nearly 600 pages into an 800-plus-page book—that the vagina was "of minimum importance in contributing to the erotic responses of the female," and actually probably contributed more to men's sexual experience than to women's. Masters and Johnson's work confirmed that this was true, and further revealed that the so-called vaginal orgasm was actually not vaginal. When it happened at all, it was the result of friction between clitoral hood and clitoris that some women experienced when the thrusts of the penis tugged at connected flesh. This, they explained, created the mistaken impression of an orgasm that was dependent on penetration. Masters and Johnson's work on masturbation further disproved the vaginal orgasm theory. Proper psychosexual adjustment, it appeared, had little to do with anything where orgasm was concerned. Proper sexual technique and adequate attention to the clitoris, on the other hand, did. What Kinsey had proposed, Masters and Johnson disposed.

These discoveries, arriving when and as they did, provided bountiful fuel for the social, political, and philosophical fires of the Sexual Revolution. Prioritizing pleasure over reproduction was a fine complement to critiques of capitalism and industrialism. Acknowledging that pleasure gave utility to non-intercourse sex acts was a powerful critique of conformity. Putting orgasm first, and making pleasure the aspect of sex that counted most, made it easier to bash "hang-ups" like monogamy, the idea that sex belonged only in marriage, and the idea that sex was only legitimate when accompanied by love. A body that was free to experience orgasm at will, it seemed to many, was a body that could be liberated from the shackles of a repressive society that wanted to control what people did with their loyalties, their energies, and their reproductive organs.

If orgasm was the thing that made sex legitimate, not the kind of activity that produced the orgasm, all kinds of possibilities for legitimate sex opened up. Oral sex in particular had been rare among male/female couples in the Kinsey reports, but became commonplace for the younger generation (those under thirty) during the 1970s. At the same time, the Pill transformed even traditional penetrative vaginal sex itself into something that could be considered from the standpoint of pleasure first, and only secondarily as a potentially reproductive act. As John D'Emilio and Estelle Freedman write in *Intimate Matters,* their landmark history of sexual life in America, "Even the supposedly immutable 'sex act' underwent redefinition in ways that weakened a male monopoly over the nature of sex."[23]

Orgasm was particularly significant to the causes of gay liberation and feminism. The rise in recreational sex and contraceptive use among straight-identified couples made it more difficult to pillory the "unproductive" sex of same-sex partners. Same-sex sexual activity also gained some legitimacy, as it became clear that different-sex couples were regularly participating in many of the same actual activities as same-sex partners. Oral sex, in particular, had become extremely popular among different-sex couples, many of whom, as studies like Kinsey's clearly showed, were also no strangers to at least occasional anal intercourse.

To women, the orgasm-centered revelations of Kinsey and of Masters and Johnson were even more important and symbolic. First and foremost, they let feminists gleefully kick the whole notion of "vaginal orgasm" to the curb. Women everywhere breathed a sigh of relief as they began to set down the Freudian baggage of "appropriate" psychosexual gender-role identification. Many were also thrilled at the prospect of legitimate female sexual pleasure that was not beholden to penetration or the penis. The pleasures of the clitoris became a rallying point for feminists and lesbian-feminists, who rapidly began to produce a number of stunning critiques of "vaginal orgasm," penetrative sexual intercourse, and heterosexuality as a whole. Anne Koedt's essay "The Myth of the Vaginal Orgasm" and Ti-Grace Atkinson's "The Institution of Sexual Intercourse" and "Vaginal Orgasm as a Mass Hysterical Survival Response" were all published in 1968, dramatically radicalizing a feminist discussion about sex that was already in a lively state of ferment.

Women's orgasms rapidly became tokens of liberation, proof that one had succeeded in throwing off, and rooting out, the psychological fetters of repressive, conformist "Victorian" and "Puritan" views of sexuality. But no sooner did the pendulum begin to swing than some women began to feel that the pressure to have orgasms was oppressive in its own way. Feminist Dana Densmore wrote, in 1971, "Our 'right' to enjoy our own bodies has not only been bestowed upon us, it is almost a duty . . . and people seem to believe that sexual freedom (even when it is only the freedom to actively offer one's self as a willing object) is freedom."[24] Some lesbian feminists, in particular, retreated from the pursuit of orgasm-focused sex, finding it too much an instrument of patriarchal, performance-oriented control. They endorsed a feminist sexuality that was whole-bodied rather than genitally focused, centered on emotions and intimacy rather than bodily sensation. Others continued to explore feminist models for overtly genital, orgasm-oriented sex predicated on physical pleasure.[25]

In the mainstream culture, too, women and men struggled to make sense of what it meant to have orgasm be a sexual raison d'être. As powerful and new as the orgasm standard was, it by no means made a clean sweep of sexual culture. Women, and men as well, had to figure out how or indeed whether the pursuit of sexual pleasure for its own sake fit in with their desires for love, romance, marriage, children, economic stability, and career goals. Books, magazine articles, and other media touted the giving and getting of sexual pleasure as a source of personal fulfillment, the ultimate in sophistication, and manifest proof of sexual desirability. But relatively few people gave up the search for love—at least in the long term—in favor of purely sexual liaisons. Clumsily, sometimes catastrophically, but also hopefully, men and women tried their best to incorporate the ethos that "good relationships are based in good sex" and the cultivation of equal-opportunity orgasm into the already demanding culture of different-sex relationships. To be heterosexual now meant to pursue relationships that encompassed, at minimum, egalitarian sexual pleasure, enthusiastic sexual desire and activity, romantic love, emotional intimacy, and companionship. In most cases, heterosexuality also encompassed economic collaboration, monogamy, kinship, shared domesticity, and parenting. It was, and still is, a lot to ask.

Making orgasm the goal of sex did not, in fact, usher in a magical era of liberation, equality, and general grooviness. Women continue to have to negotiate a sexual double standard that, even in Hollywood's fantasy factory, paints their sexual pleasure as less appropriate and less valid than men's. The film-ratings body known as the Motion Picture Association of America has been noted to apply its harshest, most commercially damaging, ratings to films featuring what it deems to be "overlong" scenes of female orgasm.[26] Women who are perceived to be overly sexual, or too sexual in the wrong ways—meaning, especially, ways that do not focus on conventional feminine receptivity to men—are still likely to be shamed, ostracized, and punished.[27]

Men, in their turn, have had to learn to contend with sexually assertive, even aggressive, women. While one might assume this would be a dream come true for men, for many it has proven to be a source of anxiety and fear. Women with the sexual experience to form critical opinions about men's sexual performance may be seen as terrifying taskmistresses whose exacting standards, as historian Angus McLaren notes, men often perceive as emasculating. Women's use of vibrators, dildos, and other tools for self-pleasuring also generate fears that the penis—and presumably the man himself—will not be able to measure up and that men will find themselves obsolete.

Women's relative freedom to have orgasms on their own, with one another, and on demand is surely an improvement over having their sexual pleasure be always and forever yoked to the movement of a husband's penis. But an expanded ethos of heterosexual pleasure options does not sweep away older mandates; it just adds to the list. Penetrative penis-in-vagina sex continues to define "sex" in the eyes of many; there is evidence that many teenagers, schooled in antipregnancy and abstinence-only rhetoric, happily engage in many other sex acts on the blithe assumption that they are "not really" sex.[28] Ejaculation also continues to hold a certain pride of place. Even in the age of HIV/AIDS—perhaps, paradoxically, partly because of it—the external ejaculation "money shot" is the standard depiction of male pleasure in pornography. The recent popularity of *bukkake* porn, in which a woman is depicted as reveling in being ejaculated on by multiple men simultaneously, also seems to tap into some very old fantasies about the source of women's "real" and "proper" sexual pleasure.

Women continue to be bombarded with exhortations to be, or become, more optimally responsive to penetrative vaginal sex. For a price, plastic surgeons will remodel a woman's vulva and vagina in a process its practitioners call "vaginal rejuvenation," with the object of rearranging tissues not only to tighten the vagina for the sake of male pleasure, but so that the thrusts of a penis create more collateral friction between clitoris and clitoral hood, and therefore in theory more female orgasms. One Los Angeles specialist has even invented a dubious procedure called "G-spot Amplification," injecting collagen into the vaginal wall structure known as the Grafenburg or G-spot on the theory that a bigger G-spot means greater arousal during penetration.[29] For men, Viagra and its relatives reinforce the hoary old shibboleth that all you need for successful sex—the kind that makes you burst into song with your buddies and makes your wife swoon—is a rock-hard penis to penetrate your partner with. Masters and Johnson may have killed the Freudian myth of the vaginal orgasm, but it seems no one has yet managed to drive a stake through its heart.

The more things change, it seems, the more things stay the same. As I write these words, the German pharmaceutical giant Boehringer Ingelheim is doing advanced testing of a drug with the uncomely name of Flibanserin, which it claims can help to alleviate the symptoms of a "disorder" of female sexuality called Hypoactive Sexual Desire Disorder (HSDD). Though the company's testing focuses on what it calls "Satisfying Sexual Events" (or SSE, in the acronymphomaniac parlance of Big Pharma), the basic dynamic is the same as the one that put countless Atomic Age wives on the analyst's couch. Women must be heterosexual in the right ways, in the right amounts, and they must experience the right degree and type of pleasure, or there is something the matter with them that demands professional treatment. This so-called "female Viagra," will, in theory, alter brain chemistry to make sure that women want what they're supposed to want, that they enjoy what they're supposed to enjoy, that they are better adjusted to the sexual demands of their men and their culture.[30] But as with Viagra itself, what does it mean when sexual—and specifically heterosexual—pleasure comes courtesy of a pill?

One thing it means is that we have not yet resolved the uneasy relationship between society and libido that Freud identified a hundred years ago. As Freud insightfully noted, the libido is a strange attractor, chaotic and amorphous, and its free reign was, and still is, antithetical to the existence of Western society as we know it. Freud claimed that sexual repression was what channeled the unruly energies of libido into useful paths, making it the engine that literally drove—and peopled, and built, and painted, and wrote, and farmed—the civilized world. But since approximately the time of Freud, the libido has made increasing claims to independence, not least, as Jonathan Ned Katz points out, through the very word and concept of "heterosexual" and its ability to give medical and intellectual legitimacy to middle-class desire.[31] The proof of concept of this new legitimization of a libido-driven pleasure ethic for male/female sex was arguably the Sexual Revolution. Its success is attested to not just in the myriad books devoted to having more and better and longer and easier orgasms, but in the most mainstream of pop culture, from the famous Katz's Deli fake-orgasm scene in *When Harry Met Sally* to the covers on the headlines of a good two-thirds of the women's magazines on the racks at any North American supermarket.

But old habits, and old doxa, endure. It is not surprising that our present landscape of heterosexual pleasure is a mixed bag of libidinous experiment and anxious rules-lawyering: the border between freedom and control is an uneasy, highly political place. We want women to be secure enough in the pursuit of their own pleasure to pick out the vibrators of their choice in friendly, feminist-owned sex shops, but we don't want them to prefer vibrators to men. We want men to be virile, experienced, and highly sexually skilled, but not to prioritize sex over love or to refuse marriage and fatherhood. We are anxious to experience sexual pleasure and plenty of it, but only if it happens to the right people, at the right ages, in the right combinations. What it seems we really want is a heterosexuality in which we can enjoy all the thrills of riding the tiger of the libido while simultaneously being kept safe from its teeth and claws. It is a goal as idealistic as the creation of a right to the pursuit of happiness. It may, in fact, be an outgrowth of the very the same thing.

CHAPTER SEVEN

Here There Be Dragons

The scene: Another doctor's office, and a man with a framed Johns Hopkins diploma hanging on the wall behind him is looking at me with an expression of irritable confusion. It's not my straightforward and minor health problem that has him bothered; it's the fact that I've just corrected his pronoun use.

" 'He,' not 'she,' " I say. "My partner is male-identified."

He thrusts a pen into the pocket of his white lab coat and shakes his head. "Then why do you use the word 'partner'? Everyone knows that 'partner' means 'same-sex partner.' You should say 'husband,' or 'boyfriend.' Just saying 'partner' like that is misleading."

Later on in the elevator, prescription in hand, I think back on the interaction. I've run into this assumption many times, that my using "partner" is code for "lesbian." But there's something about the doctor's use of the word "misleading" that grates. Had he said that my referring to my "partner" was confusing or unclear, I don't think it would have bothered me. But his use of the word "misleading" felt like an accusation. Rattled by being told that his assumptions were incorrect, he turned the tables by implying that I was lying, or at the very least breaking some unwritten rule.

And in a way, he was right. I had broken the rules, but not by using the word "partner" to describe the person who has been, in Auden's words, "my North, my South, my East and West/ My working

147

week and my Sunday rest" for nearly a decade and a half. Where I broke the rules was by correcting the doctor's assumption that I was referring to another woman, thus revealing something genuinely disturbing by the lights of our sexuality doxa: we can't always accurately guess another person's sexual orientation. My doctor *had,* I finally realized, been misled. But not by me. He was the dupe of doxa, betrayed by what he believed was true about the language of sexual orientation.

The simple fact is that no sexuality is as simple as my doctor wanted to make it. Neither is the language we use to talk about it. As Karl Ulrichs and Karl-Maria Kertbeny were well aware, sexuality is a complicated alchemy that mixes biology, gender relations, hierarchy, resources, and power. "Heterosexual" and "homosexual" were, on one level, nothing more than a smart man's attempt to use language to redefine the terms of a particularly nasty game of Us vs. Them.

Despite it, the Us vs. Them prevailed. But black-and-white approaches have a hard time staying pristine in a world that features not just the proverbial thousand shades of grey, but the full Pantone range of living and luminous color. In the past century or so, since the notion of the "heterosexual" emerged into the mainstream of Western culture and became an entrenched part of doxa, there has been a constant struggle to maintain this sense of black-or-whiteness, this convenient fiction that human beings, by their very sexual natures, divide themselves neatly into two clear and distinct sexual camps.

It is a tricky and profound struggle. The ideology of the "heterosexual" is rooted in a fairly venerable vision of human society and the human animal. As we have seen throughout these pages, heterosexuality as a concept was born to serve a particular culture at a particular time. In the milieu into which "heterosexual" emerged, Christianity still formally controlled much of the social rule-making; gender roles were considered distinct and immutable; gender itself was seen as being an inextricable component of biological sex; and the idea that men and male priorities should run the world was just beginning to be meaningfully challenged. "Heterosexual" was coined for a world in which the ideal of economically and socially viable adulthood meant marriage, children, and middle-class domestic respectability. It was a society that was fairly comfortable with hierarchy, where political and social egalitarianism had become aspirational ideals but were by no means everyday practices.

"Heterosexual" also came into being at the same moment when the underpinnings of that culture were beginning to crack under stress. Protestantism, industrialization, urbanization, abolition, colonialism, capitalism, and the rise of science as a source of wide authority all played a part, as did the pressures of egalitarian and human rights philosophies. The notion of individual human happiness began to become a recognized cultural currency, with far-reaching, fundamentally revolutionary consequences.

But massive, cultural-bedrock power structures do not simply roll over when they encounter friction. Nor do they humbly and proactively offer to give up control if it would better serve current realities. Rather, they continue to assert their power as long as possible, using a wide variety of tools that very much includes assimilation. Like the fictional Borg of *Star Trek: The Next Generation*, which assimilated the individuals and species it encountered into its own vast collective, hive-mind entity, heterosexuality often attempts to cope with disruptive influences by "adding their distinctiveness to our own." The more numerous the practices and customs encompassed by the normative authority of "heterosexual," the broader the regulatory reach of heterosexuality doxa. But assimilation has its limits. As sociologist and feminist theorist Stevi Jackson has put it, the maintenance of a particular doxa or scheme of sexuality is "not just a question of the maintenance of the heterosexual/homosexual binary, but of the multitude of desires and practices that exist on both sides of that divide."[1]

In historical hindsight, we have been able to watch "heterosexual" expand to include, however haltingly, things like contraception, divorce, women's economic autonomy, and the prioritization of orgasm over reproduction. But no entity can engulf and digest everything that is thrown at it without eventually becoming something else entirely. Categories are meaningful because they are bounded. When those boundaries become too thinly stretched—or too easily permeable, or both—the categories themselves start to lose their meaning.

This may already be starting to happen to the category of heterosexuality. The landscape of sex and gender, so central to the hetero/homo scheme, has become increasingly complex and sophisticated, thanks both to advances in biomedical technology and to a growing, and increasingly visible, transgender and transsexual culture. Options for acquiring wealth, parenting children, and for forming (and indeed dissolving and reforming) families have all undergone dramatic change that enables many options beyond the historical heterosexual nuclear-family norm. By putting a premium on psychological and physical satisfaction, we have made space to calculate the worth of sexual practices in totally nonreproductive terms: penis-in-vagina intercourse becomes only as worthwhile as it is pleasurable. And when female orgasm is made a major part of that calculus, penis-in-vagina intercourse often does not compare well to alternatives. Add to this the development of a robust queer culture and related changes in our doxa of how sexuality and sexual orientation work, and "heterosexual" becomes less and less inevitable, more vulnerable.

If the sheer weight of culture and history continues to give "heterosexual" the feel of a monolith, it is surely a monolith that has been suffering the effects of some very heavy weather. If we are to make any guesses about what the future of heterosexuality holds—and certainly if I am going to answer the question of how I might best characterize my own romantic and domestic partnership—we have to consider the impact of all these things on the nature and the future of "heterosexual."

THE WIDE STANCE

When he was arrested for lewd conduct in a men's bathroom in the Minneapolis airport in June 2007, then-senator Larry Craig, a Republican from Idaho, reportedly defended himself against charges that he had touched the foot of an undercover officer in a neighboring bathroom stall with his own by saying that he had a "wide stance" when going to the bathroom. As Craig, a hard-line social conservative with a reputation for voting against LGBT rights issues, tried ineffectually to defend himself against charges that he was secretly gay, the "wide stance" phrase rapidly became a catchphrase to use to refer to a closeted queer.

The phrase is more than apt. Craig is only one of a sizeable number of socially conservative right-wing American politicians and religious figures to have been caught up in same-sex sexual scandal in recent years.[2] Like almost all of the others—California state senator Roy Ashburn being a notable exception—Craig vociferously maintained not only that he was innocent of the crime of which he was accused (he pled guilty, then tried to retract the plea), but that he was innocent of the larger "crime" of being gay.

In a sense, he was correct. Whatever Larry Craig did or intended to do in that Minnesota bathroom, whether or not any of the several men who came forth to assert that they had had sex with Craig were telling the truth, and whatever same-sex desires might or might not have ever lurked in the former senator's thoughts really don't matter. Insofar as our modern doxa of sexual orientation involves, according to the American Psychological Association, "a person's sense of identity based on [emotional/romantic/sexual] attractions, related behaviors, and membership in a community of others who share those attractions," Larry Craig was incontrovertibly *not* gay.[3] What Craig was, metaphorically speaking if not literally, was a man with a wide stance. Like many other men have done throughout history, he straddled the border of what was permissible for a man in a position of power, with every expectation that his power, position, and privilege would insulate him from criticism.

A few decades ago, it probably would've been a pretty good bet. When a man's allegiance to the patriarchal status quo is clear and seemingly genuine—husband and father credentials are particularly relevant—there is a tendency to look the other way if, upon occasion, he indulges in a same-sex liaison. Pledging allegiance to patriarchal standards can take many forms, including that of the role the man takes vis-à-vis his male partners. From ancient Rome to present-day Latin America, men who take the insertive role in sex with other men are more likely to be perceived as masculine and sexually respectable, "normal" men who are merely making an exception in terms of the type of body on which they are doing sex. Men who take the receptive role with other men, on the other hand, are vilified for bending over, for giving up power, for being effeminate faggots. It is a crude shorthand, but demonstrative.

Such demonstrations of allegiance need not be so direct, let alone genital. For many decades, until his death from AIDS forced the issue out into the open, actor Rock Hudson successfully concealed his gay identity from the general public. Hudson's leading-man film career, and particularly his roles in the three sunnily heteronormative romantic comedies in which he was paired with the wholesome Doris Day, lent credence to a heterosexuality in which the public clearly wanted to believe. Similarly outed by his eventual AIDS death was legendary conservative lawyer Roy Cohn, best known for his roles in prosecuting the case against Julius and Ethel Rosenberg and as chief counsel to Joseph McCarthy during the Army-McCarthy hearings of 1954. During his life, Cohn was sexually active with other men, but he effectively silenced any attempted revelations of his homosexuality through staunch conservatism and a pattern of going after, in his role as McCarthy's attack dog, "communist sympathizers" who were actually often less communist than they were simply homosexual.[4]

Such privileged immunity, however, has its limits. Neither Hudson nor Cohn would be likely to pull off their double lives quite so easily today. The growth of a distinctively LGBT culture—that is, a culture created and primarily participated in by people who self-identify as some variety of non-heterosexual, and a corresponding successful creation within mainstream culture of a doxa of gayness— has made it more difficult than it used to be to enjoy the advantages of a "wide stance."

In the past fifty years or so, Westerners as a culture have come to believe that the quality of "being gay" exists naturally in a significant proportion of the population. We may be divided about the cause, or whether there even has to be one, but contemporary Westerners are reasonably firm in our belief that heterosexuality and homosexuality exist, and are neither chosen nor voluntary. People who are gay, most Westerners now believe, are not being willfully perverse, nor are they deviants. They are acting according to their natures and are, for lack of a better phrase, just being themselves. This rhetoric disguises the complicated ways that culture, doxa, experience, and relationships work together to shape our personalities, desires, and beliefs. But this is not new either. We have a long tradition of blaming (or crediting) who we are to more or less numinous, arbitrary forces like God, Nature, or Freudian psychodevelopmental mechanics. The "just being yourself" mantra is no less confounding. It implies that the development of selfhood is an unmediated, and thus authoritative, closed loop. It creates a doxa of sexual orientation that asserts that the "authentic" sexual self simply is what it is, organic and spontaneous, and whether expressed or suppressed, will always be the same.

We also have acquired a doxa of the closet and of the phenom-enon of "coming out," further testament to the effectiveness of LGBT activism and visibility. The closet has become a common idiom, used to describe any secret allegiance that seems somehow shameful or contrary to public image; currently, some members of the American political Far Right seem to adore accusing President Barack Obama of being a "closet Muslim." The fact that "closet" is now shorthand for hiding means that it has become doxic. It works because we all know what the closet is, we understand how it works, and we know what it means: to be closeted is to deny one's authentic self, an unhappy expe-rience that any sane person would want to avoid. More to the point, we believe that life in the closet is hypocritical.

Thus when someone who has self-identified publicly as hetero-sexual is revealed to have engaged in same-sex activity on the quiet, the very fact that he attempted to conceal it is instantly meaningful. The doxa of gayness and of the closet means that the revelation of a same-sex liaison appears as the revelation of a true self. Anything less than an open admission of gayness, or at least bisexuality, on the part of the person at the center of such a revelation is understood implic-itly to be an instance of "the lady doth protest too much."

The degree to which this doxa of gayness has become part of mainstream culture can be gauged by the fact that it is now typically the mainstream media, rather than specifically LGBT media, that leads the feeding frenzy when a same-sex scandal erupts. "Outing," once the controversial bailiwick of activist journalists from the queer community, has become mainstream. Queer journalists like Michel-angelo Signorile, who famously defended the practice as an explicit activist strategy after posthumously outing multimillionaire publisher Malcolm Forbes in 1990, saw outing as a way of forcibly holding the powerful and closeted accountable for their failures to support LGBT rights, which in many cases bolstered their fortune, privilege, and im-munity from homophobic criticism. The mainstream media learned from this model, and adapted it to the needs of the status quo. Main-stream media outing is done simultaneously as the policing of norma-tive boundaries and the exposure of hypocrisy.

The hypocrisy piece is critical. Our doxa of sexual orientation includes an interesting and exacting mode of personal honor. Identifying or being identified as homosexual is for the most part no longer a mortal disgrace in most of the West. The number of countries and US states legalizing same-sex marriage continues to grow. Even in America, which has come to seem somewhat backwards in terms of attitudes to LGBT people by comparison to some of its first-world neighbors, approximately 50 percent now find "gay and lesbian relations" morally acceptable, according to a 2010 Gallup report.[5] What is now seen as most shameful, with regard to homosexuality, is lying about it. "Coming out" has come to connote a certain degree of ethical rectitude, a willingness to place honesty above convenience. It is a quality many people appear to consider admirable. When celebrities come out as gay, as singer Ricky Martin did in 2010, they are applauded not just by fellow queers, but by a sizeable chunk of the mainstream that values the display of authenticity, accountability, and honesty. Certainly the excuse-making and backpedalling of many of the powerful conservative men who find themselves outed by the media—Craig's "wide stance" or Florida politician Bob Allen's incredible 2007 assertion that he offered an undercover officer money for permission to perform fellatio on him because he was afraid of black men—are viewed in the mainstream media as dishonorable, unmasculine, and ridiculous.

In this way, the mainstreaming of LGBT culture has succeeded in reducing the assimilative power of "heterosexual." The development of gayness doxa, however, succeeds partly because it too pays allegiance to a philosophy that sexuality is based on the conceit that the human species inherently sorts its sexuality neatly into, as Kinsey groused, "sheep and goats." This is a gross oversimplification, and it does us a disservice. As University of Utah psychologist Lisa Diamond's work has shown, it appears that, particularly for women, same-sex relationships and desires can genuinely be episodic. Regardless of general tendencies to be attracted to one biological sex or another, it is truly possible in some cases to love and desire a specific person regardless of plumbing.[6] Because of the either/or nature of our sexual orientation scheme, though, these both/and experiences, which are relatively common, are often erased, both from mainstream acknowledgment and from the historical record.

Certainly the doxa of gayness as it currently exists in the Western mainstream is imperfect. Its effects are limited, and the understandings it promotes are incomplete. But it is an amusing irony that heterosexuality's ability to take a wide stance with regard to assimilating same-sex liaisons has been undone, to the significant degree it has, by the very institutionalization of a clear split between homosexual and heterosexual. In an era in which we are also seeing an interesting mainstream middle ground coalesce along the borderlines of heterosexual and homosexual—the turf of "bromance," "bicurious," and "heteroflexible"—we can see the open acknowledgement of conflicting desires. In one sense, such terms represent nothing more than the same old bid to claim the emotional and erotic opportunities inherent in a "wide stance" while retaining the option of sheltering under the sturdy roof of straightness. In another way, overtly claiming a middle ground (albeit with more than a whiff of entitlement to hetero privilege) is an exciting venture beyond the binary. From the standpoint of what heterosexual has been, and will be, both bear watching.

WHERE *DO* BABIES COME FROM?

A child born today could, as Stephanie Coontz points out, fairly easily have five parents: two genetic parents who donate egg and sperm, a host mother who gestates and gives birth to the child, and two adoptive parents who raise the child and do the practical work of parenting.[7] This is a dazzling possibility, so foreign to the ways that humans have acquired children for the vast majority of our history that many people would still find it difficult, if you'll pardon the pun, to conceive. Artificial insemination of a human was documented as early as 1790 by anatomist John Hunter and was likely practiced even earlier, but the removal of sexual activity from the begetting of children was a subject fit only for science fiction as recently as 1932, when Aldous Huxley depicted the Fertilization Rooms and baby factories of his *Brave New World*. The first baby conceived via in-vitro laboratory fertilization (IVF), Louise Joy Brown, was born forty-six years after *Brave New World*, to worldwide amazement and controversy.

The Catholic Church has been particularly hostile to nonsexual methods of conception, contending that they, like contraception, separate conception from "the marriage act" in a way that was contrary to "laws written into the actual nature of man and of woman."[8] This is not surprising, since the Church's entire dogma and doctrine of sexuality has, since its inception, been predicated on the assumption that the need for children is the only thing that can rightfully trump the superiority of lifelong virginity and celibacy. But artificial insemination, IVF, and related technologies also seem to threaten many people who have no such doctrinal investment. This seems to be due in no small measure to the fact that reproductive technology exponentially multiplies the chances for people who could not do it otherwise, including same-sex couples and single parents, to have children.

Angst over reproductive technology has gone hand in hand with its medicalization and mainstreaming. Placing semen into a vagina is not exactly a complicated task, and it does not have to be done with a penis. For centuries, some people have quietly chosen a DIY approach to artificial insemination. This very much includes gay men and lesbians, for whom "turkey-baster babies" were a well-known path to parenthood well before the medical establishment was prepared to offer LGBT people access to clinical reproductive technology. Many LGBT parents still choose to handle their own artificial inseminations, surrogate pregnancies, and the like, sometimes incorporating these reproductive arrangements into their extended family structures. I have a nephew whose extended family includes his "spuncle," the man who donated the sperm and is the child's genetic father.

When clinical-grade fertility technology became available to lesbian would-be mothers, however, much of the general public reacted as if a brand new monstrosity had shown up overnight. When the UK National Health Service opened in-vitro fertilization services to LGBT prospective parents in 2006, nothing less than fatherhood itself seemed at stake. "Fathers Not Needed," wailed the *Daily Mail* headline, in a *cri du coeur* that spoke volumes.

Outsourcing the begetting and gestation of children, it seems, triggers some remarkable insecurities. On the surface this seems strange, since child *care* has traditionally been handed over to others as a matter of routine, beginning virtually at the moment of birth in the cases of wet-nurses, foundling homes, and indeed infant adoptions. But until very recently indeed for most people, the desire for a child implied the necessity of penis-in-vagina intercourse. Until, of course, it didn't. Overnight, it seemed that women could call all the reproductive shots: they could choose the sperm they wanted, get pregnant, bear their babies, and raise them, all without having to so much as shake hands with a man. What did this mean for men? What did this mean for heterosexuality?

It is not as if there is no precedent for the fatherless family or the husbandless household. These have always existed. There has never been a time when men have not abandoned women, when husbands have not died, gone to war, or been forced to leave wives and children behind when they went to sea or to some distant place to find work. Common as they have been, however, we have historically regarded husbandless households as anomalies, prone to producing problems like bossy and forward girls . . . or submissive boys effeminized by the lack of proper male role models. Single fathers get an even more focused version of this sociocultural stink-eye, the fact that they do "women's work" not quite excused by necessity. Although hands-on fatherhood and even the "stay-at-home dad" phenomenon seem to be gaining respectability currently (particularly in socially liberal countries like Sweden), the belief that women are inherently more fit to parent is so deeply entrenched that in America many people are under the mistaken impression that the law requires divorcing mothers to be given custody of any children.[9]

We have been trained for a very long time, in other words, to consider "nontraditional" families troublesome at best and actively destructive at worst. The results of the matrix of economic, social, and civic privilege that has developed around the heterosexual nuclear household have long been taken as proof that such households are somehow inherently better and more successful. There are many, including the nonprofit advertising agency Campaign for Our Children, who continue to claim, using billboards, bus-side advertisements, radio, and more, that children of married parents are better off simply because their parents are married.[10] But as the work of sociologists Timothy Biblarz and Judith Stacey indicates, much of the research that supposedly proves that unique benefits derive from having a parent of each biological sex—the traditional set of married heterosexual parents—mistakenly conflates parental sexes with parental numbers.

It is more important that there be enough parents to go around than it is that those parents be of particular biological sexes.[11] A recent study by Nanette Gartrell and Henny Bos in *Pediatrics* appears to confirm this, showing that the children of lesbian families seem, if anything, to be better adjusted and more successful than their peers who grow up with conventional, different-sex parents.[12] Having same-sex parents, in other words, does not appear to be a liability for children's development.

This could be welcomed as a liberating moment, the confirmation that the biologically critical, socially central, and symbolically enormous task of parenting the next generation doesn't have to be limited to a particular kind of parent. Yet even in the pages of the fairly reserved *Atlantic,* male fear trumped egalitarian possibility: in its June/July 2010 issue, the *Atlantic* headlined its coverage of Biblarz and Stacey's research "Are Fathers Necessary?"

It might as well have been headlined "Is Heterosexuality Necessary?" The father-headed family has historically been the standard in Western culture, and practically the insignia of middle-class normalcy. The desire to mate with an opposite-sex partner to form such a family was, according to Krafft-Ebing, what made a person "heterosexual." The father-headed nuclear family has a long track record of being the version of the family that is considered socially, politically, and scientifically correct. But when gametes can be harvested by needle and the spark of life transmitted in a petri dish, when children can be successfully and happily reared by parents who are not parts of a male-female dyad, then the monolith of heterosexuality loses two large blocks from its foundation. As the title of Robin Marantz Henig's 2004 book on the history of IVF, *Pandora's Baby,* suggests, modern innovations in the ways we can and do create new families have opened a culture-changing can of worms. What these brave new families will mean to the future of heterosexuality, of course, it is much too soon to say. Nevertheless, it is no longer really plausible, if indeed it ever was, to claim that heterosexuality is necessary for the creation of families and for the generation and rearing of children. Does heterosexuality need families and children to help validate its existence more than families and children need heterosexuality to validate theirs? It seems likely.

A TALE OF TWO SPOUSES

When jazz pianist and father of three Billy Tipton died in Spokane, Washington, in 1989, the American media exploded in shock: the seventy-five-year-old man was a woman. No one, it seems, knew this except Tipton himself. His children, informally adopted, had only ever known Tipton as their father. Tipton's five common-law wives, including his last wife, a former stripper named Kitty Oakes, apparently believed—and apparently had no reason to doubt—that a car accident in Tipton's youth had mangled his ribcage and genitals, leaving him impotent and necessitating the wearing of protective bandages.

Tipton's life had its ups and downs, like any other. His marriages tended not to work out well, and his last wife was abusive enough that Tipton ended up raising his youngest child as a solo father. His career was only modestly successful, much of it spent working out of Spokane's grand dame of a Gilded Age hotel, the Davenport. He was a loving parent, though, and he managed to make a consistent living in a notoriously fickle industry, not small things. Still, Billy Tipton's most impressive performance was his seamless and completely successful life as a man.

Hindsight, of course, is 20/20. After Tipton's death and the revelation of his biological sex, journalists and biographers would look at photos of the baby-faced Tipton and wonder how people could not have known. Tipton's ex-wives' claims that they had simply accepted his car-wreck story and adjusted to the (perhaps not entirely unwelcome) idea that the man in their lives was infertile and more interested in their pleasure than his own were weighed in the balance and found only barely credible. But the fact remains that Tipton's children, upon hearing that their father was a woman, were so stunned and hurt that two of them changed their last names.

More remarkable still was the legal reaction. After Kitty Oakes died in 2007, a Spokane County probate court upheld the Tipton children's rights of inheritance. In effect, by allowing Jonathan Clark, Scott Miller, and William Tipton Jr. to inherit, the court affirmed the legitimacy of a highly unorthodox family. The three children were biologically unrelated, both to one another and to their parents, and none were ever legally adopted. The parents were never legally married and were, in fact, both of the same biological sex. But with both

Tipton and Oakes dead, the judge ruled, there was no reason to make their children accountable for the fact that their parents had chosen not to play by the rules. The (Spokane) *Spokesman-Review* headline writer had quite a job composing a headline to convey it: "Judge: Billy Tipton's 'Sons' Can Inherit Their 'Mother's' Estate."

It was a noteworthy decision. Washington law does not, ordinarily, permit illegally adopted children not named specifically in a will to inherit property. In this instance, however, the judge agreed with the attorney for Oakes's estate that, even though the three Tipton children knew they were adopted, and that Kitty Oakes was not their biological mother, "the Tiptons were a family." For Superior Court judge Michael Price, being a family—regardless of paperwork, or even the parents' biological sexes—was, in the end, enough.

In the case of Christie Lee Littleton, on the other hand, being family was nowhere near enough. Nor was having done everything, including changing legal and physical sex, strictly by the book. Born male and christened Lee Cavazos in San Antonio, Texas, in 1952, Christie Lee Littleton felt from toddlerhood that she should have been female. This distressed her parents and the doctors to whom they took the child, but the regimens of male hormones to which Littleton was subjected in attempted masculinization therapy did not change her feelings. By the time Littleton was seventeen, she had begun to seek out a sex change, and when she was twenty-three, she managed to become part of a program at the University of Texas Health Science Center that would finally assist her in changing her hormones and her anatomy. In 1977, she changed her name to Christie Lee; in 1979, the genital surgeries that rendered her medically female were completed. In 1989, the happily female Christie Lee Cavazos, radiant in white lace, married Jonathan Mark Littleton in Kentucky, where they met and settled down to a pleasant, unremarkable life together, later moving back to Texas.

It should have been a "happily ever after" story, the kind of gender-normative, heterosexual marriage that conservative pundits praise as the backbone of traditional society. For seven years, it was. Then, tragically, Jonathan Mark Littleton died before his time. After a period of mourning her husband, Christie decided to open a case against her late husband's physician, Mark Prange, for medical malpractice leading to wrongful death.

Was there actual medical malpractice involved in Mr. Littleton's death? We may never know. Certainly there has never been a verdict on the issue, for almost immediately, Mrs. Littleton's attempts to seek redress in the matter of her husband's death were derailed by something she surely thought she had put well behind her: her previous life of being identified as a man. Prange's lawyers' counterargument in the suit was a simple one. Christie Littleton, they argued, was not entitled to file suit as Jonathan Mark Littleton's next-of-kin, for the simple reason that the marriage between the two could not possibly have been valid. Because Mrs. Littleton had begun life as a boy, because her cells carried XY chromosomes, and because, as they argued, sex reassignment only changed the appearance and not the facts of biology, she could not be in a valid marriage to a biological man.

Determined to get her case heard, Christie Littleton and her lawyers pursued the case through multiple appeals. After the Texas Fourth Court of Appeals refused to acknowledge the validity of the Littleton marriage, Mrs. Littleton and her legal team took the case to the Texas State Supreme Court, in hopes that a review of the law being invoked in the case would have a positive result.

It failed. The US Supreme Court refused to review the case. For all intents and purposes, Christie Littleton has no recourse with regard to the death of her spouse, a state of affairs of which the federal judiciary apparently approves. Where things rest—at least in Texas—is that it is possible for a US state to decide that sex is determined solely by chromosomes, that it comes in two and only two types, and that it cannot be meaningfully legally changed, regardless of medical intervention.

This, as Christie Littleton and many commentators on the case have pointed out, is not only mean-spirited and reductive, but ignorant. The law, of course, is not obligated to be kind, and it is certainly not obligated to recognize the quality of "familyness" that appears to have moved the judge in the Tipton case. But one could make the argument, as indeed Christie Littleton and her legal team have tried to do, that the state should recognize the evidence that clearly demonstrates that sex is nowhere near a binary affair.

Biology, as it happens, agrees with Christie Littleton. Although the majority of people have sex chromosomes that match one of two primary types—XY for males, XX for females—a sizeable minority of people, including my own partner, as you may recall, have sex chromosomes of some other type. Or types: not only can an individual have a single set of sex chromosomes that are neither XX or XY and can have, for instance, XXY or XYY or XO, but they may also have different sets of sex chromosomes in different cells due to the phenomena known as mosaicism and chimerism.[13] My partner, who is both genetically intersex and an example of genetic mosaicism, has some cells with XY sex chromosomes and others with XXY. One wonders which one the court would consider authoritative? If my partner and I married in Texas, would our marriage be valid? It might, if the court, in its Solomonic wisdom, were to take the opinion that a single person's chromosomes could be split in half.

But even this would only make our marriage legally binding if my own sex chromosomes are what I assume them to be. Like most people, I do not actually know my own karyotype. It is quite possible that I, like hundreds of thousands of other people, have been intersex all my life and simply do not know it. No government, including that of Texas, has yet made getting a karyotype a prerequisite for applying for a marriage license. If Texas, or any other locality, is going to limit marriage to people whose genes conform to a particular pattern, this is a problem. People don't fall in love with chromosomes, after all. They don't have sex with chromosomes, and they certainly don't get married to chromosomes. Sex is more than genetics. Much more.

As medical technology gets more sophisticated, and we learn about even more varieties and variations of human biological sex, it becomes ever clearer that thinking of biological sex as binary may be convenient, but it is not accurate. This is also true when it comes to thinking of biological sex as fixed and unchanging. While it is true that, as the Texas Appeals Court wrote in October 1999, "The male chromosomes do not change with either hormonal treatment or sex reassignment surgery. Biologically a postoperative female transsexual is still a male," it is also true that the scalpel cuts both ways. Anatomically, a transwoman who has undergone a vaginoplasty—the surgical removal of penis, scrotum, and testicles and the creation of a vagina and vulva—has functionally the same genital anatomy as any biological female who has had a hysterectomy. Two such women may also be very hormonally similar, given the tendency for post-hysterectomy patients to be given hormone replacement therapy.

Biology is not destiny. It isn't even necessarily permanent. Even if medical expertise and technology did not provide us with the means to identify and understand nature's biological bounty and to create our own, gender would still be complex, multifarious, and unpredictable. As the historical record bears out, there have always been Billy Tiptons. Male privilege can be quite motivating: women have lived as men in order to follow God, obtain educations, join the professions, support their families, and go to war, in addition to doing it so that they could love other women without being persecuted. Historical examples of men living as women are thinner on the ground, probably in part because to abandon masculinity is to abandon power. Still, we know that men have lived as women, either temporarily or long-term, in order to escape from danger, to go undercover, and, in rare cases like that of the legendary eighteenth-century diplomat and spy the Chevalier d'Eon, apparently just because they wanted to.

Our culture has yet to come to grips with this. The hopeless hodgepodge of Western legal approaches to sex and gender is just one result of our incomplete grasp of sexuality. It makes no logical sense that Christie Littleton has been denied, rather vindictively it would seem, the same humane legal consideration of her social identity and marriage that Billy Tipton received posthumously.[14]

Would lifting the heavy hand of the binary sex/gender system from the law really mean, as conservative critics sometimes warn it will, the end of marriage and the traditional family? It doesn't seem likely that it would. Nor would it necessarily spell the end of heterosexuality. Surely, if male and female are two of a variety of sexes, and masculine and feminine two of a variety of genders, then heterosexual and homosexual are two of a variety of ways to combine them. Egalitarianism, human rights, and civil rights are slowly but surely forcing the hand of the law. The law may not eagerly embrace the complexities of sex and gender, but the more that human beings continue to exist in ways that challenge the borders and dynamics of "heterosexual" and "homosexual," the more the law will be compelled to find some way to answer.

AND IN THE END . . .

Recently, over the kitchen table, I asked my partner what he thought the answer was. How did he think our relationship should be characterized, in terms of sexual orientation? He prodded his dinner with his chopsticks for a moment, looking thoughtful.

"I think," he ventured, "it depends on who's asking."

He's right. Whether we are perceived as heterosexual or nonheterosexual depends a great deal on who's looking at us. How, and even whether, we name the dynamic of our relationship for others depends a great deal on who we're talking to.

It comes down to context and safety. As a couple, we qualify in many ways to identify as nonheterosexual. Individually, we both have our queer credentials well in hand. But as a couple, it's not so clear . . . or so queer. My femmeness tends to make my queerness less obvious; his geekiness tends to make his androgyny less striking. To the casual observer, we may appear to be a few bubbles off plumb, but still pretty safely within the tolerances of "male/female couple, kissing, presumed straight." The qualities of our relationship that make "heterosexual" a less than completely appropriate adjective are not necessarily obvious to someone seeing us bickering over what kind of salad dressing to buy or laughing together as we walk our dog.

What this means is that, if we want it, heterosexual privilege is ours for the taking. We have the unparalleled privilege of being able to go about our lives without our relationship attracting notice. It may not seem like much, but it is. When you are unlikely to experience any negative consequences for doing what you do and being who you are, you can do what you need and want to do in the world with no more than an average amount of fuss, bother, oppression, and stress. It's what life should be like for everyone, but isn't. For those easily identified as not being heterosexual, it is often invasively, annoyingly, inequitably, harassingly, even violently otherwise. Having your sexuality and your relationships be perceived as "normal" provides unearned privilege. It accrues automatically and invisibly to everyone who is perceived as being heterosexual for as long as they continue to be perceived that way. The phenomenon is so automatic and so basic, both to doxa and experience, that most of the people who have this privilege don't perceive it, let alone perceive it as a privilege. They assume—as indeed doxa tells them—that it's just the way things are.

But of course it's not. Heterosexual privilege is the result of an enormous cultural machine. Parts of the apparatus existed long before the concept of "heterosexual" was so much as a twinkle in Karl-Maria Kertbeny's eye; parts were machined by the urban industrialist nineteenth century, and still other parts have been cobbled together over time by psychiatrists and statisticians, ad executives, lawyers, and a veritable army of moony, June-y songwriters. It is a complex and frankly monumental cultural inheritance, accreted over decades, filtering in from every direction and thus seemingly none at all. Our art is steeped in it; our media are driven by it. We remember our most classic stories through its tunnel vision—Antony and Cleopatra's tale is a political thriller and a bloodbath, not a swoony romance. Regardless of whom we desire or have sex with, no matter whom we form our households or raise our children with, heterosexuality influences how we keep house, how we spend our money, and how we build our families. The models we have, and the standards we are expected to maintain, come to us via heterosexuality as a normative state. Heterosexuality—whatever the current version of that concept happens to be—is unremarkable because it is the standard by which everything else is measured. *That* is heterosexual privilege.

Whether my partner and I are willing to give up the protective camouflage of being presumed to be straight, therefore, depends on a lot of things. Who wants to know? The waitress at the diner does not care; to her we're just the two-top by the window that ordered the BLT and the Cobb salad. But sometimes people do ask, and when they do we have to evaluate whether their interest seems friendly. Someone who seems like a kindred spirit can likely get us talking openly about intersex issues, femme identity politics, or our adorable baby nephew and his gay trans daddies. We don't necessarily announce ourselves as queer in those conversations, but we don't generally need to. But if questions about our sexuality arrive with sneers or snarls, or we're stared at like circus freaks? That's a little tougher. Sometimes we try to turn it into a teaching moment, a chance to inform and enlighten. Sometimes we swallow our pride and pick up another heavy sack of privileged guilt as we point solemnly to our hetero-passable façade, hoping that the jerk du jour will just go away.

The fact that how my partner and I answer the question of whether we're straight or not isn't cut-and-dried, and that it *does* matter who's asking is what ultimately gives me an answer to my question about my own sexual orientation: if I were heterosexual, I'd only have one answer.

I had hoped, when I set out to write this book, that somewhere in the history of heterosexuality I would find a master key, a one-size-fits-all definition of "heterosexual" that I could use once and for all to characterize my own relationship. What I found instead was a mouse that roared, a modern term of art posing as an eternal verity dressed in Classical-language garb, and an assimilative juggernaut. Trying to determine whether my life partnership was heterosexual by probing the history of heterosexuality was like asking questions of a Magic 8-Ball "Did our falling in love follow a traditionally heterosexual pattern?" *It is decidedly so.* "Does the fact that we aren't legally married make us less straight than we would be if we were?" *Reply hazy, try again later.* "Does my attraction to my partner's androgynous body characteristics make me nonheterosexual?" *Signs point to yes.* "Would Sigmund Freud characterize our sex life as heterosexual?" *My sources say no.* "How about the American Psychological Association?" *Reply hazy, try again.* Perhaps I will just alternate which box I check off on those clinic forms, a different one each time.

Fortunately, I am not dismayed to discover that in the end, I cannot really lay claim to the much-vaunted label of heterosexual. It bothers me much more, in fact, that I sometimes claim it, or have it claimed for me, without intending to. To lay claim to heterosexuality, it seems to me at the end of all my explorations into its history and its nature, is not so much to claim any upper hand as it is to pledge allegiance to a particular configuration of sex and power in a particular historical moment. There isn't much in that configuration, or its heritage of classism and misogyny, that I find appealing enough to want to claim as my own.

Heterosexuality seems to be bigger than we are, independent, more powerful. It is not. In reality, we are the ones whose imaginations created the heterosexual/homosexual scheme, and we are also the ones whose multitudes that scheme ultimately cannot contain. Eventually as a culture we will imagine our way into some different grand explanation, some other scheme for explaining our emotions and our desires and our passionate entanglements. For now, we believe in heterosexual. And this, too, shall pass.

ACKNOWLEDGMENTS

My heartfelt thanks and deep admiration go to many, including but definitely not limited to S. Bear Bergman, Leigh Ann Craig, Anne Gwin, Lesley A. Hall, Patrick Harris, Arianna Iliff, Laura Waters Jackson, Benjamin Lee Buckley, Keridwen Luis, China Martens, Judith McLaughlin, Kelly Morris, Moira Russell, Danya Ruttenberg, Christopher Schelling, Jordan Stein, Mary Sykes, Elizabeth Tamny, and Rhetta Wiley. I also salute and thank those academics and researchers without whose work this book would have been completely impossible, including Stephanie Coontz, Peter Gay, Chrys Ingraham, Stevi Jackson, Angus McLaren, Steven Seidman, Edward Stein, Lawrence Stone, Jeffrey Weeks, Marilyn Yalom, and the late, much-missed Vern Bullough and Roy Porter. Especial intellectual thanks are due to the redoubtable Jonathan Ned Katz, to whose *The Invention of Heterosexuality* this book owes so much. Much that is good and right about this book is owed to these people, either directly or indirectly. Whatever faults or errors may remain are mine alone.

Thanks are also due to the Creative Baltimore Fund, and to Edenfred and its sponsoring organization, the Terry Family Foundation, for a bit of world enough and time.

Finally, there is not enough gratitude to convey my thanks to my beautiful and bold (and now, former) partner, Malcolm Gin, for everything, very much including being such a good sport about being made into a framing device for a history book.

NOTES

INTRODUCTION

1. Some XXY people discover that, unlike genotypical men but exactly like many genotypical women, they are sensitive to fluctuations in the hormones of the women around them, tagging along biochemically with the menstrual cycles of nearby women. My partner and I thus suffer through PMS symptoms together—breast tenderness, food cravings, emotional volatility, the works. It makes for some spectacular fights, but typically heterosexual it's not.

2. Or for that matter call someone else one. The same is true of "homosexual." The terms were coined at the same time.

3. "Hetero" and "homo" are both Greek, while "sexual" is from the Latin. The decidedly unorthodox—and terribly uneducated-sounding, to the Classically trained—combinations have been the butt of jokes among dead-language nerds for a long time now.

4. Money became infamous for his mishandling of the David Reimer case, also known as the "John/Joan" case, which ultimately culminated in Reimer's suicide. The case is detailed in Colapinto's biography of Reimer, *As Nature Made Him.*

5. The idea that women and men might operate with different sexual orientation models also offers a big temptation to social Darwinists and evolutionary biologists given, as they sometimes are, to leaps of logic. We would do well to beware the overly tidy explanation. This is messy and largely unexplored stuff.

CHAPTER ONE: THE LOVE THAT COULD NOT SPEAK ITS NAME

1. The idea that there might be something called a "sexual orientation" would not arise until after the turn of the twentieth century.

2. The story behind the increased age of consent in the last quarter of the nineteenth century is a fabulous and lurid tale that includes muckraker journalism, shameless politicking, and the kidnapping of a minor. See my *Virgin: The Untouched History* for an overview.

3. Electrolux brand vacuum cleaners and demonic phalluses are, after all, both members of a class of objects loosely defined as "things invented wholesale by human beings." Expressions of human bias were rampant in other scientific fields besides taxonomy. Schiebinger's *Nature's Body* provides a vivid survey of Enlightenment and nineteenth-century imposition of very human values on the natural world, including claims that female orangutans modestly covered their genitals when approached by human men, and the telling process by which the unusually large and imposing insect that had for generations been attributed with supreme and lordly power as the "king of the hive" became the grotesquely fat, totally passive, brainless, mechanically reproductive "queen bee" as soon as it was realized that it laid eggs.

4. Stone, *The Family, Sex, and Marriage in England, 1500–1800.*

5. That this happened extremely rarely does not make it less horrifying that it happened at all. Nineteenth-century men and women alike had their genitals operated upon, sometimes disastrously, in the name of curbing masturbation and improper sexual appetites.

6. Guernsey, quoted in Seidman, "The Power of Desire," p. 49.

7. Maurice, "Where to Get Men."

8. James's essay was prompted, as were so many other illuminating writings on the subject of sexual deviance and social order, by the trials of Oscar Wilde. See Ellmann's 1988 biography of Wilde for more on the trials and on their fallout.

9. For the content of the Prussian Penal Code of 1851, see Drage, *The Criminal Code of the German Empire*, p. 225.

10. Ulrichs's essentialist inversion theory was also swiftly embraced. We still see it today in many of the rhetorical and medical strategies that explain and legitimize transsexuality: the "man trapped in a woman's body" trope is undiluted Ulrichs.

11. The debut of the word "hetero-sexual" was in Mary Keyt Isham's review of Freud's *Beyond the Pleasure Principle* and *Group Psychology and the Analysis of the Ego* in the *New York Times Book Review*, September 7, 1924.

CHAPTER TWO: CARNAL KNOWLEDGE

1. From the diary of James Blake, December 27, 1851. Cited in Rotundo, "Romantic Friendship."
2. From a letter written by Daniel Webster to J. Hervey Bingham, January 2, 1805. Cited in ibid.
3. The word "doxa" was first coined and used this way in social anthropologist Pierre Bourdieu's 1972 book *Outline of a Theory of Practice.*
4. Reijneveld et al. "Infant Crying and Abuse."
5. Freud, *A Case of Hysteria,* p. 146.
6. See, for example, Hartmann, "Sigmund Freud and His Impact on Our Understanding of Male Sexual Dysfunction."
7. As British philosopher of science Karl Popper put it in a 1963 essay, " 'Clinical observations,' like all other observations, are interpretations in the light of theories; and for this reason alone they are apt to seem to support those theories in the light of which they were interpreted." (See Popper, "Science: Conjectures and Refutations.") The astute Popper also recognized the mythic power of Freudian ideas, writing of the Ego, the Super-Ego, and the Id that "no substantially stronger claim to scientific status can be made for it than for Homer's collected stories from Olympus. These theories describe some facts, but in the manner of myths."
8. See Fredric Wertham's infamous 1954 *Seduction of the Innocent* or, for more context, Wright's *Comic Book Nation.* On "abstinence-only" education, see Valenti, *The Purity Myth.*
9. The theory of marking was first developed by linguist Roman Jakobson and elaborated by other linguists and sociolinguists of the Prague school.
10. Tanenbaum, *Slut,* p. 10.
11. Karras, *Sexuality in Medieval Europe,* p. 17.
12. "Reparative therapy" is psychotherapy intended to convert a homosexually identified person to heterosexuality. This controversial form of therapy was denounced as harmful in August 2009 by the American Psychological Association.
13. I have always wondered whether people who make these arguments about sexuality feel the same way about religious faith. So far as I am aware, there is no genetic or biological basis for that, either.
14. James Owen, "Homosexual Activity Among Animals Stirs Debate," *National Geographic News,* July 23, 2004, http://news.nationalgeographic.com/news/pf/56958719.html.
15. This is called hypodermic insemination, and is reasonably common among invertebrates. The male injects spermatophores, sperm-carrying

packets, into the body of the female, where eventually the sperm enter the lymphatic system and are conveyed to the ovaries, where fertilization takes place. In some species, such as the African bat bug *Afrocimex constrictus,* males do this to other males, as well.

16. Sometimes these mass-market periodical surveys are cosponsored by health or medical organizations, such as the Kaiser Family Foundation's collaboration with *Seventeen* magazine.

17. The research on the reliability of self-reporting in sexological studies is at least as enlightening as the sexological studies themselves. See, for instance, Gillmore, "Comparison of Daily and Retrospective Reports of Vaginal Sex in Heterosexual Men and Women."

18. Halperin, "Is There a History of Sexuality?," p. 257

CHAPTER THREE: STRAIGHT SCIENCE

1. Lavoisier's proof lay in demonstrating that, in the absence of a specific gas (oxygen), whose presence could be measured by weight, combustible items would not burn and oxidizable items would not rust. Thus it was revealed that combustion was an interaction between a substance and the gases in proximity to it, and not an interaction between the essential matter of a substance and the phlogiston also contained in the same substance.

2. Robie, *Sex and Life,* p. 359.

3. A fine brief review of the available history on masturbation and its "cures" is Darby, "The Masturbation Taboo and the Rise of Routine Male Circumcision."

4. Gillis, "Bad Habits and Pernicious Results." Small children often self-soothe by touching their genitals, as well as by thumb-sucking, sometimes simultaneously. One does not cause the other, and neither is typically considered to pose medical problems. Currently, the American Dental Association asserts that thumb-sucking may cause issues for dental development if it is still going on at the time that the permanent teeth are coming in, but that most children spontaneously stop thumb-sucking well before this point.

5. Clitoridectomy, or the surgical excision of the clitoris, enjoyed a mercifully brief vogue in the 1860s as a masturbation preventative. More hay has been made of this than is perhaps warranted, as it was never a mainstream practice and was hotly controversial even in its era. Although both this form of genital cutting and the many other forms of female genital cutting practiced indigenously in various cultures around the world con-

stitute efforts to control female sexual behavior, there is no known direct relationship between Victorian clitoridectomy and other forms of female genital cutting.

6. Across the Atlantic, where routine circumcision never particularly caught on, eminent surgeon Sir Jonathan Hutchinson wrote an influential article, "On Circumcision as a Preventative of Masturbation," recommending the same and saying that "measures more radical than circumcision would, if public opinion permitted their adoption, be a true kindness to many parents of both sexes."

7. Carroll, *Through the Looking-Glass* (1871).

8. Greenspan, "Courtship in *Drosophila*.".

9. Haumann, "Homosexuality, Biology, and Ideology," p. 69.

10. The same critics pointed out that, for similar reasons, the usefulness of "homosexual" was likewise suspect.

11. For example, see Ordover, *American Eugenics*.

12. To say nothing of the persistent belief in the hymen and its putative meanings. See my *Virgin: The Untouched History*.

13. Montegazza is quoted in Herrn, "On the History of Biological Theories of Homosexuality," p. 41.

14. The possibility that a researcher's opinion might introduce bias was, it seems, not entertained.

15. Masculinized femaleness was also a problem, but was both seen and acknowledged more rarely than its obverse.

16. From Stein, *The Mismeasure of Desire*, p. 234.

17. Darwin, *On the Origin of Species*, p. 57.

18. Schiebinger, *Nature's Body*.

19. Russett, *Sexual Science*, p. 27.

20. Ricketts, "Biological Research on Homosexuality," p. 90.

21. Stein, "Deconstructing Sexual Orientation," pp. 84–85.

CHAPTER FOUR: THE MARRYING TYPE

1. The *Satyr* is discussed at some length in Lanser, "Singular Politics," pp. 297–324.

2. Hill, *Women Alone*, especially chapter 9.

3. Cotton, *A Meet Help*, pp. 14–15.

4. I don't specify that this applies only to different-sex relationships here because it doesn't. This is something we tend to believe is true of all romantic and sexual relationships, regardless of the sexes or genders of the participants.

5. "Life, liberty, and the pursuit of happiness" is a revision; the original read "life, liberty, and property." A telling difference.
6. Porter, *Flesh in the Age of Reason*, p. 9.
7. Astell, "Some Reflections Upon Marriage."
8. The notion that Christianity would be better served by a priesthood of all believers rather than by tiers of increasingly powerful clergy topped by an infallible Supreme Pontiff is very like the notion that nations would be better off with a government of their own citizenry rather than layers of increasingly powerful hereditary aristocrats atop whom perched an emperor or king.
9. Proof that a marriage was unconsummated would do the trick, as would proof that a marriage was in some degree incestuous or that one's spouse was a heretic.
10. Jewish marriage, then and now, is highly contractual in nature and centers around the writing and signing of a ketubah, or marriage contract, which specifies, among other things, the settlement a woman may expect to receive if her husband divorces her.
11. There are still some holdout localities that do not permit no-fault divorce, and indeed there are some, like the island nation of Malta, that do not permit divorce at all. *Caveat nupturus.*
12. Kirchberg v. Feenstra, 450 U.S. 455 (1981).
13. Gay, *The Education of the Senses*, p. 193.
14. Smith-Rosenberg, *Disorderly Conduct*, p. 253.
15. See US Department of Labor website, http://www.dol.gov/wb/stats/main.htm.
16. See UN website, http://www.un.org/ecosocdev/geninfo/women/women96.htm#labour.
17. Quoted in Moscucci, *The Science of Woman*, p. 28.
18. Ellis, "The Psychic State in Pregnancy," p. 229.
19. What Russell meant by this was that couples might have sexual intercourse without being married and only needed to concern themselves with marriage if the woman became pregnant.
20. The Quiverfull movement is an originally American movement within fundamentalist Protestantism that eschews all forms of contraception and family planning and has a strong focus on large family sizes as a gift from God. The name comes from Psalm 127, where having a large number of children is compared to having a quiver full of arrows. For a critical overview, see Joyce, *Quiverfull.*
21. Gillis, *A World of Their Own Making*, p. 153.
22. Stone, *The Family, Sex, and Marriage in England*, p. 64.

23. Hall, *Conceiving Parenthood*, pp. 123–211.

24. Cited in Reed, *From Private Vice to Public Virtue*, p. 426. Moore later contributed materially to the passage of family-planning legislation under the Nixon administration whose eugenic underpinnings were quite plain: the intended end-users of the family-planning funding that the bill provided were to be the mentally ill, the indigent, Cuban refugees, migrant workers, and Native Americans.

25. In British mill towns, Malthusian and socialist activists were also running direct educational efforts; Ittmann notes that some towns were known for the quantity of family-planning pamphlets to be found decorating the walls of the communal privies. Ittmann, "Family Limitation and Family Economy."

26. Marks, *Sexual Chemistry*, p. 35.

27. Watkins, *On the Pill*, p. 50.

28. Cook, *The Long Sexual Revolution*, p. 88; Office for National Statistics, "Rise in UK Fertility Continues," http://www.statistics.gov.uk/cci/nugget.asp?ID=951, viewed on March 17, 2010.

29. "Births: Preliminary Data for 2007," National Vital Statistics Reports 57, no. 12 (March 18, 2009), US Department of Health and Human Services, Centers for Disease Control and Prevention, National Center for Health Statistics, National Vital Statistics System. Released as file nvsr57_12.pdf from http://www.cdc.gov/nchs/births.htm.

30. Goodwin, "Who Marries and When?"

CHAPTER FIVE: WHAT'S LOVE GOT TO DO WITH IT?

1. The use of music to deliver these themes, in Disney, makes them all the more powerful and memorable. "Someday My Prince Will Come" was listed, in 2004, as nineteenth in the American Film Institute's TV special *100 Years . . . 100 Songs*, which presented a ranking of the best songs from the history of film.

2. These figures have undoubtedly risen. My statistics come from Walt Disney World's publicly released data at http://wdwnews.com/view pressrelease.aspx?pressreleaseid=99882&siteid=1 (access date April 2010).

3. Huet, *The History of Romances*, pp. 3–4.

4. Ibid., p. 129.

5. Ibid., p. 145.

6. Ibid., pp. 142–43.

7. Stone, *The Family, Sex, and Marriage in England*, p. 284.

8. Government programs have generously made *The Ogilvies* and many other novels of the period available for free reading online. They make for an interesting and illuminating reading experience. A list of available texts is at the Literary Heritage (UK) website, http://www3.shropshire-cc .gov.uk/eauthors.htm.

9. In Gay, *The Tender Passion*, p. 142.

10. Bloch, "Changing Conceptions of Sexuality and Romance in Eighteenth-Century America," p. 22.

11. From Thomas Shepard, *The Parable of the Ten Virgins Opened and Applied* (1656). Quoted in Winship, "Behold the Bridegroom Cometh!"

12. Berend, "'The Best Or None!'" p. 937.

13. Farrar (writing as "A Lady"), *The Young Lady's Friend*.

14. Albertine, "Heart's Expression"; Eustace, "'The Cornerstone of a Copious Work.'"

15. Kingsley, letter to Grenfell, October 1, 1843, quoted in Gay, *The Tender Passion*, p. 307.

16. Kingsley, letter to Grenfell, October 4, 1843, quoted in ibid., p. 308.

17. Weld, *Letters of Theodore Dwight Weld, Angelina Grimke Weld, and Sarah Grimke*.

18. Ibid.

19. Brown, "The Action for Alienation of Affections," p. 472. Alienation of affections, as a tort, is no longer recognized by most American states. No-fault divorce superseded it.

20. The term "date" starts appearing in print referring to a courtship context around this time, according to Marilyn Yalom, *A History of the Wife*.

21. Rothman, "Sex and Self-Control."

22. See Jacobson's brilliant *Whiteness of a Different Color* for more on this process.

23. The trope of the "beauty secret" persists to this day. Women are not supposed to betray the fact that beauty very often requires quite a bit of work, as well as expense.

24. Public houses, taverns, bars, and so on were still mostly male preserves, although that was to change in time.

25. Bailey, *From Front Porch to Back Seat*, p. 28.

26. Ibid., p. 23.

27. Royden, *Sex and Common-Sense*, pp. 54–55.

28. Rothman, "Sex and Self-Control."

29. Bailey, *From Front Porch to Back Seat*.

30. From Alison Neilans, *Changes in Sex Morality* (1936), pp. 223–24, quoted in Hall, *Outspoken Women*, p. 202.

31. Hall borrowed the concept of Sturm und Drang from the late eighteenth-century early Romantic movement of the same name.

32. Hall, *Adolescence*, p. 97.

33. Hall knew Freud, with whose theories on adolescence Hall's have considerable overlap, and brought him to speak at Clark University, where Hall was president from 1889 to 1920.

34. Hall, *Adolescence*, p. 579.

35. Bailey, *From Front Porch to Back Seat,* p. 26.

36. Ibid., p. 48.

37. Kornitzer, *The Modern Woman and Herself* (1932), p. 77, quoted in Hall, *Outspoken Women,* p. 191.

38. Indeed, for the more conservative, going steady without romantic love was likewise a moral pitfall.

39. Cicely Hamilton, *Marriage as a Trade.*

40. Atkinson, *Amazon Odyssey,* p. 105.

41. Shelley, "Lesbianism and the Women's Liberation Movement."

42. To which radicals like writer Joanna Russ replied, "*But what is so dreadful about abandoning men to their own resources?* Haven't they got any? Men as a group at every class level have relatively more disposable income than women, more command over institutions, more leisure, more immunity from sexual violence, and more control over community resources than women." (Russ, "For Women Only, Or, What Is That Man Doing under My Seat?," p. 92.) The schism between mainstream and separatist feminisms continues to this day.

CHAPTER SIX: THE PLEASURE PRINCIPLE

1. Mondaini, "Sildenafil Does Not Improve Sexual Function in Men."

2. Joby Warrick, "Little Blue Pills Among the Ways CIA Wins Friends in Afghanistan," *Washington Post,* December 26, 2008, http://www.washingtonpost.com/wp-dyn/content/article/2008/12/25/AR2008122500931.html (access date June 1, 2010).

3. Sales figures are Pfizer's, from Viagra.com (accessed May 2010).

4. PDE5 drugs do have another clinical indication, but it is by far less common. They are used to treat the disorder known as pulmonary hypertension. Sildenafil, the same drug marketed as Viagra, is also marketed for pulmonary treatment use under a different name (Revatio) and at a far lower price.

5. Karras, *Sexuality in Medieval Europe,* p. 4.

6. Ibid., p. 69.

7. Laqueur, *Making Sex,* p. 44.

8. Stopes, *Enduring Passion,* p. 52. Stopes also expressed the hope that unmarried women who suffered from unsatisfied "hunger" of this sort could be helped by supplements of glandular extracts (hormones).

9. Men were in part genuinely afraid of what might happen if they found themselves overtaxed in such a way; the humoral medical understanding of the body common at the time held that serious depletions caused serious problems. But at the same time one gets the impression that the fear was a way of masking a certain delight at the subversive idea of being "forced" to submit to sex.

10. Cavender, "White-Livered Widders and Bad-Blooded Men."

11. Hanchett, *Sexual Health,* p. 62.

12. Hollick, *The Marriage Guide,* p. 356.

13. Ellis, *Analysis of the Sexual Impulse,* p. 189.

14. Ellis, *Sex in Relation to Society,* p. 531.

15. Robie, *Sex Histories,* pp. 15–16.

16. Ellis, *Little Essays of Love and Virtue,* p. 125.

17. Laipson, "'Kiss without Shame,'" p. 517; Holtzman, "The Pursuit of Married Love," p. 46.

18. Stockham's 1897 book, *Karezza,* instructed the reader in a form of quasitantric, prolonged sensual play without orgasm that went by the same name.

19. Katz, *Invention of Heterosexuality,* p. 66.

20. Jane Gerhard, "Revisiting 'The Myth of the Vaginal Orgasm,'" p. 457.

21. It is instructive that the fact that 50 percent of Kinsey's male subjects—twice as many as the women—had also reported extramarital sex did not raise the same furor.

22. Much hay has been made of Mosher's surveys since Carl Degler discovered them, not least by Degler. As late as 2010, popular geek-culture website BoingBoing.net stumbled upon coverage of the Mosher papers and proclaimed them, as many had done before, as proof positive that the Victorians weren't prudes. True enough, as far as it goes, since Mosher's data does indicate that most of the women who answered her questions seem to have felt positively about sexual relations and experienced orgasms at least sometimes. However, forty-six surveys representing forty-five respondents, all patients of the same doctor, can hardly be claimed to represent the whole of Victorian womanhood. The Mosher papers are certainly tantalizing, but in the end, only a tease.

23. D'Emilio, *Intimate Matters,* p. 337.

24. Densmore, quoted in Gerhard, "Revisiting 'The Myth of the Vaginal Orgasm,'" p. 468.

25. These competing feminist approaches to sexuality would come to a head at a conference, "The Scholar and the Feminist," held at Barnard College in 1982, where many years of feminist factional tension turned into open conflict. The ensuing "sex wars" in feminist and lesbian-feminist communities lasted for the better part of another decade.

26. This observation is made by award-winning director Kimberly Peirce in Kirby Dick's 2006 documentary *This Film Has Not Yet Been Rated*. Peirce's *Boys Don't Cry* (1999), based on the 1993 murder of transgendered man Brandon Teena, depicts the vicious rape and graphic murder of its protagonist, yet the MPAA's initial NC-17 rating was due to the film's depiction of a lengthy, smiling, and thoroughly consensual female orgasm.

27. As the horrific rape and murder of Brandon Teena certainly demonstrates.

28. See, for instance, Remez, "Oral Sex among Adolescents."

29. Whether this can possibly be anything more than placebo-effect snake oil is debatable. The G-spot's role in female pleasure is not particularly well understood, to the point that its very existence is still under biomedical debate. It is furthermore unknown whether size has anything to do with its functioning. In any event, collagen injected into the body is slowly dispersed and eventually eliminated over the course of several months, so any effects of such a procedure would be temporary at best.

30. Flibanserin was originally developed and tested as an antidepressant, and affects norepinephrine and dopamine levels while decreasing serotonin. Its mechanism is therefore quite different to that of vasodilators like Viagra. The difference in mechanism follows the hoary old supposition that men's sexuality is mechanical and bodily while women's is dependent on emotion and psychology. This is only one of the many criticisms being leveled at the drug.

31. Katz, *Invention of Heterosexuality*, p. 181.

CHAPTER SEVEN: HERE THERE BE DRAGONS

1. Jackson, "Sexuality, Heterosexuality, and Gender Hierarchy."

2. It's a sizeable list, and it keeps getting longer. Readers may recall names like Ted Haggard and George Rekers (leading religious authorities in the Christian Right), Mark Foley (Republican congressman from Florida), and Bob Allen (former Florida state representative).

3. "Answers to Your Questions: For a Better Understanding of Sexual Orien-

tation and Homosexuality," American Psychological Association website (2008), www.apa.org/topics/sorientation.pdf.

4. Cohn maintained to the end that he was not homosexual and claimed that he was dying of liver cancer, not of AIDS-related causes.

5. Gallup, Inc., and Lydia Saad, "Americans' Acceptance of Gay Relations Crosses 50% Threshold: Increased Acceptance by Men Driving the Change," press release, May 25, 2010, http://www.gallup.com/poll/135764/Americans-Acceptance-Gay-Relations-Crosses-Threshold.aspx (accessed June 4, 2010).

6. Diamond, *Sexual Fluidity*.

7. Coontz, *Marriage, a History*, p. 275.

8. Pope Paul VI, *Humana Vitae,* 1968.

9. Katrin Bennhold, "In Sweden, Men Can Have It All," *New York Times,* June 9, 2010; it is not, although until fairly recently a legal principle called the "tender years doctrine," based on an 1830 precedent, held that all other factors being equal, the mother was better suited to raise a child than the father. The "tender years doctrine" is now, according to *West's Encyclopedia of American Law,* generally considered to violate the Equal Protection Clause of the Fourteenth Amendment of the Constitution and is thus no longer explicitly invoked.

10. The Campaign for Our Children's ongoing "Marriage Works" campaign, which also includes statements like "Married people make more money" and "Married people are happier," has been running since 1987. If it weren't already obvious that this is a political campaign, I note that in my home city of Baltimore, "Marriage Works" advertisements tend to be concentrated in low-income, majority African American neighborhoods.

11. Biblarz, "How Does the Gender of Parents Matter?" p. 3.

12. Gartrell, "US National Longitudinal Lesbian Family Study."

13. Normally, organisms have a single genetic code or DNA, an identical copy of which appears in every cell in the organism. Chromosomal mosaicism means that an organism with a single set of DNA nevertheless has some cells that contain only certain subsets of the complete code, while other cells contain either a different subset or a complete set. Chromosomal chimerism means that a single organism possesses two (or more) different complete sets of DNA, one complete set of genetic code showing up in some parts of the body and another completely different set of DNA showing up in other parts.

14. That this was a probate case probably had something to do with the judicial attitude. Letting bygones be bygones is simpler when the troublemaker is dead.

BIBLIOGRAPHY

Abelove, Henry. "Freud, Male Homosexuality, and the Americans." *Dissent* 33 (Winter 1986): 59–69.

———. "Some Speculations on the History of 'Sexual Intercourse' During the 'Long Eighteenth Century' in England." *Genders* 6 (November 1989): 125–30.

Abramson, Paul R. "Sexual Science: Emerging Discipline or Oxymoron?" *Journal of Sex Research* 127, no. 2 (May 1990): 147–65.

Abramson, Paul R., and Steven D. Pinkerton. *Sexual Nature, Sexual Culture.* Chicago Series on Sexuality, History, and Society. Chicago: University of Chicago Press, 1995.

———. *With Pleasure: Thoughts on the Nature of Human Sexuality.* Rev. ed. New York: Oxford University Press, 2002.

Adams, Christine "A Choice Not to Wed? Unmarried Women in Eighteenth-Century France." *Journal of Social History* 29, no. 4 (Summer 1996): 883–94.

Adams, Mary Louise. *The Trouble with Normal: Postwar Youth and the Making of Heterosexuality.* Studies in Gender and History Series 7. Toronto: University of Toronto Press, 1997.

Adams, Michael C. C. *The Great Adventure: Male Desire and the Coming of World War I.* Bloomington: Indiana University Press, 1990.

Adkins, Lisa, and Vicki Merchant. *Sexualizing the Social: Power and the Organization of Sexuality.* New York: St. Martin's Press, 1996.

Albertine, Susan. "Heart's Expression: The Middle-Class Language of Love in Late Nineteenth-Century Correspondence." *American Literary History* 4, no. 1 (Spring 1992): 141–64.

Albright, Julie M. "Sex in America Online: An Exploration of Sex, Marital Status, and Sexual Identity in Internet Sex Seeking and Its Impacts." *Journal of Sex Research* 45, no. 2 (May 2008): 175–86.

Altman, Dennis. *The Homosexualization of America.* Boston: Beacon Press, 1983.

American Psychological Association. "Sexual Orientation and Homosexuality." APA HelpCenter online. http://www.apahelpcenter.org/articles/article.php?id=31.

Anderson, Eric. "'Being Masculine Is Not about Who You Sleep With . . . ': Heterosexual Athletes Contesting Masculinity and the One-Time Rule of Homosexuality." *Sex Roles* 58, nos. 1–2 (January 2008): 104–15.

Anderson, Marty. "Is Heterosexuality 'Natural'?" *Ladder* (July 1969): 4–7.

Astell, Mary. "Reflections upon Marriage." In *Astell: Political Writings,* edited by Patricia Springborg, 18. Cambridge, UK: Cambridge University Press, 1996.

Atkinson, Ti-Grace. *Amazon Odyssey.* New York: Links Books, 1974.

Bach, Rebecca Ann. *Shakespeare and Renaissance Literature before Heterosexuality.* New York: Palgrave Macmillan, 2007.

Badgett, Lee, and Jeff Frank. *Sexual Orientation Discrimination: An International Perspective.* New York: Routledge, 2007.

Bailey, Beth. *From Front Porch to Back Seat: Courtship in Twentieth-Century America.* Baltimore: Johns Hopkins University Press, 1988.

———. "Prescribing the Pill: Politics, Culture, and the Sexual Revolution in America's Heartland." *Journal of Social History* 30 (1997): 827–56.

Banks, Amy, and Nanette K. Gartrell. "Hormones and Sexual Orientation: A Questionable Link." *Journal of Homosexuality* 28, nos. 3/4 (June 1995): 247–68.

Banner, Lois W. *In Full Flower: Aging Women, Power, and Sexuality, A History.* New York: Knopf, 1992.

Barash, David P. *Gender Gap: The Biology of Male-Female Differences.* New Brunswick, NJ: Transaction Publishers, 2002.

Barlow, D. H., and Jennifer C. Jones. "Self-Reported Frequency of Sexual Urges, Fantasies, and Masturbatory Fantasies in Heterosexual Males and Females." *Archives of Sexual Behavior* 19, no. 3 (June 1990): 269–79.

Bayer, Ronald. *Homosexuality and American Psychiatry: The Politics of Diagnosis.* Princeton, NJ: Princeton University Press, 1987.

Beard, Daniel Carter. *Hardly a Man Is Now Alive.* New York: Doubleday, Doran & Company, 1939.

Bederman, Gail. *Manliness and Civilization: A Cultural History of Gender and Race in the United States, 1880–1917.* Women in Culture and Society. Chicago: University of Chicago Press, 1995.

Beemyn, Brett, and Michael J. Eliason. *Queer Studies: A Lesbian, Gay, Bisexual, and Transgender Anthology.* New York: New York University Press, 1996.

Bell, David, and Gill Valentine. *Mapping Desire: Geographies of Sexualities.* London: Routledge, 1995.

Bem, Sandra L. "Dismantling Gender Polarization and Compulsory Heterosexuality: Should We Turn the Volume Down or Up?" *Journal of Sex Research* 32, no. 4 (1995): 329–34.

Berglund, Hans, Per Lindström, and Ivanka Savic. "Brain Response to Putative Pheromones in Lesbian Women." *Proceedings of the National Academy of Sciences of the United States of America* 103, no. 21 (May 23, 2006): 8269–74.

Berend, Zsuzsa. "'The Best or None!' Spinsterhood in Nineteenth-Century New England." *Journal of Social History* 33, no. 4 (Summer 2000): 935–57.

Berlant, Lauren Gail. *The Female Complaint: The Unfinished Business of Sentimentality in American Culture.* Durham, NC: Duke University Press, 2008.

———. *The Queen of America Goes to Washington City: Essays on Sex and Citizenship.* Durham, NC: Duke University Press, 1997.

Biblarz, Timothy J., and Judith Stacey. "How Does the Gender of Parents Matter?" *Journal of Marriage and Family* 72 (February 2010): 3–22.

Birken, Lawrence. *Consuming Desire: Sexual Science and the Emergence of a Culture of Abundance, 1871–1914.* Ithaca, NY: Cornell University Press, 1988.

Blanchard, Ray. "Older-Sibling and Younger-Sibling Sex Ratios in Frisch and Hviid's (2006) National Cohort Study of Two Million Danes." *Archives of Sexual Behavior* 36 (2007): 860–63.

Bland, Lucy, Laura Doan, eds.. *Sexology in Culture: Labelling Bodies and Desires.* Oxford, UK: Polity Press, 1998.

Blank, Hanne. *Virgin: The Untouched History.* New York: Bloomsbury, 2007.

Blinn-Pike, Lynn. "Why Abstinent Adolescents Report They Have Not Had Sex: Understanding Sexually Resilient Youth." *Family Relations* 48, no. 3 (July 1999): 295–301.

Bloch, Ruth Howard. "Changing Conceptions of Sexuality and Romance in Eighteenth-Century America." Sexuality in Early America, third series. *William and Mary Quarterly* 60, no. 1 (January 2003): 13–42.

———. *Medieval Misogyny and the Invention of Western Romantic Love.* Chicago: University of Chicago Press, 1991.

Blumberg, Eric S. "The Lives and Voices of Highly Sexual Women." *Journal of Sex Research* 40, no. 2 (May 2003): 146–57.

Blumin, Stuart M. *The Emergence of the Middle Class: Social Experience in the American City, 1760–1900*. Interdisciplinary Perspectives on Modern History. Cambridge, UK: Cambridge University Press, 1989.

Bogaert, Anthony F. "Birth Order and Sexual Orientation in a National Probability Sample." *Journal of Sex Research* 37, no. 4 (November 2000): 361–68.

Bogaert, Anthony F., Lesley E. Crosthwait, Ray Blanchard. "Interaction of Birth Order, Handedness, and Sexual Orientation in the Kinsey Interview Data." *Behavioral Neuroscience* 121, no. 5 (2007): 845–53.

Bogart, Laura M., et al. "Is It 'Sex'? College Students' Interpretations of Sexual Behavior Terminology." *Journal of Sex Research* 37, no. 2 (May 2000): 108–16.

Boswell, John. "Toward the Long View: Revolutions, Universals, and Sexual Categories." *Salmagundi* 58–59 (Fall–Winter 1982–1983): 89–113.

Bouma, Beverly Ann. "Coming Out Straight: Role Exit and Sexual Identity (Re)Formation." Thesis. University of Victoria (Canada), 2007.

Bourdieu, Pierre. *Outline of a Theory of Practice*. Translated by Richard Nice. New York: Cambridge University Press, 1977 (orig. published 1972).

Boyarin, Daniel. *Unheroic Conduct: The Rise of Heterosexuality and the Invention of the Jewish Man*. Berkeley: University of California Press, 1997.

Breslow, Norman, Linda Evans, and Jill Langley. "Comparisons Among Heterosexual, Bisexual, and Homosexual Male Sado-Masochists." *Journal of Homosexuality* 13, no.1 (August 1986): 83–107.

Brill, A. A. "The Introduction and Development of Freud's Work in the United States." *American Journal of Sociology* 45, no. 3 (November 1939): 318–25.

Brooks, Kelly. "Sexual Identity Construction among Lesbian, Bisexual, and Unlabeled Women." PhD diss, University of Rhode Island, 2006.

Brown, Robert C. "The Action for Alienation of Affections." *University of Pennsylvania Law Review and American Law Register* 82, no. 5 (March 1934): 472–506.

Browning, James R., Debra Kessler, Elaine Hatfield, and Patricia Choo. "Power, Gender, and Sexual Behavior." *Journal of Sex Research* 36, no. 4 (November 1999): 342–47.

Brozyna, Martha A. *Gender and Sexuality in the Middle Ages: A Medieval Source Documents Reader*. Jefferson, NC: McFarland, 2005.

Buchbinder, Howard. *Who's on Top? The Politics of Heterosexuality*. Toronto: Garamond, 1987.

Bullough, Bonnie, and Vern Bullough. "Are Transvestites Necessarily Heterosexual?" *Archives of Sexual Behavior* 26, no. 1 (1997): 1–12.

Bullough, Vern. "Homosexuality and the Secret Sin in Nineteenth Century America." *Journal of the History of Medicine* 28 (1973): 143–54.

Bullough, Vern L. *Science in the Bedroom: A History of Sex Research.* New York: BasicBooks, 1994.

———. "Sex and the Medical Model." *Journal of Sex Research* 11, no. 4 (November 1975): 291–303.

Bunch, Charlotte. *Passionate Politics: Essays, 1968–1986: Feminist Theory in Action.* New York: St. Martin's Press, 1987.

Burger, Glen, and Steven F. Kruger. *Queering the Middle Ages.* Medieval Cultures 27. Minneapolis: University of Minnesota Press, 2001.

Bush, M. L. *What Is Love? Richard Carlile's Philosophy of Sex.* London: Verso, 1998.

Buss, David M. *The Evolution of Desire: Strategies of Human Mating.* Rev. ed. New York: BasicBooks, 2003.

Butler, Jack. "Before Sexual Difference: The Art and Science of Genital Embryogenesis." *Leonardo* 26, no. 3 (1993): 193–200.

Butler, Judith. *Bodies That Matter: On the Discursive Limits of "Sex."* Oxford, UK: Routledge, 1993.

———. *Undoing Gender.* New York: Routledge, 2004.

Cacchione, Thea. "Heterosexuality and 'the Labour of Love': A Contribution to Recent Debates on Female Sexual Dysfunction." *Sexualities* 10, no. 3 (July 2007): 299–320.

Call, Vaughn, Susan Sprecher, and Pepper Schwartz. "The Incidence and Frequency of Marital Sex in a National Sample." *Journal of Marriage and Family* 57, no. 3 (August 1995): 639–52.

Campbell, Colin. *The Romantic Ethic and the Spirit of Modern Consumerism.* Oxford, UK: B. Blackwell, 1987.

Cantarella, Eva. *Bisexuality in the Ancient World.* New Haven, CT: Yale University Press, 1992.

Caplan, Patricia. *The Cultural Construction of Sexuality.* London: Tavistock, 1987.

Carter, Julian B. *The Heart of Whiteness: Normal Sexuality and Race in America, 1880–1940.* Durham, NC: Duke University Press, 2007.

Carver, Priscilla R., David G. Perry, and Susan K. Egan. "Children Who Question Their Heterosexuality." *Developmental Psychology* 40, no. 1 (January 2004): 43–53.

Case, Mary Anne C. "Disaggregating Gender from Sex and Sexual Orientation: The Effeminate Man in the Law and Feminist Jurisprudence." *Yale Law Journal* 105, no. 1 (October 1995): 1–105.

Case, Sue Ellen, Philip Brett, and Susan Leigh Foster. *Cruising the Performative: Interventions into the Representation of Ethnicity, Nationality, and Sexuality.* Unnatural Acts Series. Bloomington: Indiana University Press, 1995.

Cate, Rodney M., and James E. Koval. "Heterosexual Relationship Development: Is It Really a Sequential Process?" *Adolescence* 18 (Fall 1983): 507–14.

Cavender, Anthony, and Steve Crowder. "White-Livered Widders and Bad-Blooded Men: Folk Illness and Sexual Disorder in Southern Appalachia." *Journal of the History of Sexuality* 11, no. 4 (October 2002): 637–49.

Chambers, Wendy C. "Oral Sex: Varied Behaviors and Perceptions in a College Population." *Journal of Sex Research* 44, no. 1 (February 2007): 28–42.

Chauncey, George. "From Sexual Inversion to Homosexuality: Medicine and the Changing Conceptualization of Female Deviance." *Salmagundi* 56–59 (Fall–Winter 1983): 114–46.

———. *Gay New York: Gender, Urban Culture, and the Makings of the Gay Male World, 1890–1940.* New York: Basic Books, 1994.

Chodorow, Nancy. *Femininities, Masculinities, Sexualities: Freud and Beyond.* Lexington: University Press of Kentucky, 1994.

Clausen, Jan. *Apples & Oranges: My Journey through Sexual Identity.* Boston: Houghton Mifflin, 1999.

Cody, Lisa Forman. *Birthing the Nation: Sex, Science, and the Conception of Eighteenth-Century Britons.* Oxford, UK: Oxford University Press, 2005.

Cohen, Ed. "The Double Lives of Man: Narration and Identification in the Late Nineteenth-Century Representation of Ec-Centric Masculinities." Victorian Sexualities, *Victorian Studies* 36, no. 3, (Spring 1993): 353–76.

Colapinto, John. *As Nature Made Him: The Boy Who Was Raised as a Girl.* New York: HarperCollins, 2000.

Coleman, Eli. "Bisexual Women in Marriages." *Journal of Homosexuality* 11, nos. 1/2 (Spring 1985): 87–99.

Coleman, Eli, Louis Gooren, and Michael Ross. "Theories of Gender Transpositions: A Critique and Suggestions for Further Research." *Journal of Sex Research* 26, no. 4 (November 1989): 525–38.

Coleman, Emily M., Peter W. Hoon, and Emily F. Hoon. "Arousability and Sexual Satisfaction in Lesbian and Heterosexual Women." *Journal of Sex Research* 19, no. 1 (February 1983): 58–73.

Collier, Richard. *Masculinities, Crime and Criminology: Men, Heterosexuality and the Criminal(ised) Other.* Thousand Oaks, CA: Sage Publications, 1998.

Collins, Marcus. *Modern Love: Personal Relationships in Twentieth-Century Britain.* Newark: University of Delaware Press, 2006.

Cook, Hera. *The Long Sexual Revolution: English Women, Sex, and Contraception, 1800–1975.* New York: Oxford University Press, 2004.

Coontz, Stephanie. *Marriage, a History: From Obedience to Intimacy, or How Love Conquered Marriage.* New York: Viking Penguin, 2006.

Cornell, Drucilla. "The Shadow of Heterosexuality." *Hypatia* 22, no. 1 (Winter 2007): 229–42.

Cossman, Brenda. *Sexual Citizens: The Legal and Cultural Regulation of Sex and Belonging.* Stanford, CA: Stanford University Press, 2007.

Costello, John. *Love, Sex, and War: Changing Values, 1939–45.* London: Collins, 1985.

Cott, Nancy F. "Passionlessness: An Interpretation of Victorian Sexual Ideology." *Signs* 4, no. 2 (Winter 1978): 219–36.

Cotton, John. *A Meet Help.* Boston: B. Green & J. Allen, 1699.

Coward, Rosalind. *Patriarchal Precedents: Sexuality and Social Relations.* London: Routledge & Kegan Paul, 1983.

Curtis, Bruce, and Alan Hunt. "The Fellatio 'Epidemic': Age Relations and Access to the Erotic Arts." *Sexualities* 10, no. 1 (February 2007): 5–28.

Darby, Robert. "The Masturbation Taboo and the Rise of Routine Male Circumcision: A Review of Historiography." *Journal of Social History* 36, no. 3 (2003): 737–57.

Darwin, Charles. *On the Origin of Species by Means of Natural Selection, or the Preservation of Favoured Races in the Struggle for Life.* London: Grant Richards, 1902.

Davidson, Arnold Ira. *The Emergence of Sexuality: Historical Epistemology and the Formation of Concepts.* Cambridge, MA: Harvard University Press, 2001.

Davidson, Roger, and Lesley A. Hall. *Sex, Sin and Suffering: Venereal Disease and European Society Since 1870.* London and New York: Routledge, 2001.

Davis, Katharine Bement. *Factors in the Sex Life of Twenty-Two Hundred Women.* New York: Harper & Brothers, 1929.

Dean, Carolyn J. *Sexuality and Modern Western Culture.* Twayne's Studies in Intellectual and Cultural History. New York: Twayne Publishers, 1996.

De Cecco, John P. "Homosexuality's Brief Recovery: From Sickness to Health and Back Again." *Journal of Sex Research* 23, no. 1 (February 1987): 106–14.

De Cecco, John P., and David Allen Parker. "The Biology of Homosexuality: Sexual Orientation or Sexual Preference?" *Journal of Homosexuality* 28, nos. 1/2 (June 1995): 1–28.

Degler, Carl. "What Ought To Be and What Was: Women's Sexuality in the Nineteenth Century." *American Historical Review* 79 (1974): 1480–90.

DeLora, Joann S., and Jack R. DeLora. *Intimate Life Styles: Marriage and Its Alternatives.* Pacific Palisades, CA: Goodyear Publishing Co., 1972.

D'Emilio, John, and Estelle Freedman. *Intimate Matters: A History of Sexuality in America.* New York: Harper & Row, 1988.

Demos, John, and Virginia Demos. "Adolescence in Historical Perspective." *Journal of Marriage and Family* 31, no. 4 (November 1969): 632–38.

de Rooij, Susanne R., et al. "Sexual Orientation and Gender Identity After Prenatal Exposure to the Dutch Famine." *Archives of Sexual Behavior* 38 (2009): 411–16.

Deutsch, Helen. *The Psychology of Women.* New York: Gruene and Stratton, 1944.

Devor, Holly. "Sexual Orientation Identities, Attractions, and Practices of Female-to-Male Transsexuals." *Journal of Sex Research* 30, no. 4 (November 1993): 303–15.

Diamant, Louis, and Richard D. McAnulty, eds. *The Psychology of Sexual Orientation, Behavior, and Identity: A Handbook.* Westport, CT: Greenwood Press, 1995.

Diamond, Jared M. *Why Is Sex Fun? The Evolution of Human Sexuality.* New York: HarperCollins, 1997.

Diamond, Lisa M. "Emerging Perspectives on Distinctions Between Romantic Love and Sexual Desire." *Current Directions in Psychological Science* 13, no. 3 (2004): 116–19.

———. *Sexual Fluidity: Understanding Women's Love and Desire.* Cambridge, MA: Harvard University Press, 2008.

———. "What Does Sexual Orientation Orient? A Biobehavioral Model Distinguishing Romantic Love and Sexual Desire." *Psychological Review* 110, no. 1 (2003): 173–92.

Diamond, Milton. "A Critical Evaluation of the Ontogeny of Human Sexual Behavior." *Quarterly Review of Biology* 40, no. 2 (June 1965): 147–75.

———. "Sexual Identity and Sexual Orientation in Children with Traumatized or Ambiguous Genitalia." *Journal of Sex Research* 34, no. 2 (1997): 199–211.

Doan, Laura L. *Fashioning Sapphism: The Origins of a Modern English Lesbian Culture.* Between Men—Between Women. New York: Columbia University Press, 2001.

Doll, Lynda S., et al. "The Blood Donor Study Group Homosexually and Nonhomosexually Identified Men Who Have Sex with Men: A Behavioral Comparison." *Journal of Sex Research* 29, no. 1 (February 1992): 1–14.

Douglas, Carol Anne. *Love and Politics: Radical Feminist and Lesbian Theories.* San Francisco: Ism Press, 1990.

Dowbiggin, Ian. *Inheriting Madness: Professionalization and Psychiatric Knowledge in Nineteenth Century France.* Medicine and Society 4. Berkeley: University of California Press, 1991.

Dowd, James J., and Nicole R. Pallotta. "The End of Romance: The Demystification of Love in the Postmodern Age." *Sociological Perspectives* 43, no. 4 (Winter 2000): 549–80.

Drage, Geoffrey. *The Criminal Code of the German Empire*. London: Chapman and Hall, 1885.

Drescher, Jack, and Kenneth J. Zucker, eds. *Ex-Gay Research: Analyzing the Spitzer Study and Its Relation to Science, Religion, Politics, and Culture*. New York: Harrington Park Press, 2006.

Druckerman, Pamela. *Lust in Translation: The Rules of Infidelity from Tokyo to Tennessee*. New York: Penguin Press, 2007.

Dubé, Eric M. "The Role of Sexual Behavior in the Identification Process of Gay and Bisexual Males." *Journal of Sex Research* 37, no. 2 (May 2000): 123–32.

Dubinsky, Karen. *Improper Advances: Rape and Heterosexual Conflict in Ontario, 1880–1929*. Chicago Series on Sexuality, History, and Society. Chicago: University of Chicago Press, 1993.

Duggan, Lisa. "From Instincts to Politics: Writing the History of Sexuality in the U.S." *Journal of Sex Research* 27, no. 1 (February 1990): 95–109.

Dyhouse, Carol. *Feminism and the Family in England, 1880–1939*. Oxford, UK: Basil Blackwell, 1989.

Earle, John R., and Philip J. Perricone. "Premarital Sexuality: A Ten-Year Study of Attitudes and Behavior on a Small University Campus." *Journal of Sex Research* 22, no. 3 (August 1986): 304–10.

Echols, Alice. *Daring to Be Bad: Radical Feminism in America, 1967–1975*. Minneapolis: University of Minnesota Press, 1989.

Edwards, Jonathan. *Some Thoughts Concerning the Present Revival of Religion*. Boston, 1742.

Ehrenreich, Barbara. *Re-Making Love: The Feminization of Sex*. Garden City, NY: Anchor Press/Doubleday, 1986.

Ellis, Havelock. *Analysis of the Sexual Impulse, Love and Pain, the Sexual Impulse in Women*. Vol. III, *Studies in the Psychology of Sex*. Philadelphia: F. A. Davis Company, 1903.

———. *The Evolution of Modesty, the Phenomena of Sexual Periodicity, Auto-Erotism*. 3rd ed. Vol. I, *Studies in the Psychology of Sex*. Philadelphia: F. A. Davis Company, 1920.

———. *Little Essays of Love and Virtue*. New York: George H. Doran, 1922.

———. "The Psychic State in Pregnancy" (1906). In *Erotic Symbolism, the Mechanism of Detumescence, the Psychic State in Pregnancy*. Vol. V, *Studies in the Psychology of Sex*, by Havelock Ellis. Philadelphia: F. A. Davis Company, 1912.

————. *Sex in Relation to Society.* Vol. VI, *Studies in the Psychology of Sex.* Philadelphia: F. A. Davis Company, 1910.

Ellis, Lee, et al. "Eye Color, Hair Color, Blood Type, and the Rhesus Factor: Exploring Possible Genetic Links to Sexual Orientation." *Archives of Sexual Behavior* 37 (2008): 145–49.

Ellmann, Richard. *Oscar Wilde.* New York: Knopf, 1988.

Epstein, Debbie, and Deborah Lynn Steinberg. "All Het Up! Rescuing Heterosexuality on the 'Oprah Winfrey Show.'" *Feminist Review* 54 (Autumn 1996): 88–115.

Epstein, Debbie, Richard Johnson, Deborah Lynn Steinberg, and Politics of Sexuality Group. *Border Patrols: Policing the Boundaries of Heterosexuality.* London: Cassell, 1997.

Epstein, Julia, and Kristina Straub, eds. *Body Guards: The Cultural Politics of Gender Ambiguity.* New York: Routledge, 1991.

Escoffier, Jeffrey. "Gay-for-Pay: Straight Men and the Making of Gay Pornography." *Qualitative Sociology* 26, no. 4 (Winter 2003): 531–55.

Estep, Rhoda E., Martha R. Burt, and Herman J. Milligan. "The Socialization of Sexual Identity." *Journal of Marriage and Family* 39, no. 1 (February 1977): 99–112.

Etorre, Betsy. "Compulsory Heterosexuality and Psych/Atrophy: Some Thoughts on Lesbian Feminist Theory." *Women's Studies International Forum* 8, no. 5 (1985): 421–28.

Eustace, Nicole. "'The Cornerstone of a Copious Work': Love and Power in Eighteenth-century Courtship." *Journal of Social History* 34, no. 3 (Spring 2001): 517–46.

Faderman, Lillian. *Surpassing the Love of Men: Romantic Friendship and Love Between Women, from the Renaissance to the Present.* New York: Morrow, 1981.

Falomir-Pichastor, Juan M., and Gabriel Mugny. "'I'm not gay. . . . I'm a real man!': Heterosexual Men's Gender Self-Esteem and Sexual Prejudice." *Personality and Social Psychology Bulletin* 35, no. 9 (2009): 1233–43.

Farnham, Marynia, and Ferdinand Lundberg. *Modern Woman: The Lost Sex.* New York: Harper & Brothers, 1947.

Farrar, Eliza W. [writing as A Lady]. *The Young Lady's Friend: A Manual of Practical Advice and Instruction to Young Females on Entering upon the Duties of Life after Quitting School.* London: John W. Parker, 1837.

Farvid, Panteá, and Virginia Braun. "'Most of Us Guys Are Raring to Go Anytime, Anyplace, Anywhere': Male and Female Sexuality in *Cleo* and *Cosmo.*" *Sex Roles* 55, nos. 5/6 (2006): 295–310.

Fass, Paula S. *The Damned and the Beautiful: American Youth in the 1920's.* New York: Oxford University Press, 1977.

Fausto-Sterling, Anne, et al. "Genetics and Male Sexual Orientation." New series, *Science* 261, no. 5126 (September 3, 1993): 1257–59.

Fellman, Anita Clair, and Michael Fellman. "The Rule of Moderation in Late Nineteenth-Century American Sexual Ideology." *Journal of Sex Research* 17, no. 3 (1981): 238–55.

Filene, Peter G. *Him/Her/Self: Gender Identities in Modern America.* 3rd ed. Baltimore: Johns Hopkins University Press, 1998.

Finger, Frank W. "Changes in Sex Practices and Beliefs of Male College Students Over 30 Years." *Journal of Sex Research* 11, no. 4 (November 1975): 304–17.

Fisher, Helen E. *Why We Love: The Nature and Chemistry of Romantic Love.* New York: Henry Holt and Company, 2004.

Fisher, Kate. *Birth Control, Sex and Marriage in Britain, 1918–1960.* Oxford, UK: Oxford University Press, 2006.

Flood, Michael. "Men, Sex, and Homosociality." *Men & Masculinities* 10, no. 3 (April 2008): 339–59.

Forgas, Joseph P., and Barbara Dobosz. "Dimensions of Romantic Involvement: Towards a Taxonomy of Heterosexual Relationships." *Social Psychology Quarterly* 43, no. 3 (September 1980): 290–300.

Foster, Thomas A., ed. *Long Before Stonewall: Histories of Same-Sex Sexuality in Early America.* New York: New York University Press, 2007.

Foucault, Michel. *The History of Sexuality.* New York: Pantheon Books, 1978.

Fout, John C., and Maura Shaw Tantillo, eds. *American Sexual Politics: Sex, Gender, and Race since the Civil War.* Chicago: University of Chicago Press, 1993.

Fox, Ronald C. *Current Research on Bisexuality.* Binghamton, NY: Harrington Park Press, 2004.

France, David. "The Science of Gaydar—New Research on Everything from Voice Pitch to Hair Whorl." *New York,* June 17, 2007.

Francoeur, Robert T., Patricia Barthalow Kock, and David L. Weis. *Sexuality in America: Understanding Our Sexual Values and Behavior.* New York: Continuum, 1998.

Freedman, Estelle B. "The Prison Lesbian: Race, Class, and the Construction of the Aggressive Female Homosexual, 1915–1965." *Feminist Studies* 22, no. 2 (Summer 1996): 397–423.

———. "Sexuality in Nineteenth-century America: Behavior, Ideology, and Politics." *Reviews in American History* 10, no. 4 (December 1982): 196–215.

———. "'Uncontrolled Desires': The Response to the Sexual Psychopath, 1920–1960." *Journal of American History* 74, no. 1 (June 1987): 83–106.

Freud, Sigmund. *A Case of Hysteria, Three Essays on Sexuality and Other Works.* Vol. VII, *The Standard Edition of the Complete Works of Sigmund*

Freud. Translated and edited by James Strachey. London: Hogarth Press, 1954.

Friedan, Betty. *The Feminine Mystique.* New York: W. W. Norton, 1997.

Frost, Ginger S. *Promises Broken: Courtship, Class, and Gender in Victorian England.* Victorian Literature and Culture Series. Edited by Karen Chase, Jerome J. McGann, and Herbert Tucker. Charlottesville: University Press of Virginia, 1995.

Froyum, Carissa M. "'At Least I'm Not Gay': Heterosexual Identity Making among Poor Black Teens." *Sexualities* 10, no. 5 (December 2007): 603–22.

Frye, Marilyn. "Lesbian 'Sex'" In *Feminist Philosophies,* edited by Janet Kourany, James Sterba, and Rosemarie Tong, 72–77. 2nd ed. New York: Prentice Hall, 1999.

Gallup, Gordon G., and S. D. Suarez. "Homosexuality as a By-Product of Selection for Optimal Heterosexual Strategies." *Perspectives in Biology and Medicine* 26, no. 2 (Winter 1983): 315–22.

Gardella, Peter. *Innocent Ecstasy: How Christianity Gave America an Ethic of Sexual Pleasure.* New York: Oxford University Press, 1985.

Garton, Stephen. *Histories of Sexuality.* New York: Routledge, 2004.

Gartrell, Nanette, and Henny Bos. "US National Longitudinal Lesbian Family Study: Psychological Adjustment of 17-Year-Old Adolescents." *Pediatrics.* Published online June 7, 2010. DOI: 10.1542/peds.2009–3153. Accessed June 10, 2010.

Gay, Peter. *Education of the Senses.* Vol. 1, *The Bourgeois Experience: Victoria to Freud.* New York: Oxford University Press, 1984.

———. *The Tender Passion.* Vol. 2, *The Bourgeois Experience: Victoria to Freud.* New York: Oxford University Press, 1986.

Geddes, Patrick, and J. Arthur Thomson. *The Evolution of Sex.* London: W. Scott, 1889.

Gerhard, Jane. "Revisiting 'The Myth of the Vaginal Orgasm': The Female Orgasm in American Sexual Thought and Second Wave Feminism." Women and Health issue, *Feminist Studies* 26, no. 2 (Summer 2000): 449–76.

Giddens, Anthony. *The Transformation of Intimacy: Sexuality, Love and Eroticism in Modern Societies.* Stanford, CA: Stanford University Press, 1992.

Gilbert, Margaret. "Modeling Collective Belief." *Synthese* 73, no. 1 (1987): 185–204.

———. *On Social Facts.* London: Routledge, 1989.

Gillis, John R. *A World of Their Own Making: Myth, Ritual, and the Quest for Family Values.* New York: Basic Books, 1996.

———. *Youth and History: Tradition and Change in European Age Relations, 1770–Present.* Studies in Social Discontinuity. New York: Academic Press, 1974.

Gillis, Jonathan. "Bad Habits and Pernicious Results: Thumb Sucking and the Discipline of Late-Nineteenth-Century Pediatrics." *Medical History* 40 (1996): 55–73.

Gillmore, M. R., et al. "Comparison of Daily and Retrospective Reports of Vaginal Sex in Heterosexual Men and Women." *Journal of Sex Research* 47, no. 4 (2009).

Gilman, Sander L. *The Case of Sigmund Freud: Medicine and Identity at the Fin De Siècle*. Baltimore: Johns Hopkins University Press, 1993.

———. *Difference and Pathology: Stereotypes of Sexuality, Race, and Madness*. Ithaca, NY: Cornell University Press, 1985.

Gladue, Brian A. "The Biopsychology of Sexual Orientation." *Current Directions in Psychological Science* 3, no. 5 (October 1994): 150–54.

Glenn, Norval D., and Charles N. Weaver. "Attitudes Toward Premarital, Extramarital, and Homosexual Relations in the U.S. in the 1970s." *Journal of Sex Research* 15, no. 2 (May 1979): 108–18.

Goldberg, Richard L. "Heterosexual Panic." *American Journal of Psychoanalysis* 44, no. 2 (Summer 1984): 209–11.

Goodwin, Paula, et al. "Who Marries and When? Age at First Marriage in the United States, 2002." NCHS data brief, no 19. Hyattsville, MD: National Center for Health Statistics, 2009.

Gooren, Louis J. G. "Biomedical Concepts of Homosexuality: Folk Belief in a White Coat." *Journal of Homosexuality* 28, nos. 3/4 (June 1995): 237–46.

Green, Katherine S. "The Heroine's Blazon and Hardwicke's Marriage Act: Commodification for a Novel Market." *Tulsa Studies in Women's Literature* 9, no. 2 (Autumn 1990): 273–90.

Greenberg, David F. *The Construction of Homosexuality*. Chicago: University of Chicago Press, 1988.

Greenspan, Ralph J., and Jean-Francois Ferveur. "Courtship in *Drosophila*." *Annual Review of Genetics* 34 (2000): 205–32.

Grello, Catherine M., Deborah P. Welsh, and Melinda S. Harper. "No Strings Attached: The Nature of Casual Sex in College Students." *Journal of Sex Research* 43, no. 3 (2006): 255–67.

Gross, Alan E. "The Male Role and Heterosexual Behavior." *Journal of Social Issues* 34, no. 1 (Winter 1978): 87–107.

Haag, Pamela S. "In Search of 'The Real Thing': Ideologies of Love, Modern Romance, and Women's Sexual Subjectivity in the United States, 1920–40." *Journal of the History of Sexuality* 2, no. 4 (April 1992): 547–77.

Hacking, Ian. "How 'Natural' Are 'Kinds' of Sexual Orientation?" *Law and Philosophy* 21, no. 1 (January 2002): 95–107.

Haley, Bruce. *The Healthy Body and Victorian Culture*. Cambridge, MA: Harvard University Press, 1978.

Hall, Amy Laura. *Conceiving Parenthood: American Protestantism and the Spirit of Reproduction.* Grand Rapids, MI: W. B. Eerdmans, 2008.

Hall, Donald E., and Maria T. Pramaggiore, eds. *RePresenting Bisexualities: Subjects and Cultures of Fluid Desire.* New York: New York University Press, 1996.

Hall, G. Stanley. *Adolescence: Its Psychology and Its Relations to Physiology, Anthropology, Sociology, Sex, Crime, Religion, and Education.* Vol. 2. New York: Appleton, 1904.

Hall, Lesley A. *Hidden Anxieties: Male Sexuality, 1900–1950.* Family Life Series. Oxford, UK: Polity Press, 1991.

———. *Outspoken Women: An Anthology of Women's Writing on Sex, 1870–1969.* London: Routledge, 2005.

———. *Sex, Gender and Social Change in Britain since 1880.* European Culture and Society Series. Basingstoke, UK: Macmillan, 2000.

Hall, Lynn S. "Dermatoglyphic Analysis of Total Finger Ridge Count in Female Monozygotic Twins Discordant for Sexual Orientation." *Journal of Sex Research* 37, no. 4 (November 2000): 315–20.

Halley, Janet E. "The Construction of Heterosexuality." In *Fear of a Queer Planet: Queer Politics and Social Theory,* edited by Michael Warner. Minneapolis: University of Minnesota Press, 1993.

———. "Reasoning about Sodomy: Act and Identity in and after *Bowers v. Hardwick.*" *Virginia Law Review* 79, no. 7 (October 1993): 1721–80.

———. "Sexual Orientation and the Politics of Biology: A Critique of the Argument from Immutability." *Stanford Law Review* 46, no. 3 (February 1994): 503–68.

Halperin, David M. "Is There a History of Sexuality?" *History and Theory* 28, no. 3 (October 1989): 257–74.

Halperin, David M., John J. Winkler, and Froma I. Zeitlin. *Before Sexuality: The Construction of Erotic Experience in the Ancient Greek World.* Princeton, NJ: Princeton University Press, 1990.

Hamer, Dean H. *The Science of Desire: The Search for the Gay Gene and the Biology of Behavior.* New York: Simon & Schuster, 1994.

Hamilton, Cicely. *Marriage as a Trade.* New York: Moffat, Yard and Company, 1909.

Hanchett, Henry G. *Sexual Health.* 2nd ed. New York: Böricke & Tafel, 1889.

Hanigan, James. *Heterosexuality: The Test Case for Christian Sexual Ethics.* New York: Paulist, 1988.

Hanscombe, Gillian, Diana Chapman, and Martin Humphries. *Heterosexuality.* London: GMP, 1987.

Harding, Jennifer. *Sex Acts: Practices of Femininity and Masculinity.* London: SAGE Publications, 1998.

Harth, Erica. "The Virtue of Love: Lord Hardwicke's Marriage Act." *Cultural Critique* 9 (Spring 1988): 123–54.

Hartmann, Uwe. "Sigmund Freud and His Impact on Our Understanding of Male Sexual Dysfunction." *Journal of Sex Medicine* 6, no. 8 (August 2009): 2332–39.

Hatfield, Elaine, and Richard L. Rapsen. *Love and Sex: Cross-Cultural Perspectives.* Boston: Allyn and Bacon, 1996.

Haumann, Gunter. "Homosexuality, Biology, and Ideology." *Journal of Homosexuality* 28, no. 1 (1995): 57–77.

Haynes, James D. "A Critique of the Possibility of Genetic Inheritance of Homosexual Orientation." *Journal of Homosexuality* 28, nos. 1/2 (June 1995): 91–114.

Heidenry, John. *What Wild Ecstasy: The Rise and Fall of the Sexual Revolution.* New York: Simon & Schuster, 1997.

Hekma, Gert. "'A Female Soul in a Male Body': Sexual Inversion as Gender Inversion in Nineteenth-century Sexology." In *Third Sex, Third Gender: Beyond Sexual Dimorphism in Culture and History,* edited by Gilbert Herdt. New York: Zone Books, 1994.

———. *Homosexualiteit, een Medische Reputatie: De Uitdoktering van de Homosexueel in Negentiende-Eeuws.* Nederland: SUA, 1987.

Heller, Thomas C., and Christine Brook-Rose. *Reconstructing Individualism: Autonomy, Individuality, and the Self in Western Thought.* Stanford, CA: Stanford University Press, 1986.

Hendrick, Harry. *Images of Youth: Age, Class, and the Male Youth Problem, 1880–1920.* Oxford, UK: Clarendon Press, 1990.

Herdt, Gilbert H. *Third Sex, Third Gender: Beyond Sexual Dimorphism in Culture and History.* New York: Zone Books, 1994.

Henig, Robin Marantz. *Pandora's Baby: How the First Test Tube Babies Sparked the Reproductive Revolution.* Boston: Houghton Mifflin, 2004.

Herrn, Rainer. "On the History of Biological Theories of Homosexuality." *Journal of Homosexuality* 28, nos. 1–2 (June 1995): 31–56.

Herzer, Manfred. "Kertbeny and the Nameless Love." *Journal of Homosexuality* 12, no. 1 (1985): 1–25.

Herzer, Manfred, and Jean-Claude Feray. "Homosexual Studies and Politics in the Nineteenth Century: Karl Maria Kertbeny." Translated by Glen Peppel. *Journal of Homosexuality* 19, no. 1 (1990): 23–47.

Hill, Bridget. *Women Alone: Spinsters in England, 1660–1850.* New Haven, CT: Yale University Press, 2001.

Hill, Darryl B. "'Feminine' Heterosexual Men: Subverting Heteropatriarchal Sexual Scripts?" *Journal of Men's Studies* 14, no. 2 (Spring 2006): 145–59.

Hitchcock, Tim. *English Sexualities, 1700–1800*. Social History in Perspective Series. New York: St. Martin's Press, 1997.

———. "Reading Sex in the Eighteenth Century: Bodies and Gender in English Erotic Culture." *Journal of the History of Sexuality* 15, no. 1 (January 2006): 139–43.

———. "Redefining Sex in Eighteenth-century England." *History Workshop Journal* 41 (Spring 1996): 72–90.

Hite, Shere. *The Shere Hite Reader: New and Selected Writings on Sex, Globalization, and Private Life*. New York: Seven Stories Press, 2006.

Hockey, Jennifer Lorna. *Mundane Heterosexualities: From Theory to Practices*. Basingstoke: Palgrave Macmillan, 2007.

Holland, Janet, and Lisa Adkins. *Sex, Sensibility and the Gendered Body*. London: Macmillan, 1996.

Hollick, Frederick. *The Marriage Guide or Natural History of Generations*. New York, 1885.

Holmberg, Diane, and Karen L. Blair. "Sexual Desire, Communication, Satisfaction, and Preferences of Men and Women in Same-Sex Versus Mixed-Sex Relationships." *Journal of Sex Research* 46, no. 1 (2009): 57–66.

Holtzman, Ellen. "The Pursuit of Married Love: Women's Attitudes Towards Sexuality and Marriage in Great Britain, 1918–1939." *Journal of Social History* 16 (1982): 39–52.

Huet, Pierre-Daniel. *The History of Romances: An Enquiry into their Original; Instructions for Composing them; an Account of the most Eminent Authors; with Characters, and Curious Observations upon the Best Performances of that Kind*. Translated by Stephen Lewis. London: J. Hooke and T. Caldecott, 1715.

Hughes, Charles. "Erotopathia—Morbid Eroticism." *Alienist and Neurologist* 14, no. 4 (October 1893): 531–78.

Hunt, Lynn. *The Invention of Pornography: Obscenity and the Origins of Modernity, 1500–1800*. New York: Zone Books, 1993.

Hurlbert, David Farley. "Female Sexuality: A Comparative Study Between Women in Homosexual and Heterosexual Relationships." *Journal of Sex and Marital Therapy* 19, no. 4 (Winter 1993): 315–27.

Hutchinson, Sir Jonathan. "On Circumcision as a Preventative of Masturbation." *Archives of Surgery* 2, no. 7 (January 1891): 267–69.

Ingraham, Chrys. "The Heterosexual Imaginary: Feminist Sociology and Theories of Gender." *Sociological Theory* 12, no. 2 (July 1994): 203–19.

———. *Thinking Straight: The Promise, the Power and Paradox of Heterosexuality*. New York: Routledge, 2005.

———. *White Weddings: Romancing Heterosexuality in Popular Culture*. New York: Routledge, 1999.

Irvine, Janice M. *Disorders of Desire: Sex and Gender in Modern American Sexology*. Health, Society, and Policy. Philadelphia: Temple University Press, 1990.

Ittmann, Karl. "Family Limitation and Family Economy in Bradford, West Yorkshire, 1851–1881." *Journal of Social History* 25, no. 3 (Spring 1992): 547–73.

Ivory, Yvonne. "The Urning and His Own: Individualism and the Fin-de-Siecle Invert." *German Studies Review* 26, no. 2 (May 2003): 333–52.

Jackson, Stevi. *Heterosexuality in Question*. Thousand Oaks, CA: Sage Publications, 1999.

———. "Ordinary Sex." *Sexualities* 11, nos. 1/2 (February 2008): 33–37.

———. "Sexuality, Heterosexuality, and Gender Hierarchy: Getting Our Priorities Straight." In *Thinking Straight: The Power, the Promise, and the Paradox of Heterosexuality*, edited by Chrys Ingraham, 26. New York: Routledge, 2005.

Jackson, Stevi, and Sue Scott, eds. *Feminism and Sexuality: A Reader*. Gender and Culture. New York: Columbia University Press, 1996.

Jacobson, Matthew Frye. *Whiteness of Another Color: European Immigrants and the Alchemy of Race*. Cambridge, MA: Harvard University Press, 1998.

Jaeger, C. Stephen. *Ennobling Love: In Search of a Lost Sensibility*. The Middle Ages Series. Philadelphia: University of Pennsylvania Press, 1999.

James, William H. "Biological and Psychosocial Determinants of Male and Female Human Sexual Orientation." *Journal of Biosocial Science* 37 (2005): 555–67.

Jedlicka, Davor, and Ira E. Robinson. "Fear of Venereal Disease and Other Perceived Restraints on the Occurrence of Premarital Coitus." *Journal of Sex Research* 23, no. 3 (1987): 391–96.

Joffe, Carole. *The Regulation of Sexuality: Experiences of Family Planning Workers*. Health, Society, and Policy. Philadelphia: Temple University Press, 1986.

Johnson, Paul. *Love, Heterosexuality, and Society*. Advances in Sociology 16. London: Routledge, 2005.

Joyce, Kathryn. *Quiverfull: Inside the Christian Patriarchy Movement*. Boston: Beacon Press, 2009.

Kaestle, Christine E., and Carolyn T. Halpern. "What's Love Got to Do with It? Sexual Behaviors of Opposite-Sex Couples through Emerging Adulthood." *Perspectives on Sexual and Reproductive Health* 39, no. 3 (September 2007): 134–40.

Kafer, Alison. "Compulsory Bodies: Reflections on Heterosexuality and Able-bodiedness." *Journal of Women's History* 15, no. 3 (Autumn 2003): 77–89.

Karras, Ruth Mazo. *Common Women: Prostitution and Sexuality in Medieval*

England. Studies in the History of Sexuality. New York: Oxford University Press, 1996.

———. *From Boys to Men: Formations of Masculinity in Late Medieval Europe.* The Middle Ages Series. Philadelphia: University of Pennsylvania Press, 2003.

———. *Sexuality in Medieval Europe: Doing Unto Others.* New York: Routledge, 2005.

Karras, Ruth Mazo, Joel Kaye, and E. Ann Matter. *Law and the Illicit in Medieval Europe.* The Middle Ages Series. Philadelphia: University of Pennsylvania Press, 2008.

Katz, Jonathan. *The Invention of Heterosexuality.* Chicago: University of Chicago Press, 2007.

Kett, Joseph F. *Rites of Passage: Adolescence in America, 1790 to the Present.* New York: Basic Books, 1977.

Kiernan, James. "Responsibility in Sexual Perversion." *Chicago Medical Recorder* 3 (May 1892): 185–210.

Kimmel, Michael S. *The Sexual Self: The Construction of Sexual Scripts.* Nashville, TN: Vanderbilt University Press, 2007.

King, Richard. *The Party of Eros: Radical Social Thought and the Realm of Freedom.* Chapel Hill: University of North Carolina Press, 1972.

Kinnaird, Joan K. "Mary Astell and the Conservative Contribution to English Feminism." *Journal of British Studies* 19, no. 1 (Autumn 1979): 53–75.

Kinsey, Alfred C., Wardell B. Pomeroy, and Clyde E. Martin. *Sexual Behavior in the Human Male.* Philadelphia: W. B. Saunders, 1949.

Kinsey, Alfred C. and Staff of the Institute for Sex Research, Indiana University. *Sexual Behavior in the Human Female.* Philadelphia: W. B. Saunders, 1953.

Kinsman, Gary William. "'Homosexuality' Historically Reconsidered Challenges Heterosexual Hegemony." *Journal of Historical Sociology* 4, no.2 (October 2006): 91–111.

Kitzinger, Celia, and Sue Wilkinson. *Heterosexuality: A Feminism & Psychology Reader.* London: Sage Publications, 1993.

Klein, Fred, and Timothy J. Wolf. *Two Lives to Lead: Bisexuality in Men and Women.* New York: Harrington Park Press, 1985.

Koedt, Anne, et al., eds. *Radical Feminism.* New York: Quadrangle Books, 1973.

Koven, Seth. *Slumming: Sexual and Social Politics in Victorian London.* Princeton, NJ: Princeton University Press, 2004.

Krafft-Ebing, Richard von. *Psychopathia Sexualis.* Stuttgart, Germany: F. Enke, 1890.

Kunzel, Regina G. *Fallen Women, Problem Girls: Unmarried Mothers and the Professionalization of Benevolence, 1890–1945.* New Haven, CT: Yale University Press, 1993.

Laipson, Peter. "'Kiss without Shame, for She Desires It': Sexual Foreplay in American Marital Advice Literature, 1900–1925." *Journal of Social History* 29, no. 3 (Spring 1996): 507–25.

Langland, Elizabeth. "Nobody's Angels: Domestic Ideology and Middle-Class Women in the Victorian Novel." *PMLA* 107, no. 2 (March 1992): 290–304.

Langlands, Rebecca. *Sexual Morality in Ancient Rome.* Cambridge, UK: Cambridge University Press, 2006.

Lanser, Susan S. "Singular Politics: The Rise of the British Nation and the Production of the Old Maid." In *Singlewomen in the European Past, 1250–1800,* edited by Judith M. Bennett and Amy M. Froide, 297–324. Philadelphia: University of Pennsylvania Press, 1999.

Lantz, Herman R. "Romantic Love in the Pre-Modern Period: A Sociological Commentary." Special issue on the History of Love, *Journal of Social History* 15, no. 3 (Spring 1982): 349–70.

Laqueur, Thomas. *Making Sex: Body and Gender from the Greeks to Freud.* Cambridge, MA: Harvard University Press, 1994.

Leites, Edmund. "The Duty to Desire: Love, Friendship, and Sexuality in Some Puritan Theories of Marriage." Special Issue on the History of Love, *Journal of Social History* 15, no. 3 (Spring 1982): 383–408.

Leneman, Leah, and Rosalind Mitchison. "Clandestine Marriage in the Scottish Cities 1660–1780." *Journal of Social History* 26, no. 4 (Summer 1993): 845–61.

LeVay, Simon. *The Sexual Brain.* Cambridge, MA: MIT Press, 1993.

Lever, Janet, et al. "Behavior Patterns and Sexual Identity of Bisexual Males." *Journal of Sex Research* 29, no. 2 (May 1992): 141–67.

Lewin, Miriam. *In the Shadow of the Past: Psychology Portrays the Sexes.* New York: Columbia University Press, 1984.

Lewis, Carolyn Frances. "Coitus Perfectus: The Medicalization of Heterosexuality in the Cold War United States." PhD diss. University of California at Santa Barbara, 2007.

Light, Alison. "'Returning to Manderley': Romance Fiction, Female Sexuality and Class." *Feminist Review* 16 (Summer 1984): 7–25.

Lochrie, Karma, Peggy McCracken, and James A. Schultz, eds. *Constructing Medieval Sexuality.* Medieval Cultures 11. Minneapolis: University of Minnesota Press, 1997.

Lovell, Sue. "'Wanted, a Strong Girl, Able to Milk, and Make Herself Agreeable.'" *Australian Feminist Studies* 23, no. 56 (June 2008): 195–211.

Lowe, Pam. "Contraception and Heterosex: An Intimate Relationship." *Sexualities* 8, no. 1 (February 2005): 75–92.

Luibhéid, Eithne, and Lionel Cantú. *Queer Migrations: Sexuality, U.S. Citizenship, and Border Crossings.* Minneapolis: University of Minnesota Press, 2005.

Luis, Keridwen N. "Ourlands: Culture, Gender, and Intention in Women's Land Communities in the United States." PhD diss. Brandeis University, 2009.

Lundblad, Michael Stanley. "The Progressive Animal: Evolutionary Fictions and the Discourse of the American Jungle." PhD diss. University of Virginia, 2007.

Lystra, Karen. *Searching the Heart: Women, Men, and Romantic Love in Nineteenth-Century America.* New York: Oxford University Press, 1989.

Macfarlane, Alan. *Marriage and Love in England: Modes of Reproduction, 1300–1840.* Oxford, UK: B. Blackwell, 1986.

MacKinnon, Catharine A. *Women's Lives, Men's Laws.* Cambridge, MA: Belknap Press of Harvard University Press, 2005.

MacMillan, James. *Housewife or Harlot: The Place of Women in French Society, 1870–1940.* New York: St. Martin's Press, 1981.

Mandeville, Bernard. *A Modest Defence of Publick Stews.* 1724 Series: Augustan Reprint Society. Los Angeles: William Andrews Clark Memorial Library, University of California, 1973.

Mangan, J. A., and James Malvin. *Manliness and Morality: Middle-Class Masculinity in Britain and America, 1800–1940.* New York: St. Martin's Press, 1987.

Markle, Gail. "'Can Women Have Sex Like a Man?' Sexual Scripts in *Sex and the City*." *Sexuality & Culture* 12, no. 1 (Winter 2008): 45–57.

Marks, Laura V. *Sexual Chemistry: A History of the Contraceptive Pill.* New Haven, CT: Yale University Press, 2001.

Masters, William H. *Heterosexuality: The Up-to-Date, Comprehensive Book of Male-Female Love, Pleasure, Health, and Well-Being by the World's Foremost Team of Sexual Researchers-Therapists.* New York: Harper Collins Publishers, 1994.

Maurice, Frederick. "Where to Get Men." *Contemporary Review* (January 1902): 78–86.

Maynard, Mary. *(Hetero)sexual Politics.* London: Taylor & Francis, 1995.

McCabe, Marita P. "Desired and Experienced Levels of Premarital Affection and Sexual Intercourse During Dating." *Journal of Sex Research* 23, no. 1 (February 1987): 23.

McCaughey, Martha. *The Caveman Mystique: Pop-Darwinism and the Debates Over Sex, Violence, and Science.* New York: Routledge, 2008.

McCoy, Beth A. "Dangerous Desire: Literature of Sexual Freedom and Sexual Violence since the Sixties." *Sexualities* 10, no. 1 (February 2007): 123–24.

McDaniel, Patricia. "Shrinking Violets and Caspar Milquetoasts: Shyness and Heterosexuality from The Roles of the Fifties to The Rules of the Nineties." *Journal of Social History* 34, no. 3 (Spring 2001): 547–68.

McFadden, Dennis, et al. "A Reanalysis of Five Studies on Sexual Orientation and the Relative Length of the 2nd and 4th Fingers (the 2D:4D Ratio)." *Archives of Sexual Behavior* 34, no. 3 (June 2005): 341–56.

McGuire, Terry R. "Is Homosexuality Genetic?" *Journal of Homosexuality* 28, nos. 1/2 (June 1995): 115–46.

McIntosh, Mary. "The Homosexual Role." *Journal of Social History* 16, no. 2 (Autumn 1968): 182–92.

McKelvie, Melissa, and Steven R. Gold. "Hyperfemininity: Further Definition of the Construct." *Journal of Sex Research* 31, no. 3 (1994): 219–28.

McKeon, Michael. "Historicizing Patriarchy: The Emergence of Gender Difference in England, 1660–1760." *Eighteenth-Century Studies* 28, no. 3 (Spring 1995): 295–322.

McLaren, Angus. *A History of Contraception: From Antiquity to the Present*. Oxford, UK: Blackwell, 1990.

———. *Impotence: A Cultural History*. Chicago: University of Chicago Press, 2007.

———. *Reproductive Rituals: The Perception of Fertility in England from the Sixteenth to the Nineteenth Century*. London: Methuen, 1984.

———. *The Trials of Masculinity: Policing Sexual Boundaries, 1870–1930*. Chicago Series on Sexuality, History, and Society. Edited by John C. Fout. Chicago: University of Chicago Press, 1997.

McWhirter, David P., Stephanie A. Sanders, and June Machover Reinisch, eds. *Homosexuality/Heterosexuality: Concepts of Sexual Orientation*. New York: Oxford University Press, 1990.

Meah, Angela, Jenny Hockey, and Victoria Robinson. "What's Sex Got to Do with It? A Family-Based Investigation of Growing Up Heterosexual during the Twentieth Century." *Sociological Review* 56, no. 3 (2008): 454–73.

Menasche, Ann E. *Leaving the Life: Lesbians, Ex-Lesbians and the Heterosexual Imperative*. London: Onlywomen, 1999.

Mercer, Calvin, and Thomas W. Durham. "Religious Mysticism and Gender Orientation." *Journal for the Scientific Study of Religion* 38, no. 1 (March 1999): 175–82.

Mikulincer, Mario, and Gail S. Goodman, eds. *Dynamics of Romantic Love: Attachment, Caregiving, and Sex*. New York: Guilford Press, 2006.

Miller, Stacie, Heather Hoffmann, and Brian Mustanski. "Fluctuating Asymmetry and Sexual Orientation in Men and Women." *Archives of Sexual Behavior* 37, no. 1 (February 2008): 150–57.

Mintz, Steven. *Domestic Revolutions: A Social History of American Family Life.* New York: Free Press, 1988.

Mondaini, N., et al. "Sildenafil Does Not Improve Sexual Function in Men without Erectile Dysfunction but Does Reduce the Postorgasmic Refractory Time." *International Journal of Impotence Research* 15 (2003): 225–28.

Money, John. "Bisexual, Homosexual, and Heterosexual: Society, Law and Medicine." *Journal of Homosexuality* 2, no.3 (Spring 1977): 229–33.

———. *Gay, Straight, and In-Between: The Sexology of Erotic Orientation.* New York: Oxford University Press, 1988.

———. *Principles of Developmental Sexology.* New York: Continuum, 1997.

———. "Sex Rearing and Sexual Orientation." *Journal of Sex Research* 12, no. 2 (May 1976): 152–57.

———. "To Quim and to Swive: Linguistic and Coital Parity, Male and Female." *Journal of Sex Research* 18, no. 2 (May 1982): 173.

Montagu, Ashley. *The Practice of Love.* Englewood Cliffs, NJ: Prentice-Hall, 1975.

Moore, John C. "'Courtly Love': A Problem of Terminology." *Journal of Social History* 40, no. 4 (October—December 1979): 621–32.

Mort, Frank. *Dangerous Sexualities: Medico-Moral Politics in England since 1830.* New York: Routledge, 2000.

Moscucci, Ornella. *The Science of Woman.* Cambridge, UK: Cambridge University Press, 1990.

Mosse, George L. *Nationalism and Sexuality: Respectability and Abnormal Sexuality in Modern Europe.* New York: H. Fertig, 1985.

Mulvey-Roberts, Marie. *Sex & Sexuality, 1640-1940: Literary, Medical and Sociological Perspectives. Part 1, Sources from the Bodleian Library, Oxford and the Wellcome Institute for the History of Medicine, London.* Marlborough, UK: Adam Matthew Publications, 1998.

Munck, Victor C. De. *Romantic Love and Sexual Behavior: Perspectives from the Social Sciences.* Westport, CT: Praeger, 1998.

Nagel, Joane. *Race, Ethnicity, and Sexuality: Intimate Intersections, Forbidden Frontiers.* New York: Oxford University Press, 2003.

National Institute of Mental Health (US) Task Force on Homosexuality. *National Institute of Mental Health Task Force on Homosexuality: Final Report and Background Papers.* 1972.

Nelson, Claudia, and Michelle H. Martin, eds. *Sexual Pedagogies: Sex Education in Britain, Australia, and America, 1879–2000.* New York: Palgrave Macmillan, 2004.

Nelson, Robert K. "'The Forgetfulness of Sex': Devotion and Desire in the Courtship Letters of Angelina Grimke and Theodore Dwight Weld." *Journal of Social History* 37, no. 3 (Spring 2004): 663–79.

Newburn, Tim. *Permission and Regulation: Laws and Morals in Post War Britain.* London: Routledge, 1992.

Norton, Rictor. *Mother Clap's Molly House: The Gay Subculture in England, 1700–1830.* London: GMP, 1992.

Nurius, Paula S., and Walter W. Hudson. "Sexual Activity and Preference: Six Quantifiable Dimensions." *Journal of Sex Research* 24 (1988): 30–46.

Odem, Mary. "Single Mothers, Delinquent Daughters, and the Juvenile Court in Early 20th Century Los Angeles." *Journal of Social History* 25, no. 1 (Autumn 1991): 27–43.

Omoto, Allen M., and Howard S. Kurtzman, eds. *Sexual Orientation and Mental Health: Examining Identity and Development in Lesbian, Gay, and Bisexual People.* Contemporary Perspectives on Lesbian, Gay, and Bisexual Psychology. Washington, DC: American Psychological Association, 2006.

Oram, Alison. *Her Husband Was a Woman! Women's Gender-Crossing in Modern British Popular Culture.* Women's and Gender History. London: Routledge, 2007.

Ordover, Nancy. *American Eugenics: Race, Queer Anatomy, and the Science of Nationalism.* Minneapolis: University of Minnesota Press, 2003.

O'Sullivan, Lucia F., and Elizabeth Rice Allgeier. "Feigning Sexual Desire: Consenting to Unwanted Sexual Activity in Heterosexual Dating Relationships." *Journal of Sex Research* 35, no. 3 (1998): 234–43.

Parrinder, Edward Geoffrey. *Sexual Morality in the World's Religions.* Oxford, UK: Oneworld, 1996.

Pascoe, C. J. "'Dude, You're a Fag': Adolescent Masculinity and the Fag Discourse." *Sexualities* 8, no. 3 (July 2005): 329–46.

Pateman, Carole. *The Sexual Contract.* Stanford, CA: Stanford University Press, 1988.

Patrick, Megan E., Jennifer L. Maggs, and Caitlin C. Abar. "Reasons to Have Sex, Personal Goals, and Sexual Behavior During the Transition to College." *Journal of Sex Research* 44, no. 3 (2007): 240–49.

Paul, Elizabeth L., Brian McManus, and Allison Hayes. "'Hookups': Characteristics and Correlates of College Students' Spontaneous and Anonymous Sexual Experiences." *Journal of Sex Research* 37, no. 1 (February 2000): 76–88.

Peiss, Kathy. *Cheap Amusements: Working Women and Leisure in Turn-of-the-Century New York.* Philadelphia: Temple University Press, 1986.

Peiss, Kathy, and Christina Simmons, eds., with Robert A. Padgug. *Passion and Power: Sexuality in History.* Critical Perspectives on the Past. Philadelphia: Temple University Press, 1989.

Perry, Lewis. "'Progress, Not Pleasure, Is Our Aim': The Sexual Advice of an Antebellum Radical." *Journal of Social History* 12, no. 3 (Spring 1979): 354–66.

Peterson, Zoë D., and Charlene L. Muehlenhard. "What Is Sex and Why Does It Matter? A Motivational Approach to Exploring Individuals' Definitions of Sex." *Journal of Sex Research* 44, no. 3 (2007): 256–68.

Phillips, Mary Jane, and Julie R. Ancis. "The Process of Identity Development as the Parent of a Lesbian or Gay Male." *Journal of LGBT Issues in Counseling* 2, no. 2 (2008): 126–58.

Pitzulo, Carrie. "The Battle in Every Man's Bed: Playboy and the Fiery Feminists." *Journal of the History of Sexuality* 17, no. 2 (May 2008): 259–89.

Plummer, Ken. *Telling Sexual Stories: Power, Change and Social Worlds.* London: Routledge, 1995.

Popper, Karl. "Science: Conjectures and Refutations." In *Conjectures and Refutations: The Growth of Scientific Knowledge,* by Karl Popper. London: Routledge, 1963.

Porter, Roy. *Flesh in the Age of Reason: The Modern Foundations of Body and Soul.* New York: W. W. Norton & Company, 2004.

Primoratz, Igor. "Sexual Perversion." *American Philosophical Quarterly* 34, no. 2 (April 1997): 245–58.

Prince, Virginia. "Sex, Gender, and Semantics." *Journal of Sex Research* 21, no. 1 (February 1985): 92–101.

Pugh, Tison. *Sexuality and Its Queer Discontents in Middle English Literature.* 2nd ed. New York: Palgrave Macmillan, 2008.

Purnine, Daniel M., Michael P. Carey, and Randall S. Jorgensen. "Gender Differences Regarding Preferences for Specific Heterosexual Practices." *Journal of Sex and Marital Therapy* 20, no. 4 (Winter 1994): 271–87.

Raffalovich, Marc-Andre. "Uranism, Congenital Sexual Inversion, Observations and Recommendations." *Journal of Comparative Neurology* 5 (March 1895): 33–65.

Rainer, John D., et al. "Homosexuality and Heterosexuality in Identical Twins." *Psychosomatic Medicine* 22 (July–August 1960): 251–58.

Reed, James. *From Private Vice to Public Virtue: The Birth Control Movement and American Society Since 1830.* New York: Basic Books, 1978.

Regan, Pamela C., and Ellen Berscheid. *Lust: What We Know About Human Sexual Desire.* Sage Series on Close Relationships. Thousand Oaks, CA: Sage Publications, 1999.

Reijneveld, Sijmen A., et al. "Infant Crying and Abuse." *Lancet* 364, no. 9442 (October 9–15, 2004): 1340–42.

Reinisch, June Machover, and Kinsey Institute for Research in Sex, Gender, and Reproduction. *The Kinsey Institute New Report on Sex: What You Must Know to Be Sexually Literate.* New York: St. Martin's Press, 1990.

Reis, Elizabeth, ed. *American Sexual Histories.* Blackwell Readers in American Social and Cultural History 6. Malden, MA: Blackwell Publishers, 2001.

Reiss, Ira L., et al. *A Guide for Researching Heterosexual Relationships.* Technical Report 4. Minneapolis: University of Minnesota Family Study Center, 1980.

Remez, Lisa. "Oral Sex Among Adolescents: Is It Sex or Is It Abstinence?" *Family Planning Perspectives* 32, no. 6 (November/December 2000): 298–304.

Renold, Emma. " 'If You Don't Kiss Me, You're Dumped': Boys, Boyfriends and Heterosexualised Masculinities in the Primary School." *Educational Review* 55, no. 2 (June 2003): 179–94.

Rich, Adrienne. "Compulsory Heterosexuality and Lesbian Existence." *Signs: Journal of Women in Culture and Society* 5, no. 4 (Summer 1980): 631–60.

Richardson, Diane. *Rethinking Sexuality.* London: SAGE Publications, 2000.

———. *Theorising Heterosexuality: Telling It Straight.* Buckingham, UK: Open University Press, 1996.

Richetti, John, ed. *The Cambridge Companion to the Eighteenth Century Novel.* Cambridge, UK: Cambridge University Press, 1996.

Richters, Juliet. "Understanding Sexual Orientation: A Plea for Clarity." Sexuality issue, *Reproductive Health Matters* 6, no. 12 (November 1998): 144–49.

Ricketts, Wendell. "Biological Research on Homosexuality: Ansell's Cow or Occam's Razor." *Journal of Homosexuality* 9, no. 4 (1984): 65–93.

Ridley, Carl, Brian Ogolsky, Pamela Payne, Casey Totenhagen, and Rodney Cate. "Sexual Expression: Its Emotional Context in Heterosexual, Gay, and Lesbian Couples." *Journal of Sex Research* 45, no. 3 (2008): 305–14.

Risch, Neil, et al. "Male Sexual Orientation and Genetic Evidence." New series. *Science* 262, no. 5142 (December 24, 1993): 2063–65.

Robie, Walter Franklin. *Sex and Life: What the Experienced Should Teach and What the Inexperienced Should Learn.* Boston: Richard G. Badger, 1920.

———. *Sex Histories.* London: Amalgamated Medical Press, c. 1921.

Robinson, Paul A. *The Modernization of Sex: Havelock Ellis, Alfred Kinsey, William Masters, and Virginia Johnson.* New York: Harper & Row, 1976.

Romesburg, Don. "The Tightrope of Normalcy: Homosexuality, Developmental Citizenship, and American Adolescence, 1890–1940." *Journal of Historical Sociology* 21, no. 4 (December 2008): 417–42.

Rosario, Vernon A., II, ed. *Science and Homosexualities*. New York: Routledge, 1997.

Rose, June. *Marie Stopes and the Sexual Revolution*. London: Faber and Faber, 1992.

Rosenblum, Karen E., and Toni-Michelle C. Travis. *The Meaning of Difference: American Constructions of Race, Sex and Gender, Social Class, and Sexual Orientation*. 4th ed. Boston: McGraw-Hill, 2006.

Rosenzweig, Linda W. "'The Anchor of My Life': Middle-Class American Mothers and College-Educated Daughters, 1880–1920." *Journal of Social History* 25, no. 1 (Autumn 1991): 5–25.

Ross, Michael W. "Typing, Doing, and Being: Sexuality and the Internet." *Journal of Sex Research* 42, no. 4 (November 2005): 342–52.

Rothman, Ellen K. "Sex and Self-Control: Middle-Class Courtship in America, 1770–1870." *Journal of Social History* 15, no. 3 (Spring 1982): 409–25.

Rotundo, E. Anthony. *American Manhood: Transformations in Masculinity from the Revolution to the Modern Era*. New York: BasicBooks, 1993.

———. "Romantic Friendship: Male Intimacy and Middle-Class Youth in the Northern United States, 1800–1900." *Journal of Social History* 23, no. 1 (Autumn 1989): 1–25.

Roughgarden, Joan. *Evolution's Rainbow: Diversity, Gender, and Sexuality in Nature and People*. Berkeley: University of California Press, 2004.

Rowbotham, Judith. *Good Girls Make Good Wives: Guidance for Girls in Victorian Fiction*. Oxford, UK: Blackwell, 1989.

Royden, A. Maude. *Sex and Common-Sense*. 8th ed. London: Hurst and Blackett, 1922.

Rubin, Gayle S. "Thinking Sex: Notes for a Radical Theory on the Politics of Sexuality." In *The Lesbian and Gay Studies Reader*, edited by Henry Abelove et al., 3–44. New York: Routledge, 1993.

Rupp, Leila J. *A Desired Past: A Short History of Same-Sex Love in America*. Chicago: University of Chicago Press, 1999.

Russ, Joanna. "For Women Only, Or, What Is That Man Doing under My Seat?" In *What Are We Fighting For? Sex, Race, Class, and the Future of Feminism*, by Joanna Russ, 92. New York: St. Martin's Press, 1998.

Russell, Bertrand. *Marriage and Morals*. New York: Liveright, 1929.

Russett, Cynthia Eagle. *Sexual Science: The Victorian Construction of Womanhood*. Cambridge, MA: Harvard University Press, 1989.

Rust, Paula C. *Bisexuality in the United States: A Social Science Reader*. New York: Columbia University Press, 2000.

———. "The Politics of Sexual Identity: Sexual Attraction and Behavior among Lesbian and Bisexual Women." *Social Problems* 39, no. 4 (November 1992): 366–86.

Sagarin, Edward. "Sex Rearing and Sexual Orientation: The Reconciliation of Apparently Contradictory Data." *Journal of Sex Research* 11, no. 4 (November 1975): 329–34.

Saiz, Ignacio. "Bracketing Sexuality: Human Rights and Sexual Orientation: A Decade of Development and Denial at the UN." Sexuality, Human Rights, and Health issue, *Health and Human Rights* 7, no. 2 (2004): 48–80.

Sandnabba, N. Kenneth, Pekka Santtila, Niklas Nordling. "Sexual Behavior and Social Adaptation Among Sadomasochistically-Oriented Males." *Journal of Sex Research* 36, no. 3 (August 1999): 273–82.

Santow, Gigi. "Coitus Interruptus in the Twentieth Century." *Population and Development Review* 19 (1993): 767–92.

Schiebinger, Londa. *Nature's Body: Gender in the Making of Modern Science.* Boston: Beacon Press, 1996.

Schlichter, Annette. "Contesting 'Straights': 'Lesbians,' 'Queer Heterosexuals' and the Critique of Heteronormativity." *Journal of Lesbian Studies* 11, nos. 3/4 (June 2007): 189–201.

Schmersahl, Katrin. *Medizin Und Geschlecht: Zur Konstruktion Der Kategorie Geschlecht Im Medizinischen Diskurs Des 19. Jahrhunderts.* Opladen: Leske & Budrich, 1998.

Schmitt, Michael T., Justin J. Lehmiller, and Allison L. Walsh. "The Role of Heterosexual Identity Threat in Differential Support for Same-Sex 'Civil Unions' versus 'Marriages.'" *Group Processes & Intergroup Relations* 10, no. 4 (October 2007): 443–55.

Schüklenk, Udo, et al. "The Ethics of Genetic Research on Sexual Orientation." Sexuality issue. *Reproductive Health Matters* 6, no. 12 (November 1998): 134–43.

Schüklenk, Udo, and Michael Ristow. "The Ethics of Research into the Cause(s) of Homosexuality." *Journal of Homosexuality* 31, no. 3 (September 1996): 5–30.

Shulman, Alix K. "Sex and Power: Sexual Bases of Radical Feminism." Special issue: Women: Sex and Sexuality. *Signs* 5, no. 4 (Summer 1980): 590–604.

Schultz, James A. *Courtly Love, the Love of Courtliness, and the History of Sexuality.* Chicago: University of Chicago Press, 2006.

Schutte, Ofelia. "A Critique of Normative Heterosexuality: Identity, Embodiment, and Sexual Difference in Beauvoir and Irigaray." *Hypatia* 12, no. 1 (Winter 1997): 40–62.

Schwartz, Pepper, and Virginia Rutter. *The Gender of Sexuality*. The Gender Lens. Lanham, MD: AltaMira Press, 1998.

Seelow, David. *Radical Modernism and Sexuality: Freud, Reich, D. H. Lawrence and Beyond*. New York: Palgrave Macmillan, 2005.

Segal, Lynne. *Straight Sex: Rethinking the Politics of Pleasure*. Berkeley: University of California Press, 1994.

Seidman, Steven. *Embattled Eros: Sexual Politics and Ethics in Contemporary America*. Thinking Gender. New York: Routledge, 1992.

——. "The Power of Desire and the Danger of Pleasure: Victorian Sexuality Reconsidered." *Journal of Social History* 24, no. 1 (Autumn 1990): 47–67.

——. *Romantic Longings: Love in America, 1830–1980*. New York: Routledge, 1991.

Sengoopta, Chandak. "Glandular Politics: Experimental Biology, Clinical Medicine, and Homosexual Emancipation in Fin-de-Siècle Central Europe." *Isis* 89, no. 3 (September 1998): 445–73.

Shelley, Martha. "Lesbianism and the Women's Liberation Movement." In *Women's Liberation: Blueprint for the Future*, edited by Sookie Stambler, 127. New York: Ace Books, 1970.

Sherblom, Stephen A., and Michael W. Bahr. "Homosexuality and Normality: Basic Knowledge and Practical Considerations for School Consultation." *Journal of Educational & Psychological Consultation* 18, no. 1 (March 2008): 81–100.

Sigel, Lisa Z. *Governing Pleasures: Pornography and Social Change in England, 1815–1914*. New Brunswick, NJ: Rutgers University Press, 2002.

Simon, William, and John H. Gagnon. *Heterosexuality and Homosociality: A Dilemma of the Lower Class Family*. Bloomington: Institute for Sex Research, Indiana University, 1967.

Sinfield, Alan. *The Wilde Century: Effeminacy, Oscar Wilde, and the Queer Moment*. Between Men—Between Women. New York: Columbia University Press, 1994.

Smith, Alison. *The Victorian Nude: Sexuality, Morality and Art*. Manchester, UK: Manchester University Press, 1996.

Smith, Daniel Scott "Female Householding in Late Eighteenth-Century America and the Problem of Poverty." *Journal of Social History* 28, no. 1 (Autumn 1994): 83–107.

——. "'The Number and Quality of Children': Education and Marital Fertility in Early Twentieth-Century Iowa." *Journal of Social History* 30, no. 2 (Winter 1996): 367–92.

Smith-Rosenberg, Carroll. *Disorderly Conduct: Visions of Gender in Victorian America*. New York: Oxford University Press, 1986.

————. "The Female World of Love and Ritual: Relations between Women in Nineteenth-Century America." *Signs* 1, no. 1 (Autumn 1975): 1–29

————. "Puberty to Menopause: The Cycle of Femininity in Nineteenth-Century America." Special Double Issue: Women's History. *Feminist Studies* 1, nos. 3/4 (Winter–Spring 1973): 58–72.

————. "Sex as Symbol in Victorian Purity: An Ethnohistorical Analysis of Jacksonian America." Supplement: "Turning Points: Historical and Sociological Essays on the Family." *American Journal of Sociology* 84 (1978): 212–47.

Smith-Rosenberg, Carroll, and Charles Rosenberg. "The Female Animal: Medical and Biological Views of Woman and Her Role in Nineteenth-Century America." *Journal of American History* 60, no. 2 (September 1973): 332–56.

Soble, Alan, and Nicholas Power, eds. *The Philosophy of Sex: Contemporary Readings.* Lanham, MD: Rowman & Littlefield, 1997.

Social Text Collective. *Fear of a Queer Planet: Queer Politics and Social Theory.* Minneapolis: University of Minnesota Press, 1993.

Sohn, Anne-Marie "The Golden Age of Male Adultery: The Third Republic." *Journal of Social History* 28, no. 3 (Spring 1995): 469–90.

Sokolow, Jayme A. *Eros and Modernization: Sylvester Graham, Health Reform, and the Origins of Victorian Sexuality in America.* Rutherford, NJ: Fairleigh Dickinson University Press, 1983.

Somerville, Jennifer. *Feminism and the Family: Politics and Society in the UK and USA.* Houndmills, Basingstoke, Hampshire, UK: Macmillan, 2000.

Sommer, Doris. "For Love and Money: Of Potboilers and Precautions." *PMLA* 116, no. 2 (March 2001): 380–91.

Spackman, Barbara. "Fascist Women and the Rhetoric of Virility." In *Mothers of Invention: Women, Fascism, and Culture,* edited by Robin Pickering-Iazzi. Minneapolis: University of Minnesota Press, 1995.

Spurlock, John C. *Free Love: Marriage and Middle-Class Radicalism in America, 1825–1860.* American Social Experience Series 13. New York: New York University Press, 1988.

Spurlock, John C., and Cynthia A. Magistro. "'Dreams Never to Be Realized': Emotional Culture and the Phenomenology of Emotion." *Journal of Social History* 28, no. 2 (Winter 1994): 295–310.

Stanley, Liz. *Sex Surveyed, 1949–1994: From Mass Observation's 'Little Kinsey' to the National Survey and the Hite Reports.* London: Taylor and Francis, 1995.

Stansell, Christine. *City of Women: Sex and Class in New York, 1789–1860.* New York: Knopf, 1986.

Stanton, Domna C., ed. *Discourses of Sexuality: From Aristotle to AIDS.* Ann Arbor: University of Michigan Press, 1992.

Steakley, James D. *The Homosexual Emancipation Movement in Germany.* Homosexuality. New York: Arno Press, 1975.

Stearns, Peter N. "Girls, Boys, and Emotions: Redefinitions and Historical Change." *Journal of American History* 80, no. 1 (June 1993): 36–74.

Stearns, Peter N., and Mark Knapp. "Men and Romantic Love: Pinpointing a 20th-Century Change." *Journal of Social History* 26, no. 4 (Summer 1993): 769–95.

Stein, Edward. *The Mismeasure of Desire: The Science, Theory, and Ethics of Sexual Orientation.* Ideologies of Desire. Oxford, UK: Oxford University Press, 1999.

———. "The Relevance of Scientific Research about Sexual Orientation to Lesbian and Gay Rights." *Journal of Homosexuality* 27, nos. 3/4 (November 1994): 269–308.

Stein, Terry S. "Deconstructing Sexual Orientation." *Journal of Homosexuality* 34, no. 1 (September 1997): 81–86.

Stokes, Mason Boyd. *The Color of Sex: Whiteness, Heterosexuality, and the Fictions of White Supremacy.* Durham, NC: Duke University Press, 2001.

Stone, Lawrence. *The Family, Sex, and Marriage in England, 1500–1800.* New York: Harper and Row, 1979.

Stopes, Marie. *Enduring Passion.* London: G. P. Putnam's Sons, 1928.

———. *Married Love.* London: A. C. Fifield, 1918.

Storr, Merl. "Postmodern Bisexuality." *Sexualities* 2, no. 3 (1999): 309–25.

Strock, Carren. *Married Women Who Love Women.* New York: Doubleday, 1998.

Suppe, Frederick. "Explaining Homosexuality: Philosophical Issues, and Who Cares Anyhow?" *Journal of Homosexuality* 27, nos. 3/4 (November 1994): 223–68.

Surkis, Judith. *Sexing the Citizen: Morality and Masculinity in France, 1870–1920.* Ithaca, NY: Cornell University Press, 2006.

Szuchman, Lenore T., and Frank Muscarella, eds. *Psychological Perspectives on Human Sexuality.* New York: Wiley, 2000.

Tanenbaum, Leora. *Slut! Growing Up Female with a Bad Reputation.* New York: Seven Stories Press, 1999.

Terry, Jennifer. "Lesbians Under the Medical Gaze: Scientists Search for Remarkable Differences." *Journal of Sex Research* 27, no. 3 (1990): 317–39.

Terry, Jennifer, and Jacqueline Urla, eds. *Deviant Bodies: Critical Perspectives on Difference in Science and Popular Culture.* Race, Gender, and Science. Bloomington: Indiana University Press, 1995.

Thomas, Calvin, ed. *Straight with a Twist: Queer Theory and the Subject of Heterosexuality.* Urbana: University of Illinois Press, 2000.

Thompson, Elisabeth Morgan, and Elizabeth M. Morgan. "'Mostly Straight' Young Women: Variations in Sexual Behavior and Identity Development." *Developmental Psychology* 44, no. 1 (January 2008): 15–21.

Tiefer, Leonore. "Prognosis: More Pharmasex." *Sexualities* 11, nos. 1/2 (February 2008): 53–59.

———. *Sex Is Not a Natural Act, and Other Essays.* Boulder, CO: Westview Press, 1995.

Toulalan, Sarah. Review of *Sensible Flesh: On Touch in Early Modern Culture,* by E. D. Harvey, ed. *Sexualities* 7, no. 3 (2004): 381–83.

Travis, Cheryl Brown, and Jacquelyn W. White, eds. *Sexuality, Society, and Feminism.* Washington, DC: American Psychological Association, 2000.

Tripp, C. A. (Clarence Arthur). *The Homosexual Matrix.* 2nd ed. New York: Plume, 1987.

Trumbach, Randolph. "London's Sodomites: Homosexual Behavior and Western Culture in the 18th Century." *Journal of Social History* 11, no. 1 (Autumn 1977): 1–33.

———. *Sex and the Gender Revolution, Vol. 1: Heterosexuality and the Third Gender in Enlightenment London.* Chicago Series on Sexuality, History, and Society. Chicago: University of Chicago Press, 1998.

Turnbull, Annmarie, and Alison Oram. *The Lesbian History Sourcebook: Love and Sex between Women in Britain from 1780 to 1970.* London: Routledge, 2001.

Turner, James Grantham. *Libertines and Radicals in Early Modern London: Sexuality, Politics and Literary Culture, 1630–1685.* Cambridge, UK: Cambridge University Press, 2002.

Tweedie, Jill. *In the Name of Love: A Study of Sexual Desire.* New York: Tauris Parke, 2000.

Upchurch, Charles. "Queer London: Perils and Pleasures in the Sexual Metropolis, 1918–1957." *Sexualities* 9, no. 4 (October 2006): 497–98.

Valdes, Francisco. "Queers, Sissies, Dykes, and Tomboys: Deconstructing the Conflation of 'Sex,' 'Gender,' and 'Sexual Orientation' in Euro-American Law and Society." *California Law Review* 83, no. 1 (January 1995): 1–377.

Valenti, Jessica. *The Purity Myth: How America's Obsession with Virginity Is Hurting Young Women.* Berkeley, CA: Seal Press, 2009.

Vance, Carole S., ed. *Pleasure and Danger: Exploring Female Sexuality.* London: Pandora Press, 1992.

Van de Velde, Theodor. *Ideal Marriage: Its Physiology and Technique.* Translated by Stella Browne. London: William Heinemann, 1928.

Vicinus, Martha. *Independent Women: Work and Community for Single Women, 1850–1920.* Women in Culture and Society. Chicago: University of Chicago Press, 1985.

Waites, Matthew. "The Fixity of Sexual Identities in the Public Sphere: Biomedical Knowledge, Liberalism and Heterosexual/Homosexual Binary in Late Modernity." *Sexualities* 8, no. 5 (December 2005): 539–69.

Waterman, Caroline K., and Emil J. Chiauzzi. "The Role of Orgasm in Male and Female Sexual Enjoyment." *Journal of Sex Research* 18, no. 2 (May 1982): 146–59.

Watkins, Elizabeth Siegel. *On the Pill: A Social History of Contraceptives, 1950–1970.* Baltimore: Johns Hopkins University Press, 1998.

Watt, John D., and Jackie E. Ewing. "Toward the Development and Validation of a Measure of Sexual Boredom." *Journal of Sex Research* 33, no. 1 (1996): 57–66.

Weeks, Jeffrey. *Invented Moralities: Sexual Values in an Age of Uncertainty.* New York: Columbia University Press, 1995.

———. *Sex, Politics, and Society: The Regulation of Sexuality since 1800.* London: Longman, 1989.

———. *The World We Have Won: The Remaking of Erotic and Intimate Life.* London: Routledge, 2007.

Weeks, Jeffrey, and Janet Holland. *Sexual Cultures: Communities, Values, and Intimacy.* Basingstoke, UK: MacMillan, 1996.

Weld, Theodore Dwight, Angelina Emily Grimke, and Sarah Moore Grimke. *Letters of Theodore Dwight Weld, Angelina Grimke and Sarah Grimke, 1822–1844.* Edited by Gilbert H. Barnes and Dwight L. Dumond. Gloucester, MA: Peter Smith, 1965.

Wells, Joel W. "The Sexual Vocabularies of Heterosexual and Homosexual Males and Females for Communicating with a Sexual Partner." *Archives of Sexual Behavior* 19, no. 2 (April 1990): 139–47.

Welter, Barbara. "The Cult of True Womanhood: 1820–1860." *American Quarterly* 18, no. 2, part 1 (Summer 1966): 151–74.

Wertham, Fredric. *Seduction of the Innocent.* New York: Reinhart & Company, 1954.

West's Encyclopedia of American Law. 2nd ed. Los Angeles: West Group Publishing, 1998.

Widmer, Eric D., Judith Treas, and Robert Newcomb. "Attitudes Toward Nonmarital Sex in 24 Countries." *Journal of Sex Research* 35, no. 4 (November 1998): 349–58.

Wilkerson, Abby. "Homophobia and the Moral Authority of Medicine." *Journal of Homosexuality* 27, nos. 3/4 (November 1994): 329–47.

Wilson, Gordon. *The Third Sex: Genders of the Species.* London: Taprobane, 1990.

Wilson, W. Cody. "The Distribution of Selected Sexual Attitudes and Behaviors Among the Adult Population of the United States." *Journal of Sex Research* 11, no. 1 (February 1975): 46–64.

Winship, Michael P. "Behold the Bridegroom Cometh! Marital Imagery in Massachusetts Preaching, 1630–1730." *Early American Literature* 27, no. 3 (1992): 170–84.

Wintermute, Robert. *Sexual Orientation and Human Rights: The United States Constitution, the European Convention, and the Canadian Charter.* Oxford, UK: Clarendon Press, 1995.

Wittig, Monique. *The Straight Mind, and Other Essays.* Boston: Beacon Press, 1992.

Wollstonecraft, Mary, and Carol H. Poston. *A Vindication of the Rights of Woman: An Authoritative Text, Backgrounds, the Wollstonecraft Debate, Criticism.* New York: W. W. Norton, 1988.

Wood, Jill M., Patricia Barthalow Koch, and Phyllis Kernoff Mansfield. "Women's Sexual Desire: A Feminist Critique." *Journal of Sex Research* 43, no. 3 (2006): 236–44.

Wright, Bradford. *Comic Book Nation: The Transformation of Youth Culture in America.* Baltimore: Johns Hopkins University Press, 2001.

Yalom, Marilyn. *A History of the Wife.* New York: Harper Collins, 2002.

Zaun, Stefanie, and Jorn Steigerwald. *Imagination Und Sexualität: Pathologien Der Einbildungskraft Im Medizinischen Diskurs Der Frühen Neuzeit.* Analecta Romanica Heft 71. Frankfurt, Germany: Klostermann, 2004.

Zuckerman, Marvin, and P. L. Myers. "Sensation Seeking in Homosexual and Heterosexual Males." *Archives of Sexual Behavior* 12, no. 4 (August 1983): 347–56.